KiNG of BANDITS JiN
Title 2

inRustyNail
c/wJoshuaTree

TWILIGHTTALES ❷

KUMAKURAYUICHI

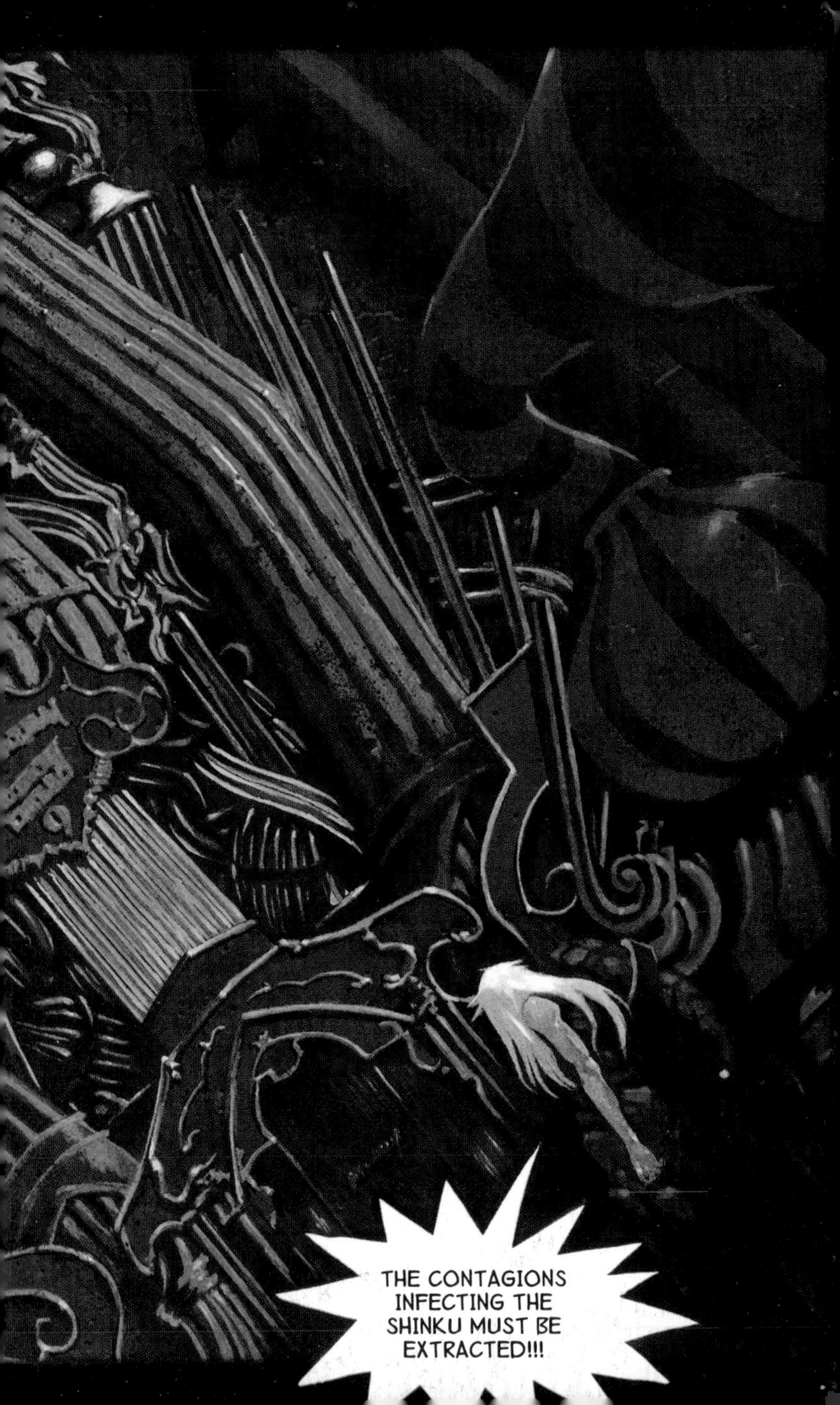
THE CONTAGIONS INFECTING THE SHINKU MUST BE EXTRACTED!!!

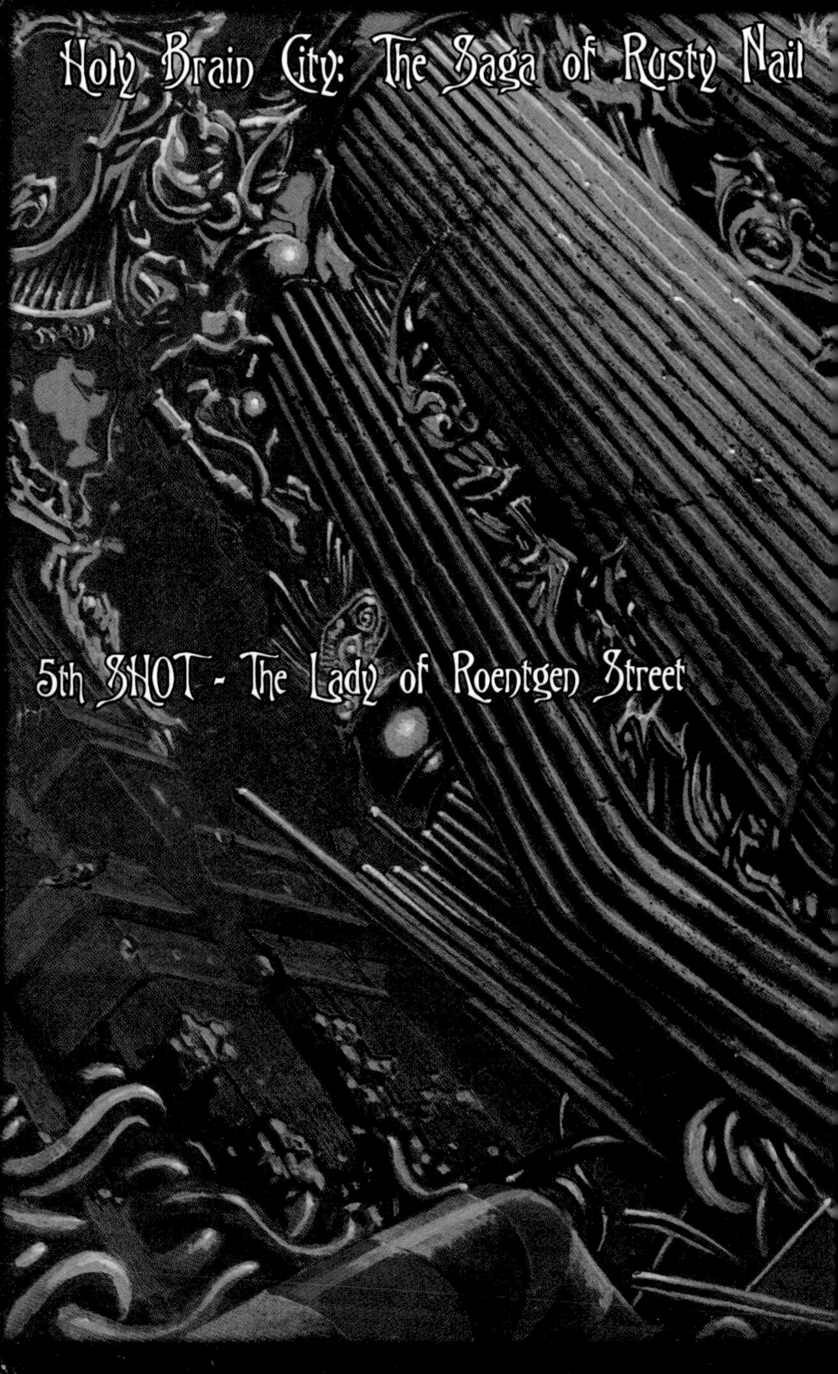
Holy Brain City: The Saga of Rusty Nail
5th SHOT - The Lady of Roentgen Street

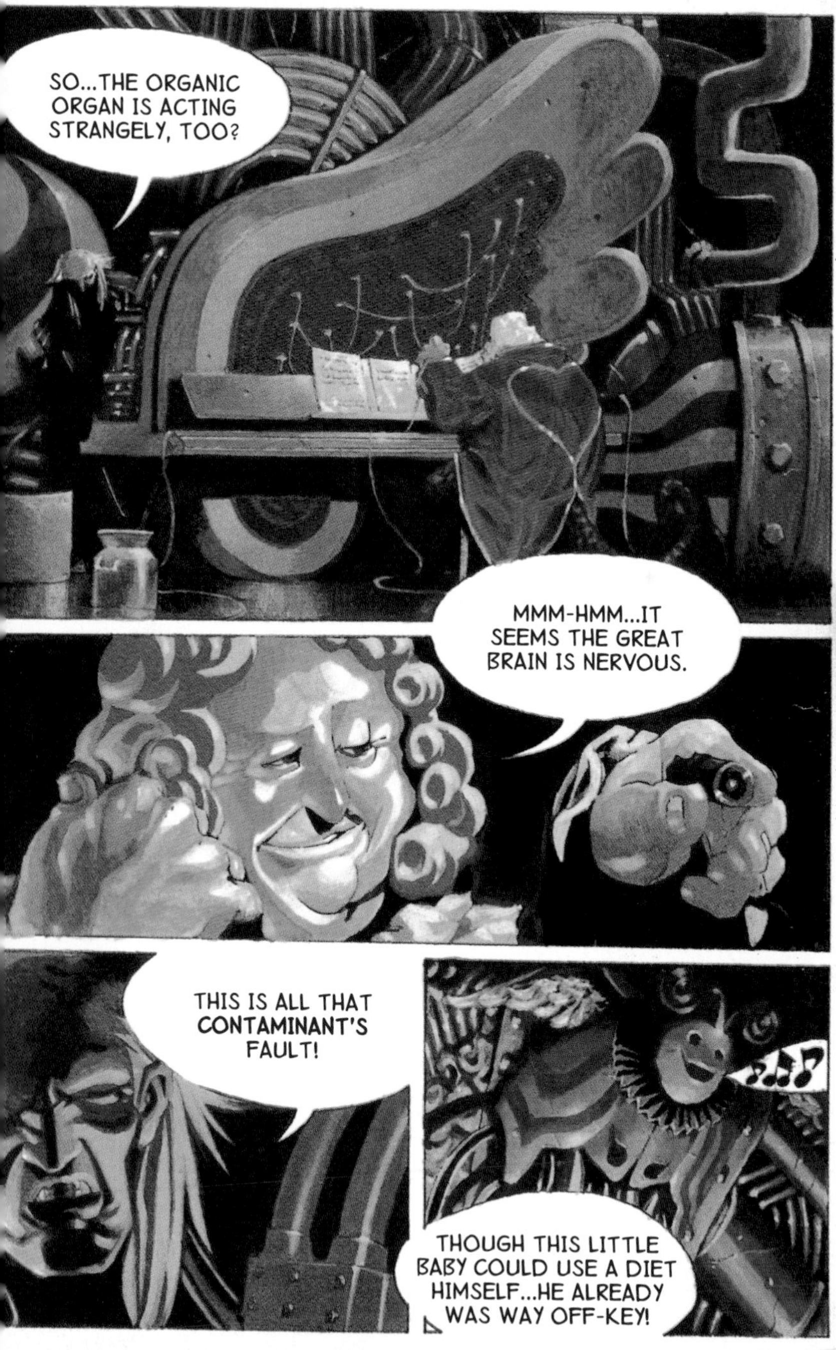
SO...THE ORGANIC ORGAN IS ACTING STRANGELY, TOO?
MMM-HMM...IT SEEMS THE GREAT BRAIN IS NERVOUS.
THOUGH THIS LITTLE BABY COULD USE A DIET HIMSELF...HE ALREADY WAS WAY OFF-KEY!
THIS IS ALL THAT CONTAMINANT'S FAULT!

All that glitters...

Even the stars

All things precious...

Even your life

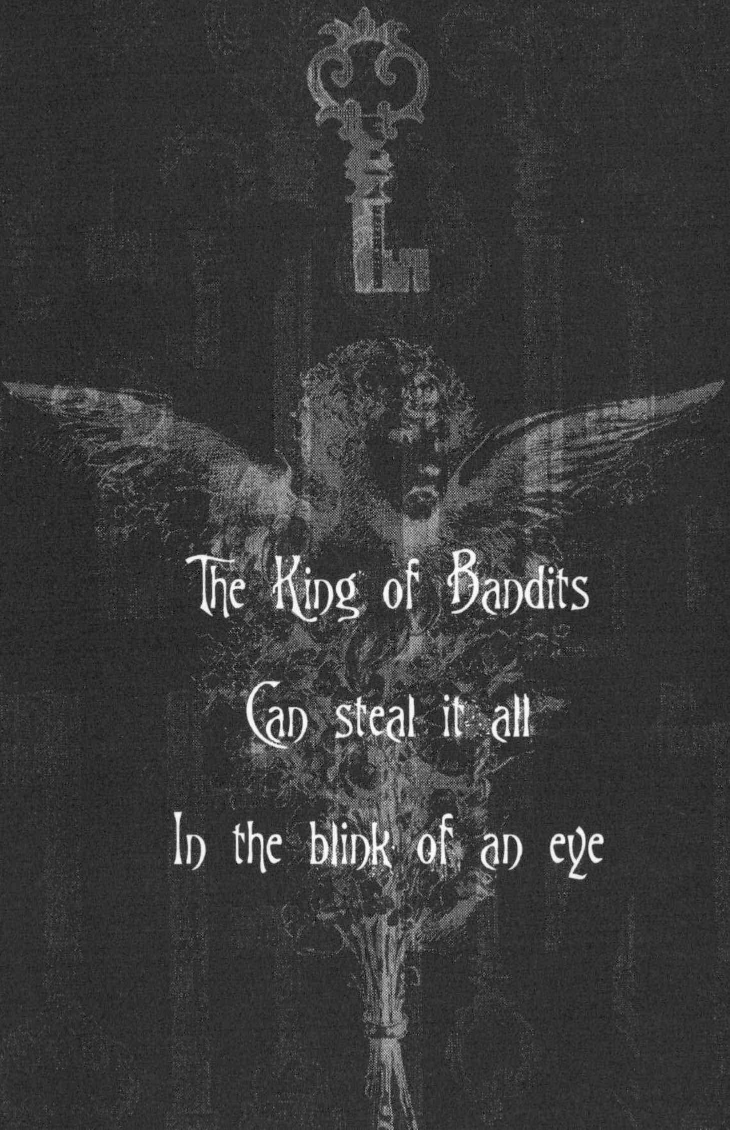
The King of Bandits
Can steal it all
In the blink of an eye

KING OF BANDITS JING

TWILIGHT TALES

VOLUME 2 OF 6

STORY AND ART BY
YUICHI KUMAKURA

HAMBURG // LONDON // LOS ANGELES // TOKYO

Jing: King of Bandits - Twilight Tales Vol. 2
Created by Yuichi Kumakura

Translation - Alexis Kirsch
English Adaptation - Carol Fox
Copy Editor - Suzanne Waldman
Retouch and Lettering - Vicente Rivera, Jr.
Cover Design - Gary Shum

Editor - Paul Morrissey
Digital Imaging Manager - Chris Buford
Pre-Press Manager - Antonio DePietro
Production Managers - Jennifer Miller and Mutsumi Miyazaki
Art Director - Matt Alford
Managing Editor - Jill Freshney
VP of Production - Ron Klamert
President and C.O.O. - John Parker
Publisher and C.E.O. - Stuart Levy

A **TOKYOPOP** Manga

TOKYOPOP Inc.
5900 Wilshire Blvd. Suite 2000
Los Angeles, CA 90036

E-mail: info@TOKYOPOP.com
Come visit us online at www.TOKYOPOP.com

ISBN: 1-59182-470-2

First TOKYOPOP printing: December 2004
10 9 8 7 6 5 4 3 2 1
Printed in the USA

Once upon a midnight dreary, a thief named Jing was weak and weary.
Many strange and forgotten lands he did traverse and did explore.
His companion was a bird, an odd one name of Kir
Who possessed a strange vocation, a less than honest occupation.
"Wake up, Jing" Kir muttered, "all around is loot galore!"

Thus this ebony bird's wiling, changed Jing's sadness into willing
As he set about to do the thing he truly did adore.
So the albatross sat proudly on Jing's placid bust sang loudly
While his beady eyes explored the treasure stacked upon the floor.
One more thing that Kir did utter, his feathers all a greedy flutter
And his voice commenced a terrible dull roar,
Quoth the albatross, "Let's steal some more!"

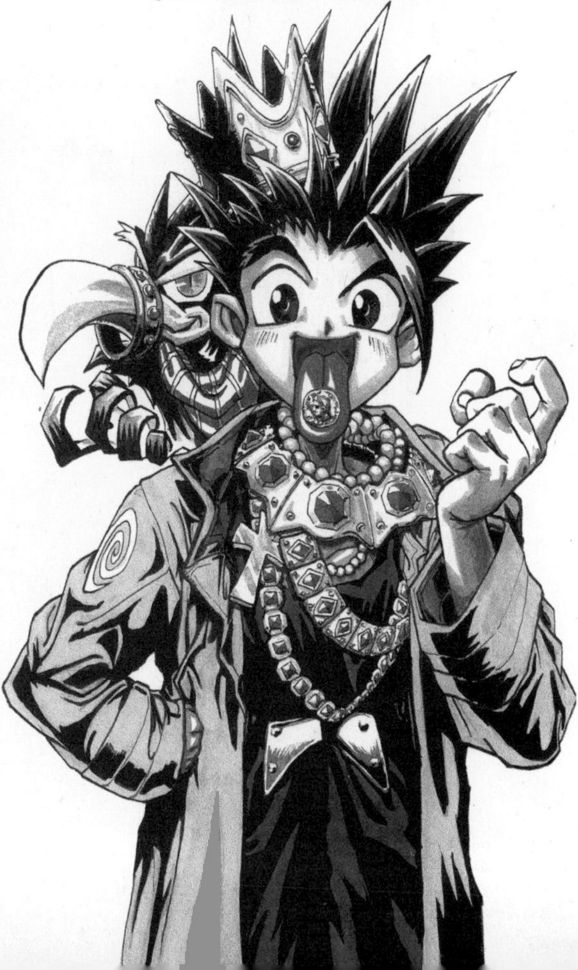

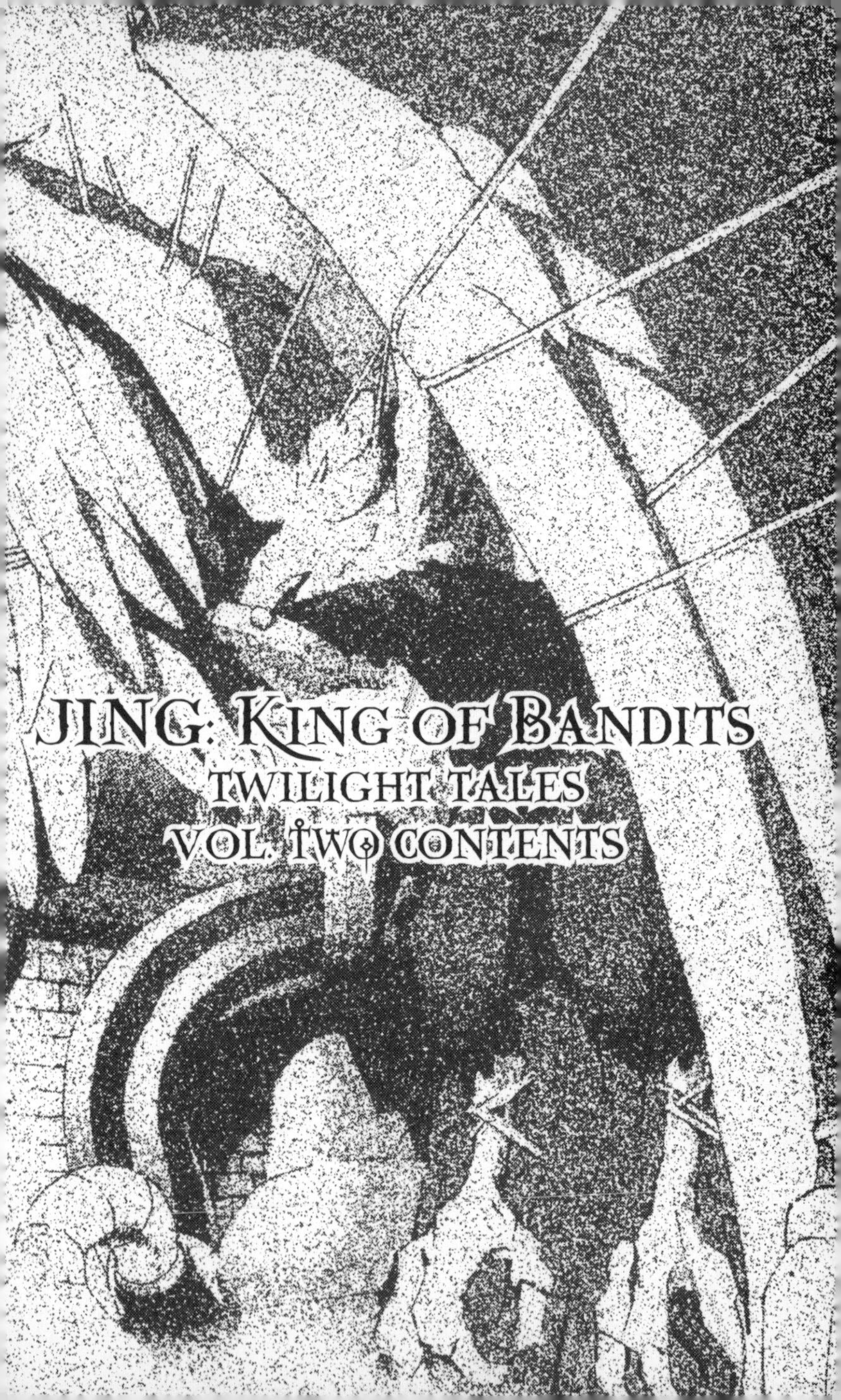
JING: KING OF BANDITS
TWILIGHT TALES
VOL. TWO CONTENTS

KING OF BANDITS
王ドロボウ JING
TWILIGHT TALES

Story So Far...

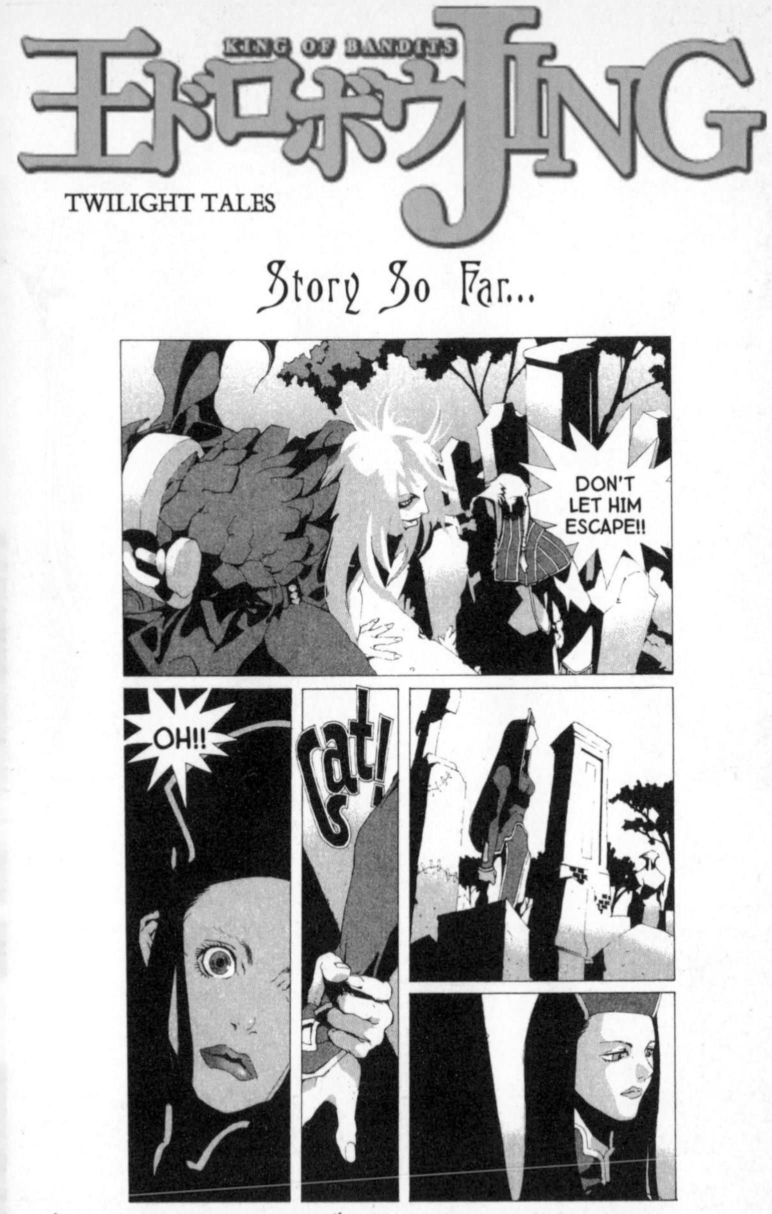
DON'T LET HIM ESCAPE!!
Cat!
OH!!

Jing and Kir arrive at a city called Rusty Nail. Supposedly this strange town is controlled by the brain of "God," which they refer to as the "Shinku." Stealing the brain seems to be on Jing's agenda, but when he's cornered by a group of killer creatures in the town's cemetery, it looks like he might be a guest at his own funeral! The quick-witted Jing is able to escape by abducting one of their associates, a nurse named Shin Lu, who has quite a sad tale to tell...

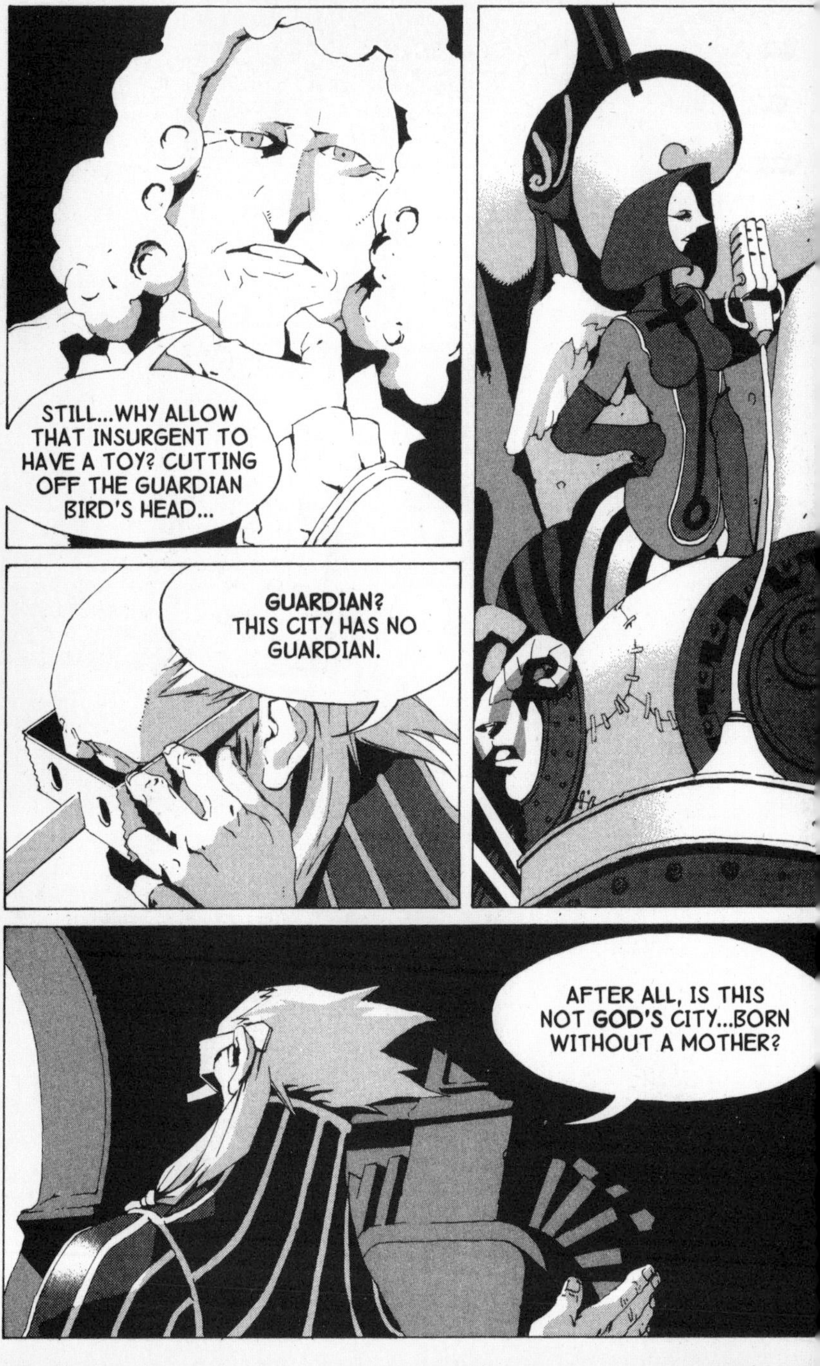
STILL...WHY ALLOW THAT INSURGENT TO HAVE A TOY? CUTTING OFF THE GUARDIAN BIRD'S HEAD...
GUARDIAN? THIS CITY HAS NO GUARDIAN.
AFTER ALL, IS THIS NOT GOD'S CITY...BORN WITHOUT A MOTHER?

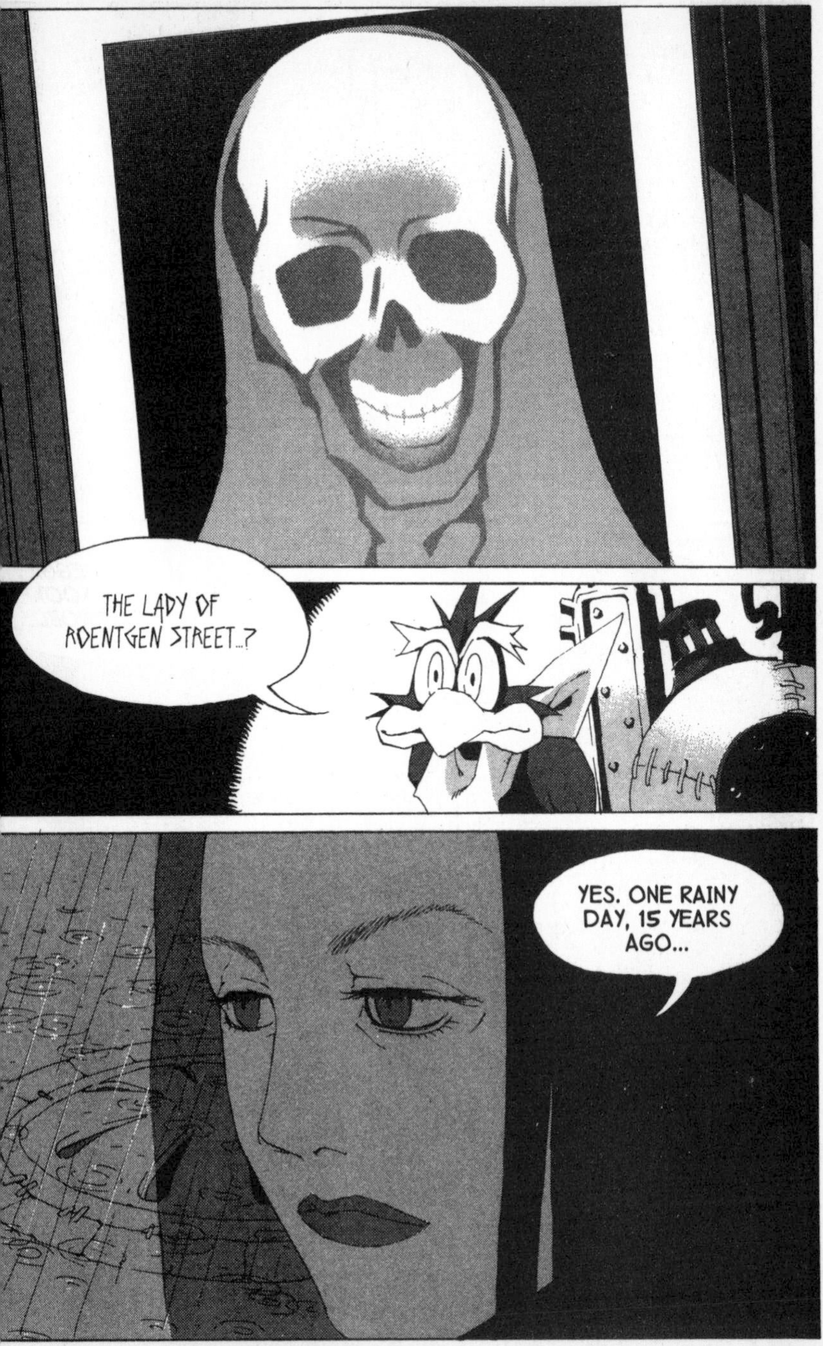
THE LADY OF ROENTGEN STREET...?
YES. ONE RAINY DAY, 15 YEARS AGO...

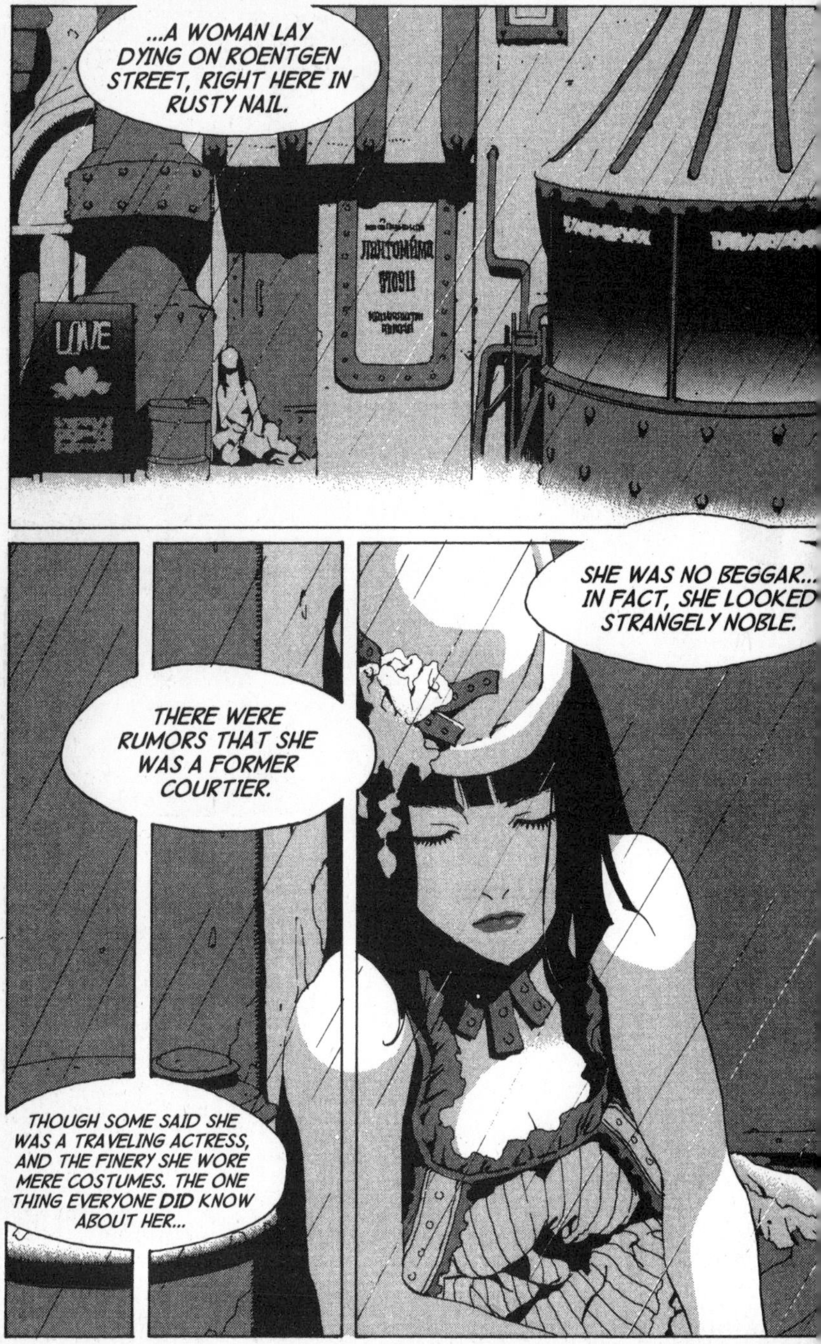
...A WOMAN LAY DYING ON ROENTGEN STREET, RIGHT HERE IN RUSTY NAIL.
SHE WAS NO BEGGAR... IN FACT, SHE LOOKED STRANGELY NOBLE.
THERE WERE RUMORS THAT SHE WAS A FORMER COURTIER.
THOUGH SOME SAID SHE WAS A TRAVELING ACTRESS, AND THE FINERY SHE WORE MERE COSTUMES. THE ONE THING EVERYONE DID KNOW ABOUT HER...

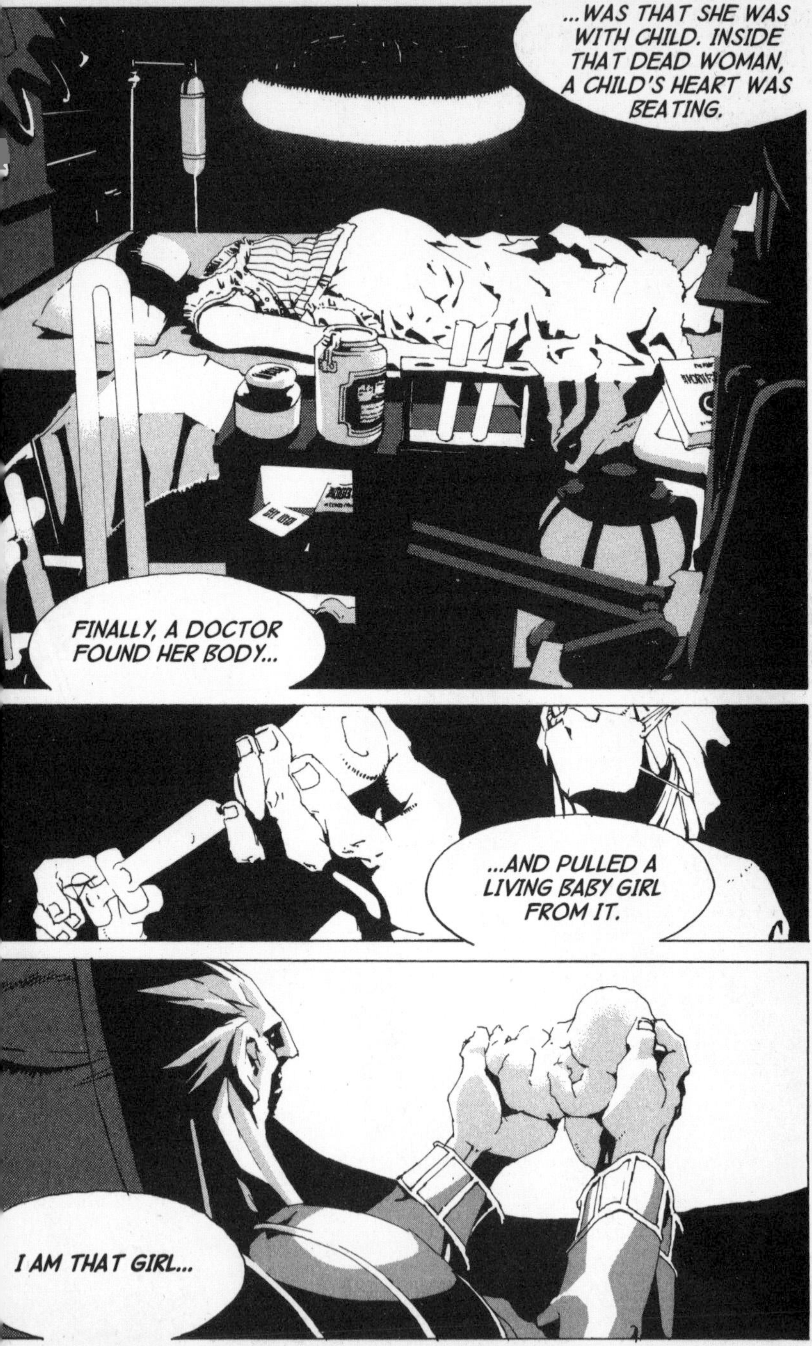
...WAS THAT SHE WAS WITH CHILD. INSIDE THAT DEAD WOMAN, A CHILD'S HEART WAS BEATING.
FINALLY, A DOCTOR FOUND HER BODY...
...AND PULLED A LIVING BABY GIRL FROM IT.
I AM THAT GIRL...

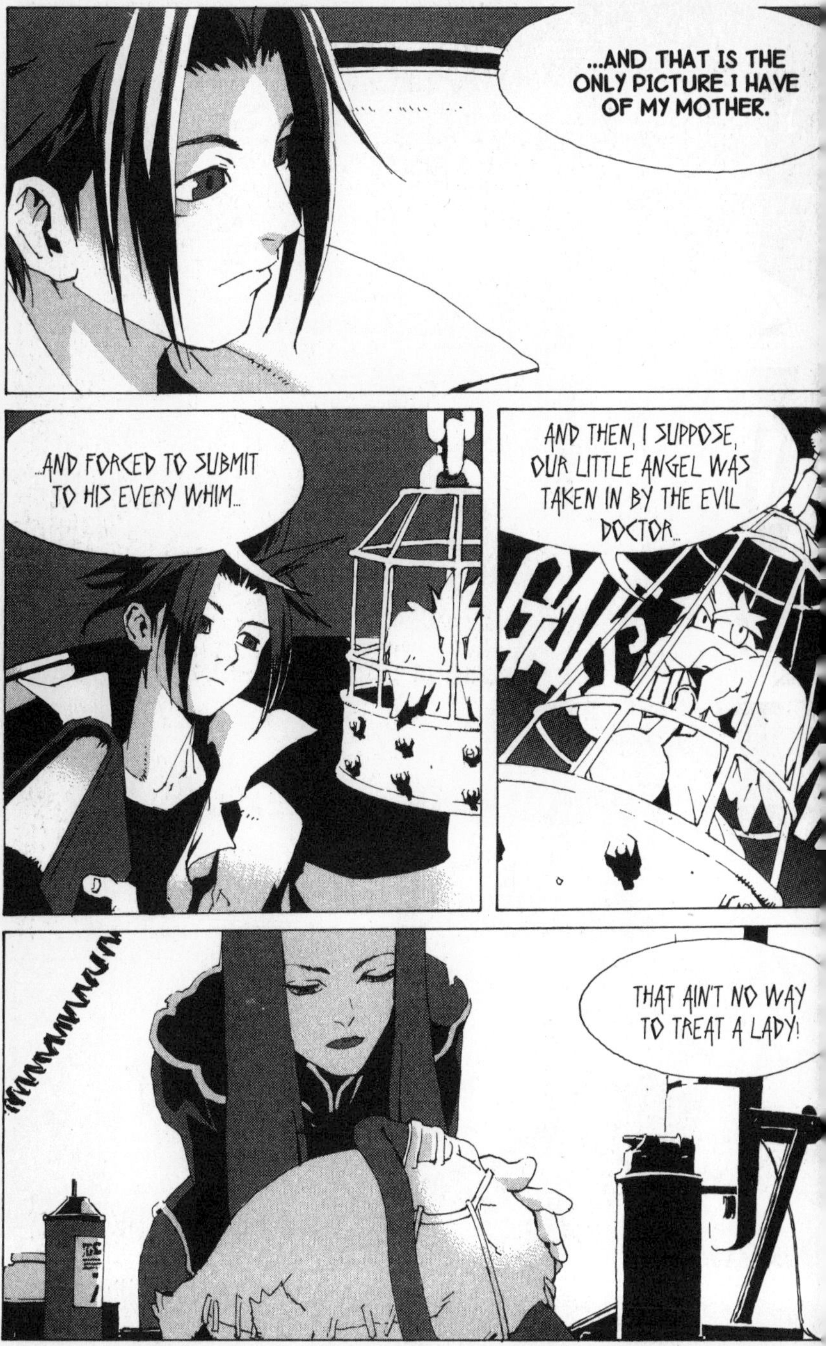
...AND THAT IS THE ONLY PICTURE I HAVE OF MY MOTHER.
AND THEN, I SUPPOSE, OUR LITTLE ANGEL WAS TAKEN IN BY THE EVIL DOCTOR...
...AND FORCED TO SUBMIT TO HIS EVERY WHIM...
THAT AIN'T NO WAY TO TREAT A LADY!

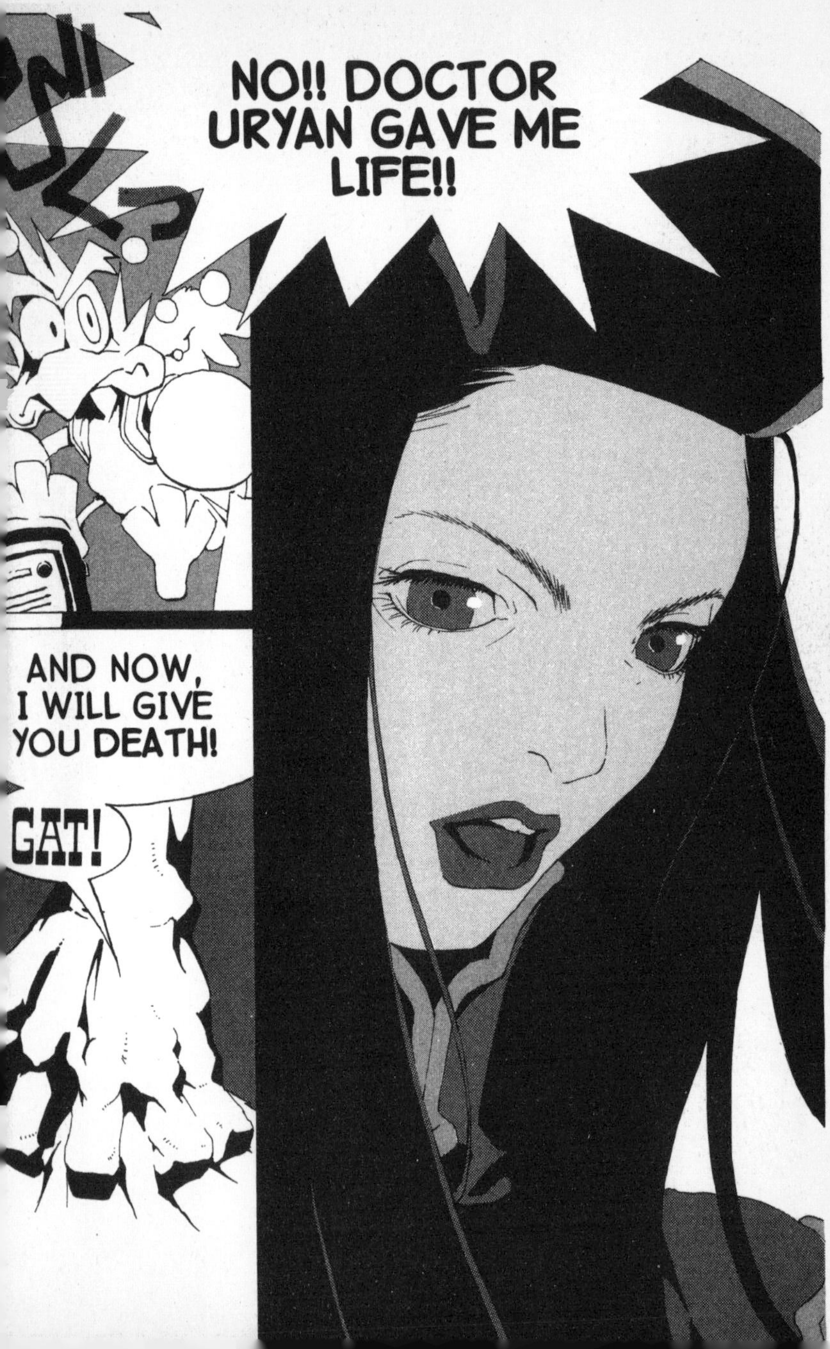
NO!! DOCTOR URYAN GAVE ME LIFE!!
AND NOW, I WILL GIVE YOU DEATH!
GAT!

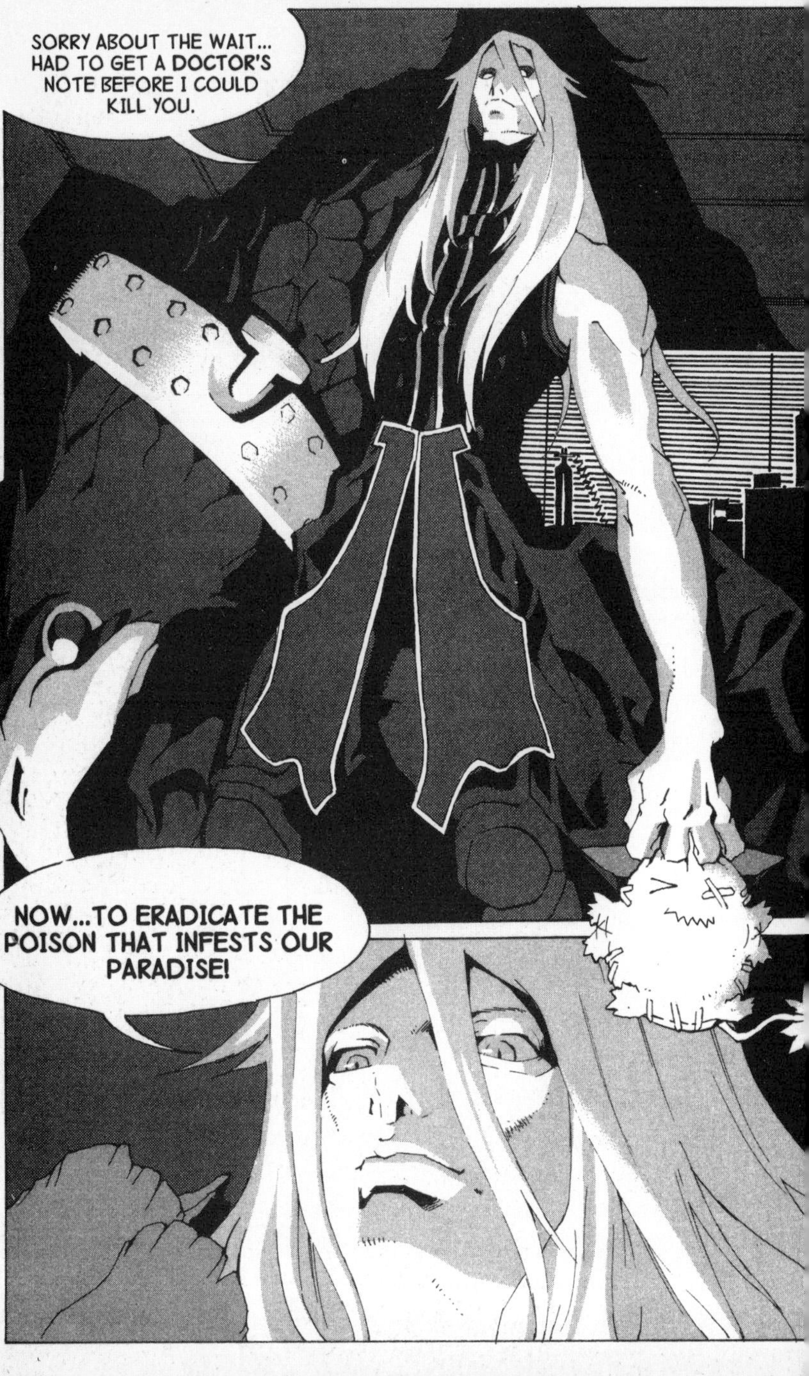
SORRY ABOUT THE WAIT... HAD TO GET A DOCTOR'S NOTE BEFORE I COULD KILL YOU.
NOW...TO ERADICATE THE POISON THAT INFESTS OUR PARADISE!

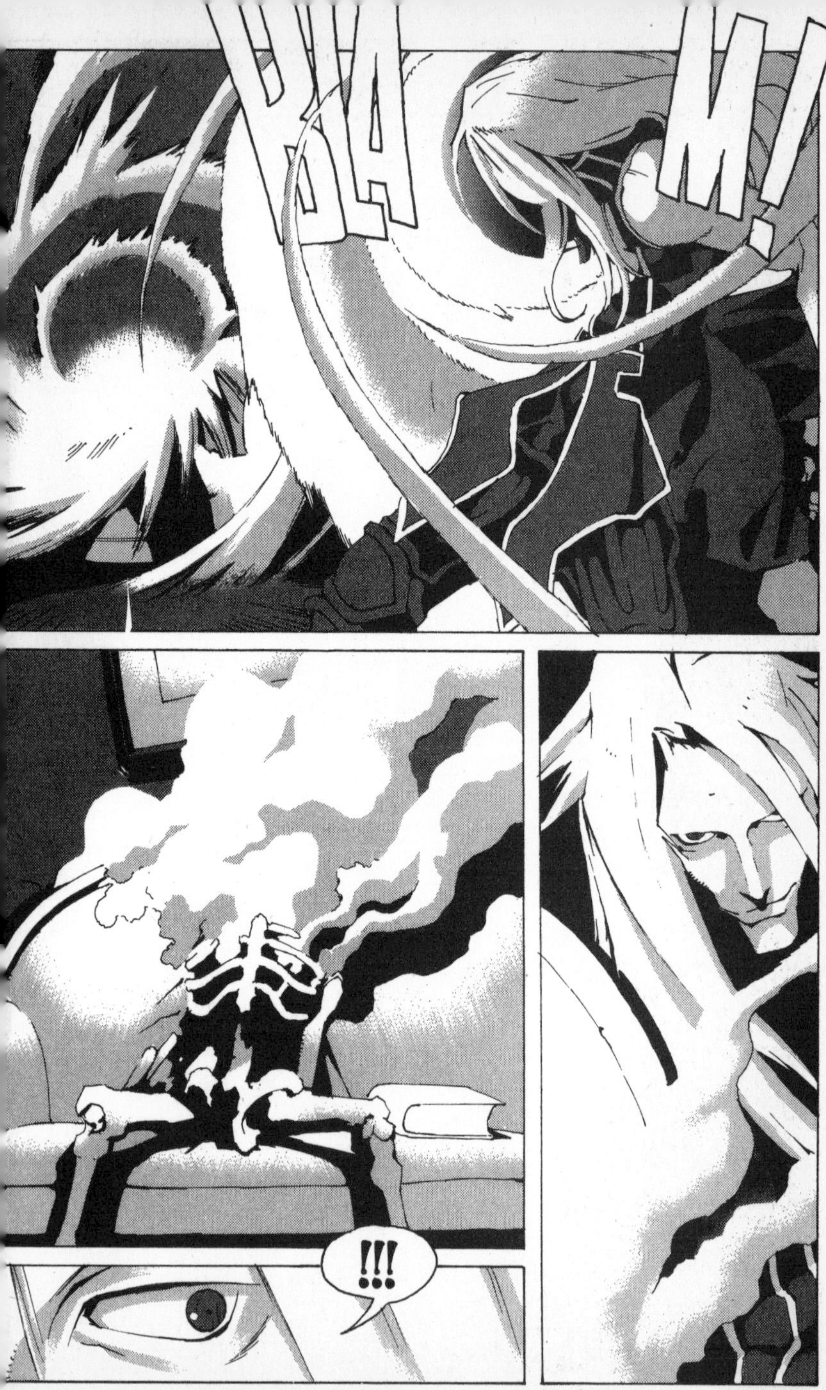
BLAM!
!!!

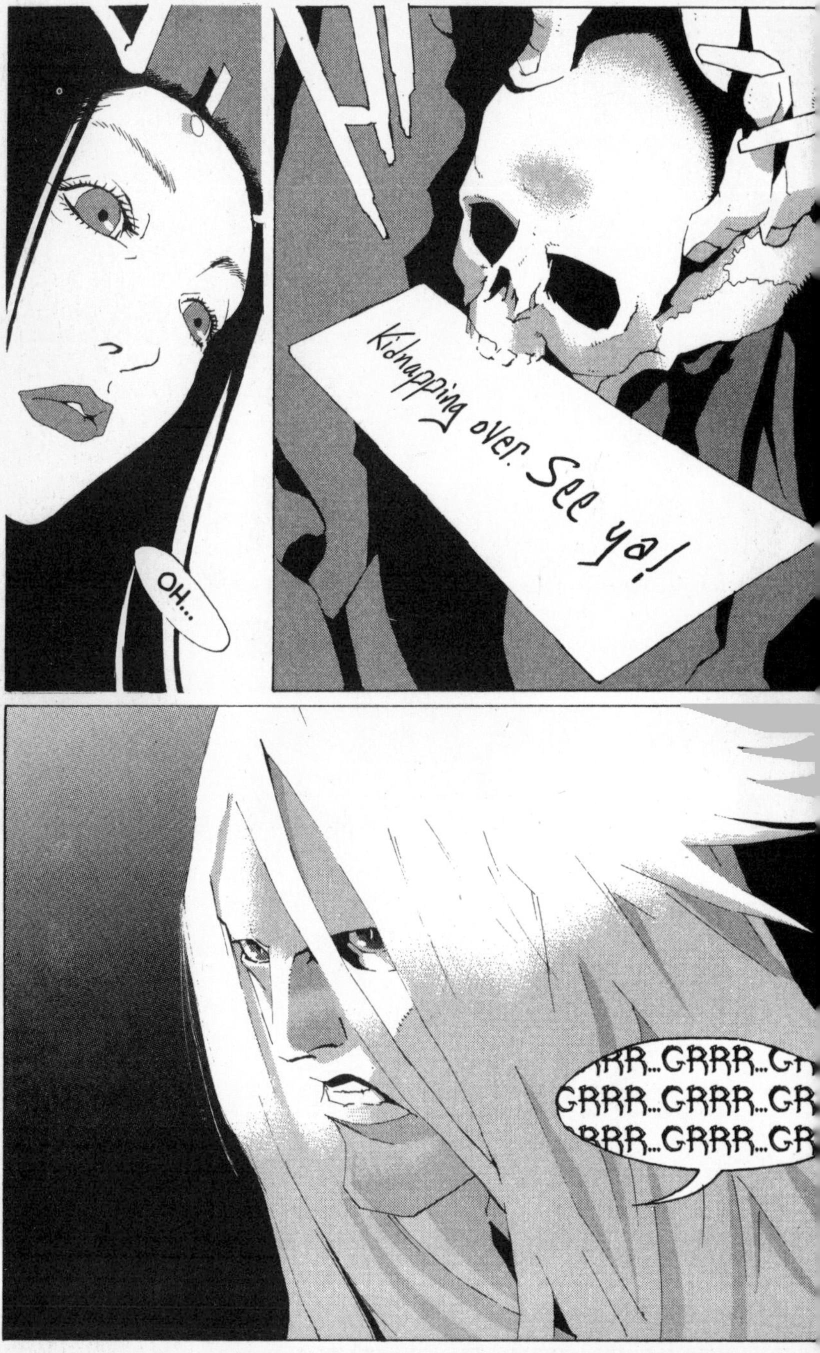
Kidnapping over. See ya!
OH...
RRR...GRRR...GR GRRR...GRRR...GR RRR...GRRR...GR

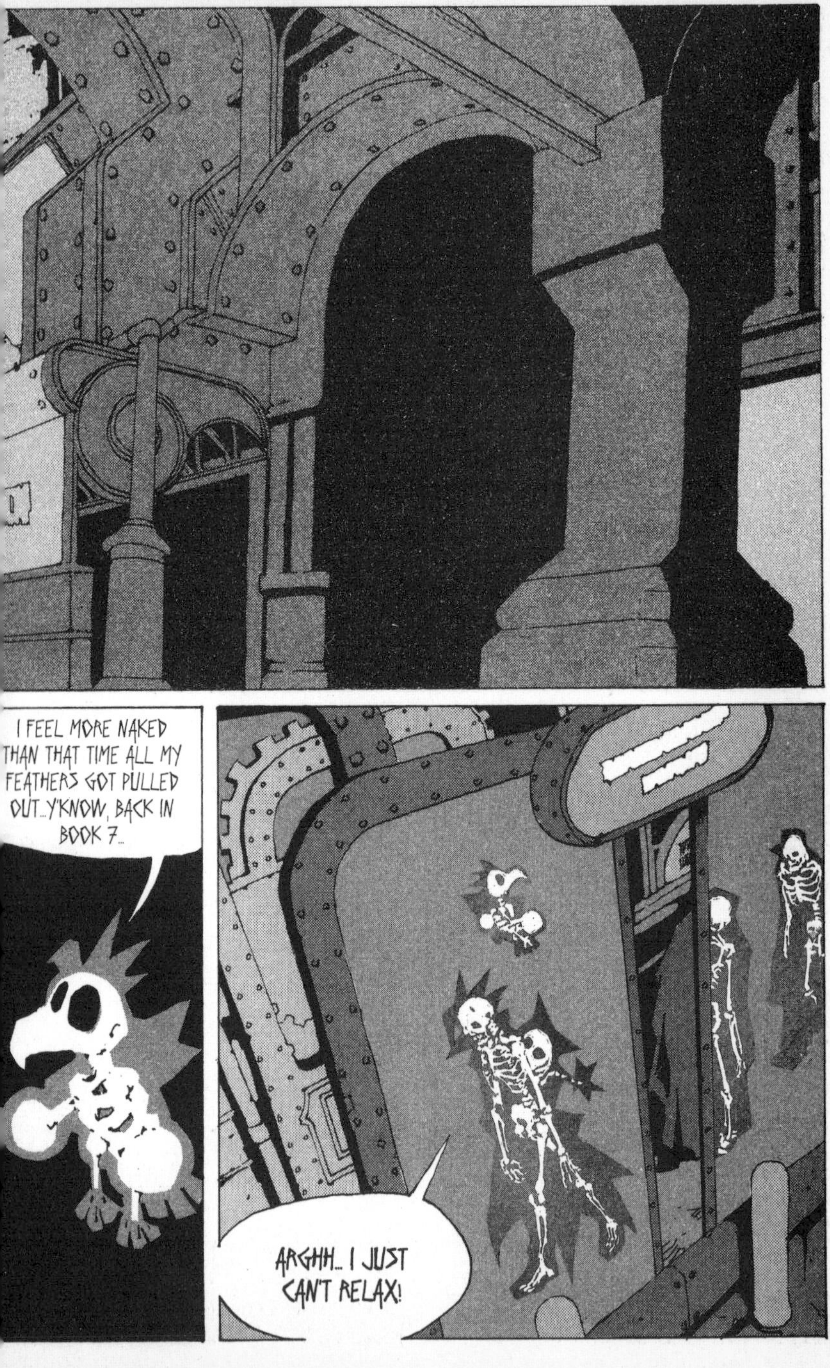
ARGHH... I JUST CAN'T RELAX!
I FEEL MORE NAKED THAN THAT TIME ALL MY FEATHERS GOT PULLED OUT...Y'KNOW, BACK IN BOOK 7...

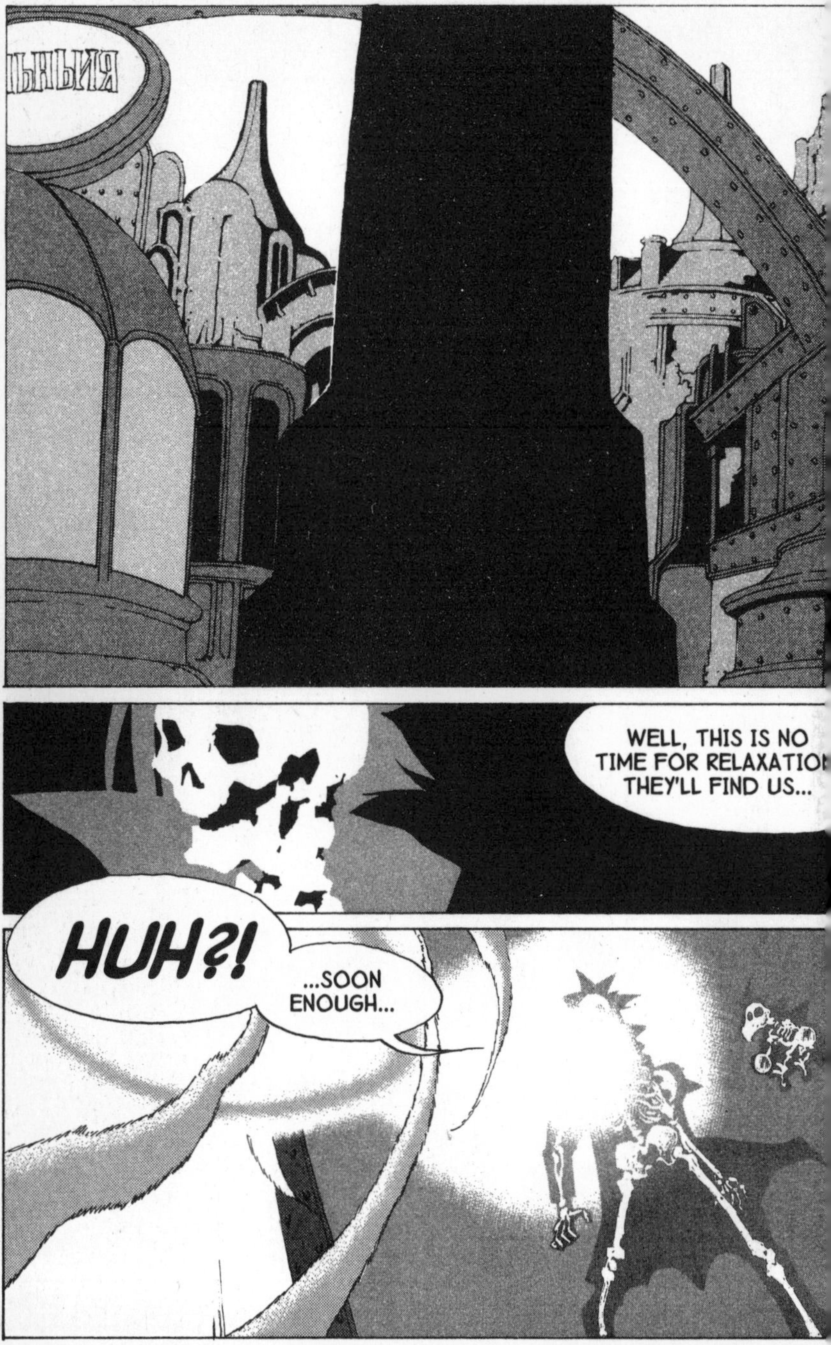
WELL, THIS IS NO TIME FOR RELAXATIO THEY'LL FIND US...
...SOON ENOUGH...
HUH?!

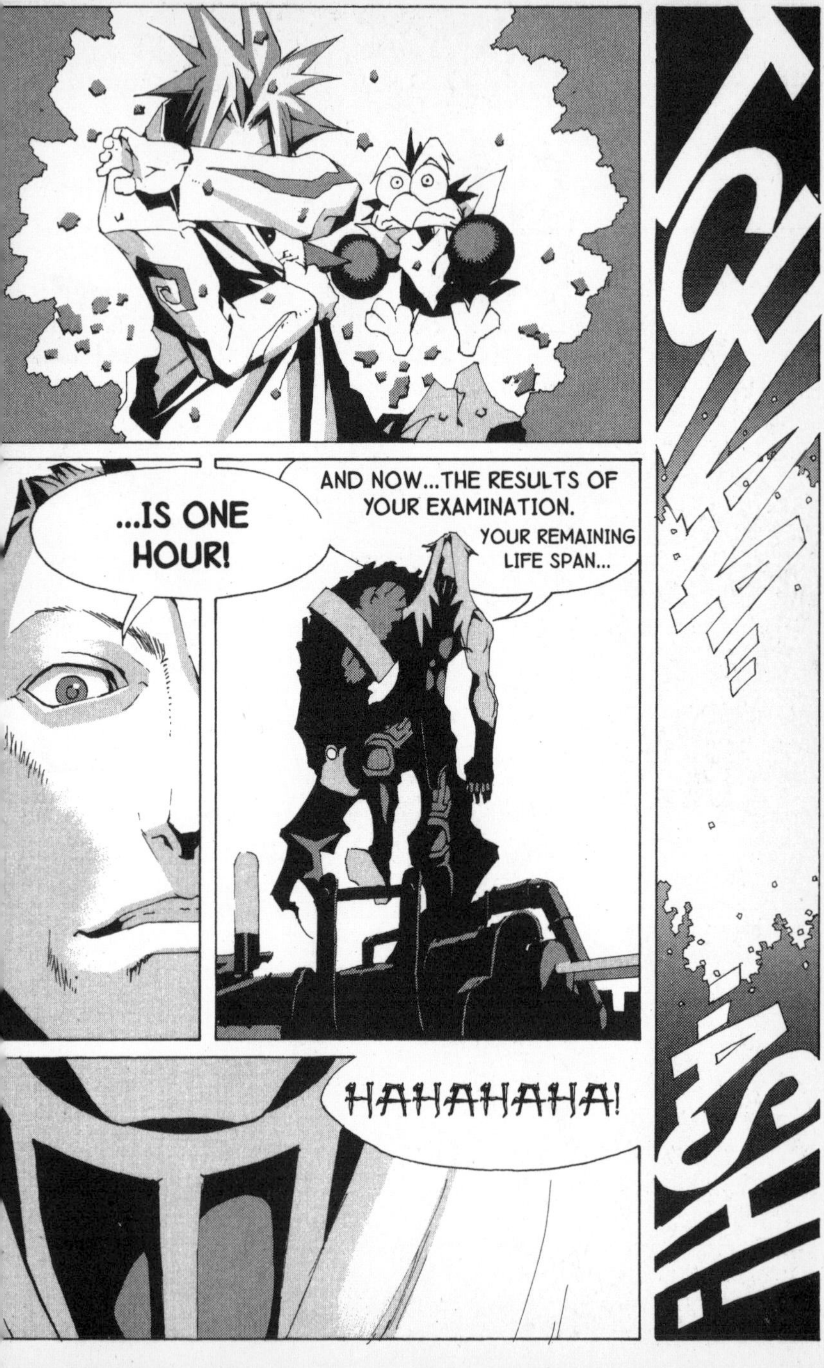
TCHA
ASH!
AND NOW...THE RESULTS OF YOUR EXAMINATION.
YOUR REMAINING LIFE SPAN...
...IS ONE HOUR!
HAHAHAHA!

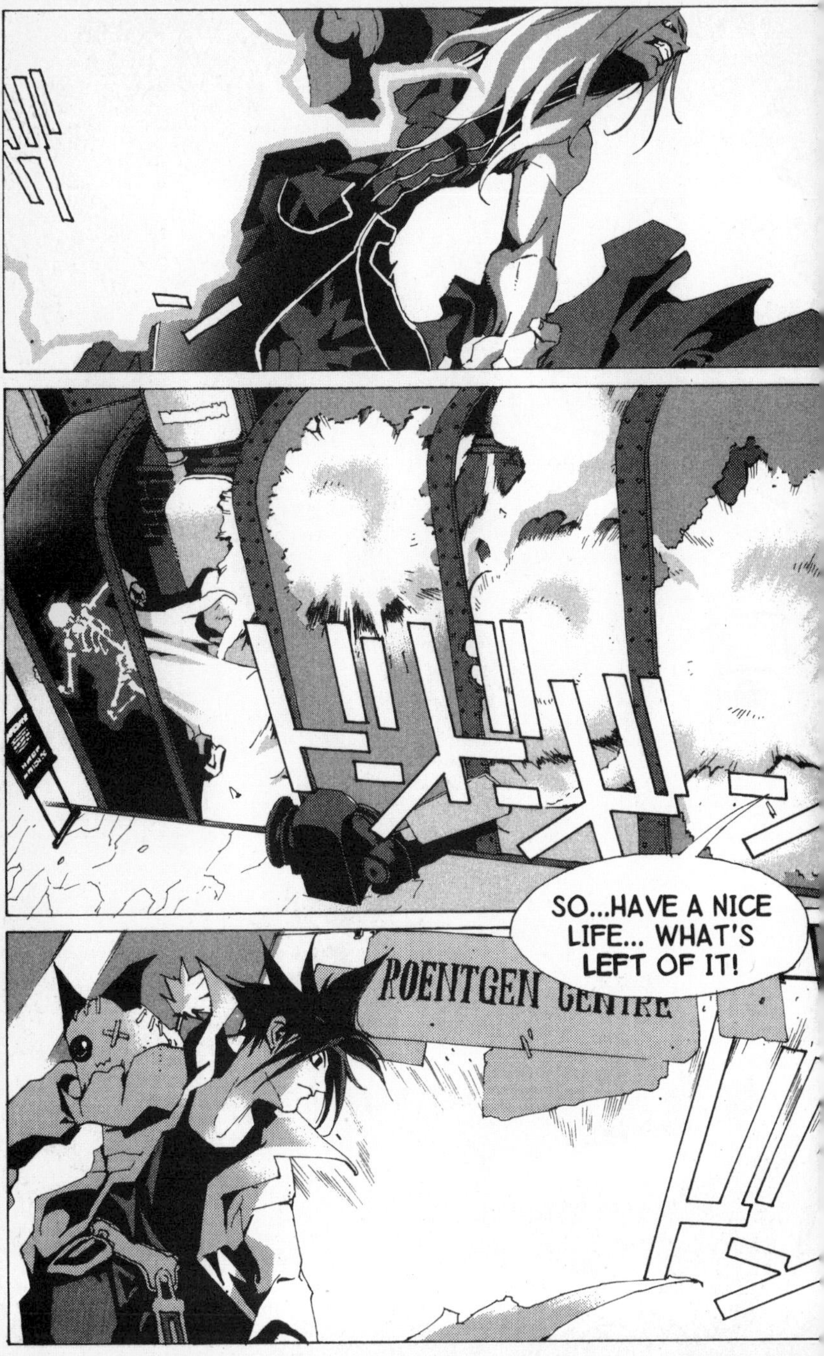

SO...HAVE A NICE LIFE... WHAT'S LEFT OF IT!
ROENTGEN CENTRE

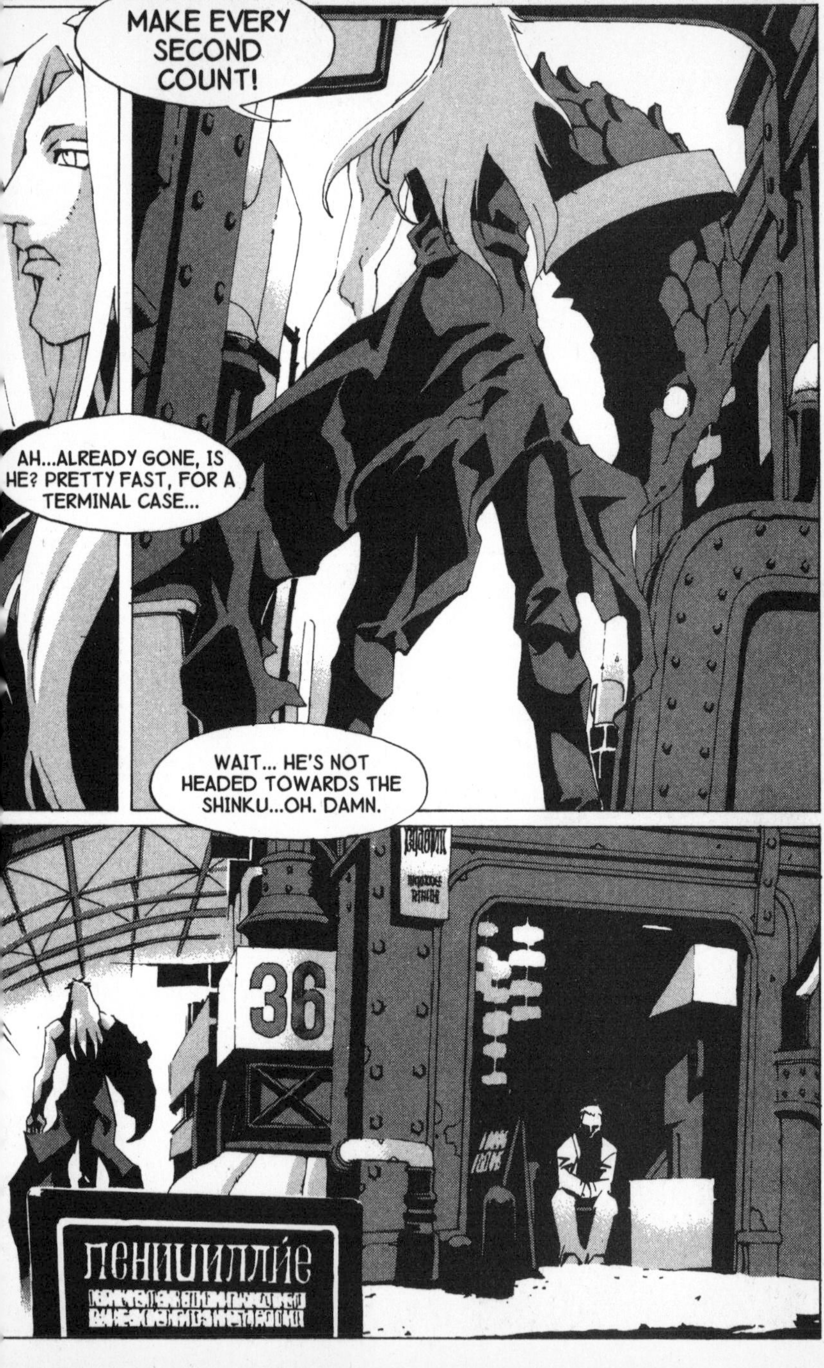
MAKE EVERY SECOND COUNT!
AH...ALREADY GONE, IS HE? PRETTY FAST, FOR A TERMINAL CASE...
WAIT... HE'S NOT HEADED TOWARDS THE SHINKU...OH. DAMN.
36

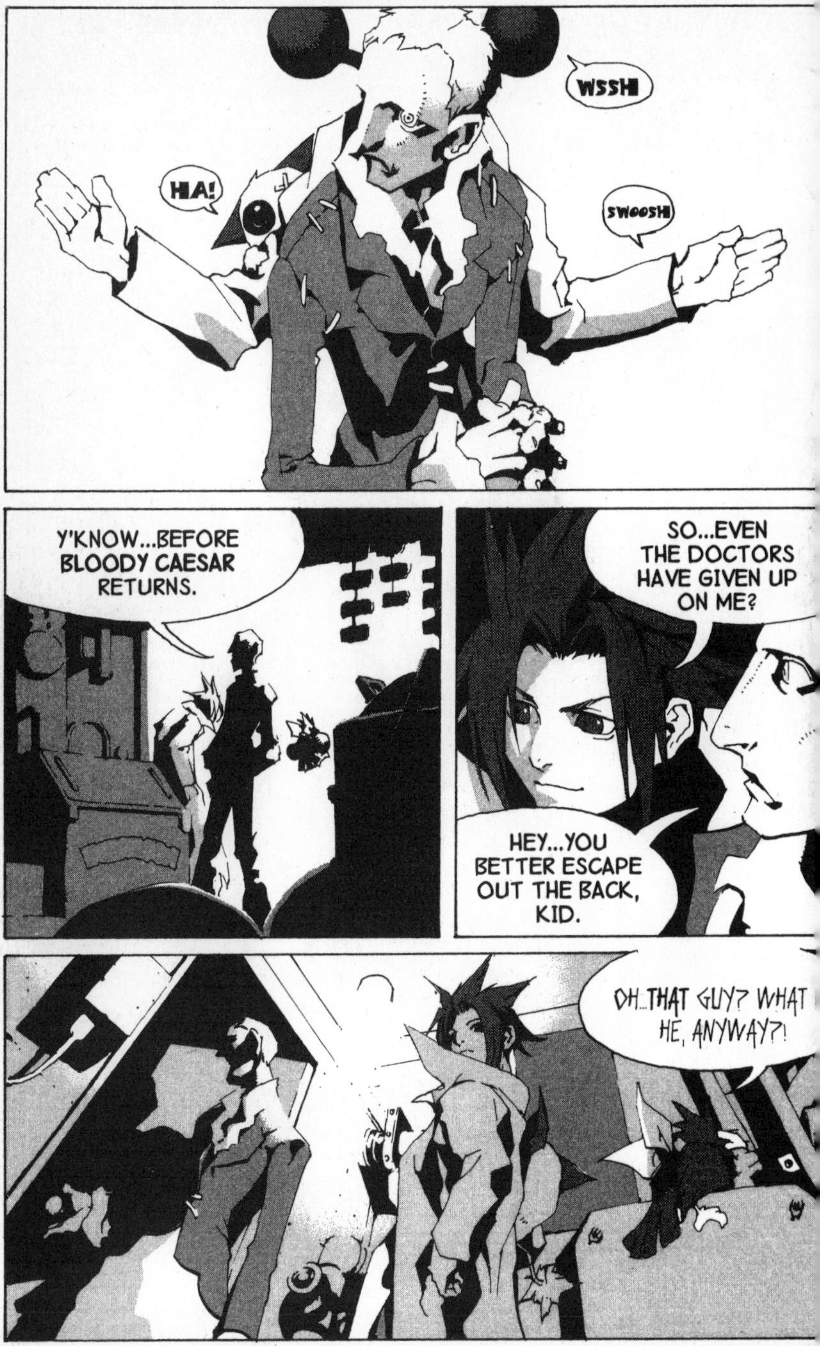
WSSH
SWOOSH
HA!
SO...EVEN THE DOCTORS HAVE GIVEN UP ON ME?
HEY...YOU BETTER ESCAPE OUT THE BACK, KID.
Y'KNOW...BEFORE BLOODY CAESAR RETURNS.
OH...THAT GUY? WHAT HE, ANYWAY?!

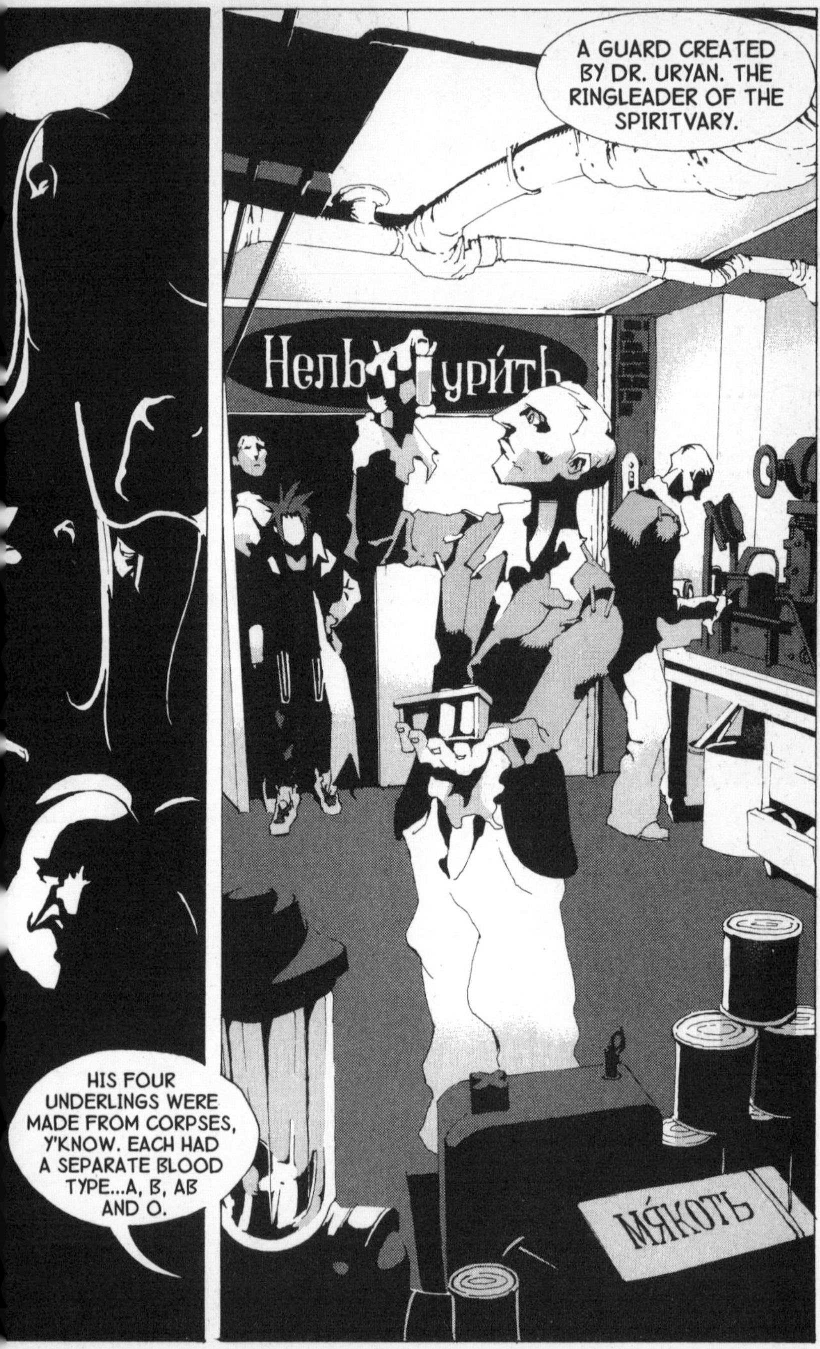

A GUARD CREATED BY DR. URYAN. THE RINGLEADER OF THE SPIRITVARY.
МЯКОТЬ
HIS FOUR UNDERLINGS WERE MADE FROM CORPSES, Y'KNOW. EACH HAD A SEPARATE BLOOD TYPE...A, B, AB AND O.

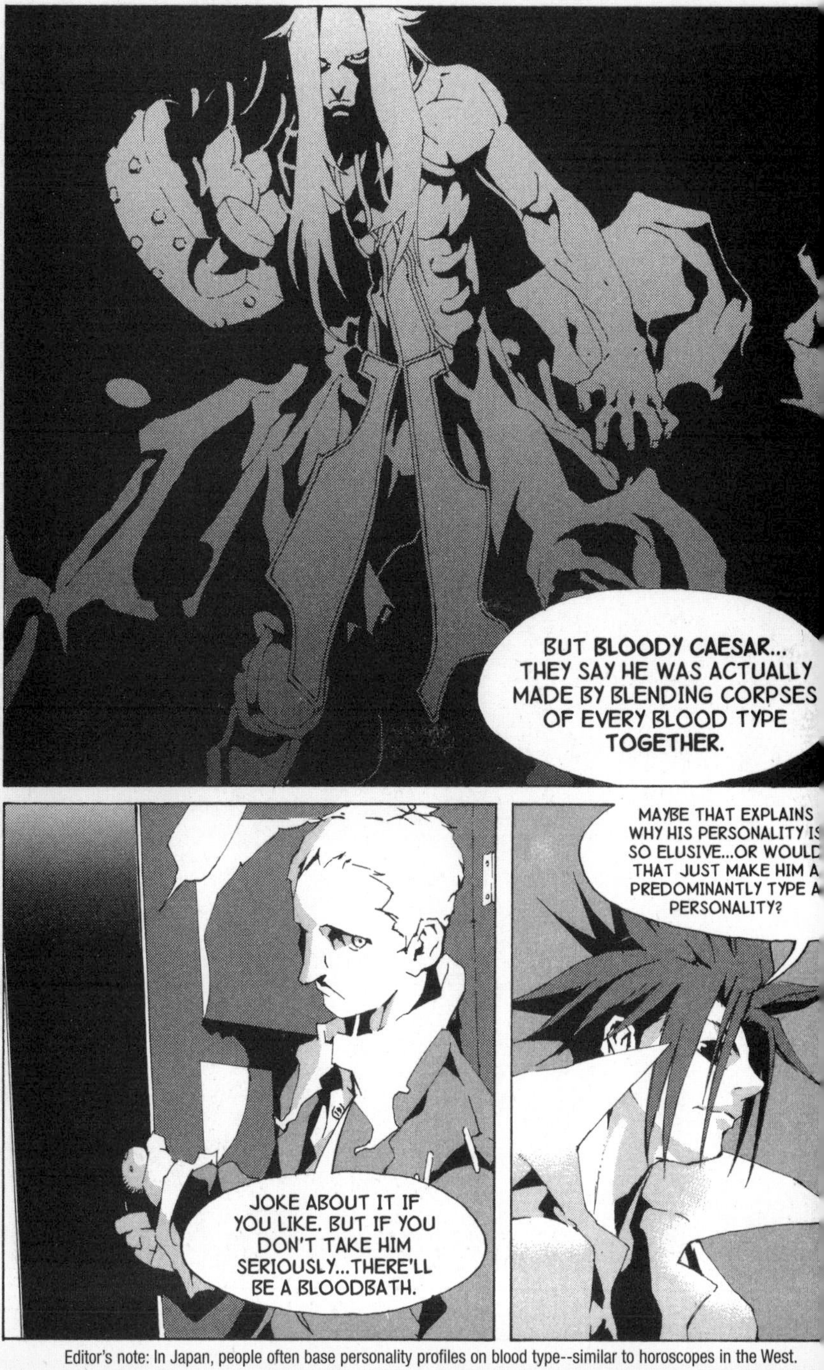
BUT BLOODY CAESAR... THEY SAY HE WAS ACTUALLY MADE BY BLENDING CORPSES OF EVERY BLOOD TYPE TOGETHER.
MAYBE THAT EXPLAINS WHY HIS PERSONALITY IS SO ELUSIVE...OR WOULD THAT JUST MAKE HIM A PREDOMINANTLY TYPE A PERSONALITY?
JOKE ABOUT IT IF YOU LIKE. BUT IF YOU DON'T TAKE HIM SERIOUSLY...THERE'LL BE A BLOODBATH.

Editor's note: In Japan, people often base personality profiles on blood type--similar to horoscopes in the West.

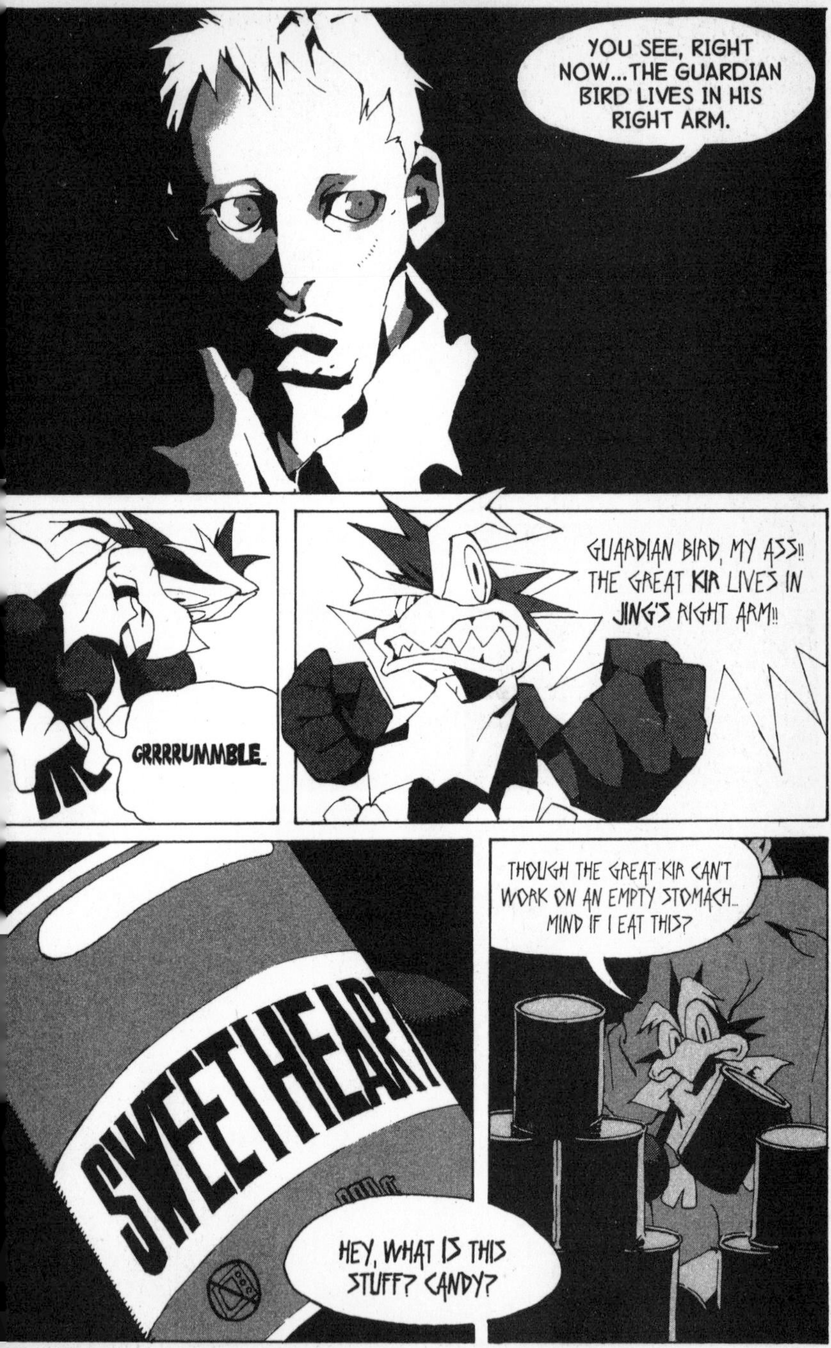
YOU SEE, RIGHT NOW...THE GUARDIAN BIRD LIVES IN HIS RIGHT ARM.
GUARDIAN BIRD, MY ASS!! THE GREAT KIR LIVES IN JING'S RIGHT ARM!!
GRRRRUMMBLE
THOUGH THE GREAT KIR CAN'T WORK ON AN EMPTY STOMACH... MIND IF I EAT THIS?
SWEETHEART
HEY, WHAT IS THIS STUFF? CANDY?

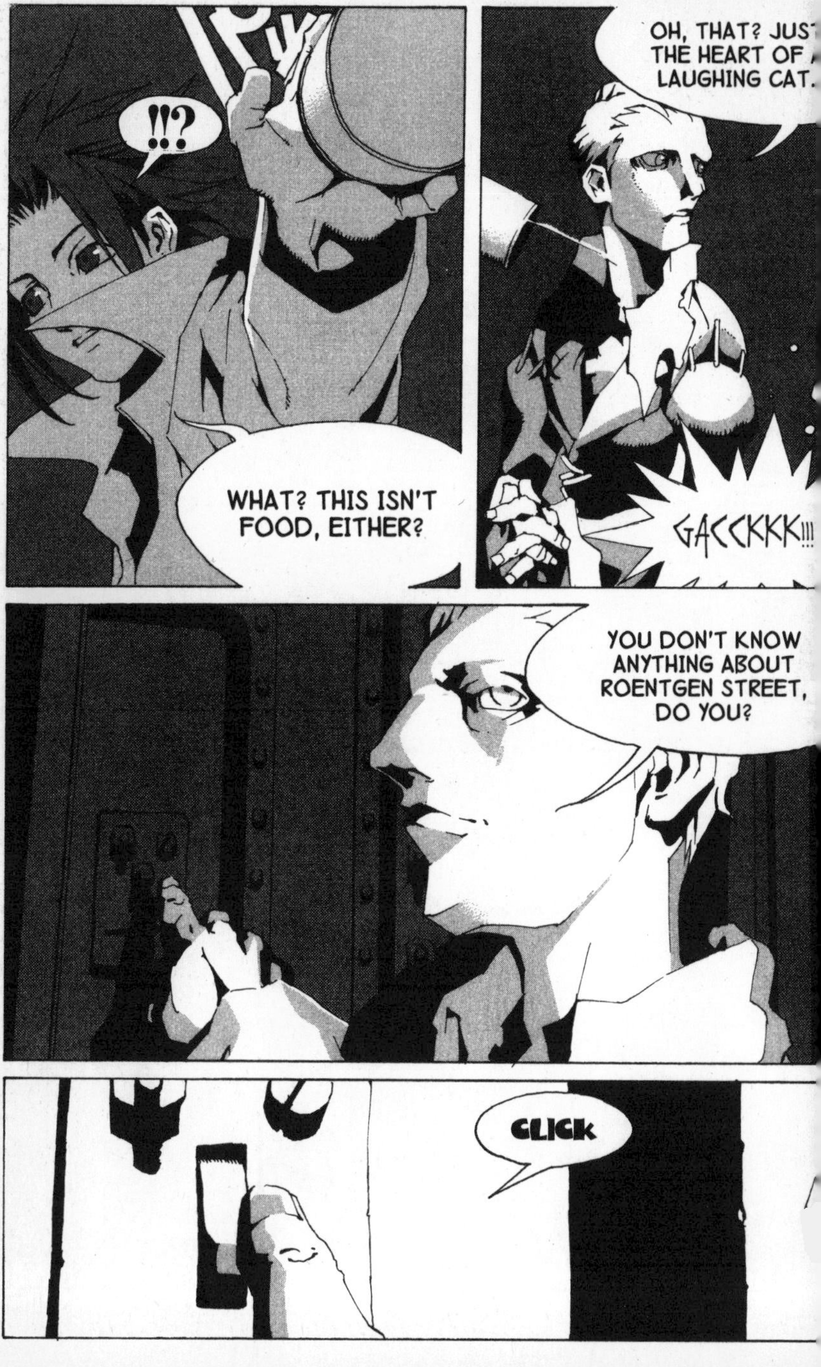
OH, THAT? JUST THE HEART OF A LAUGHING CAT.
GACCKKK!!!
!!?
WHAT? THIS ISN'T FOOD, EITHER?
YOU DON'T KNOW ANYTHING ABOUT ROENTGEN STREET, DO YOU?
CLICK

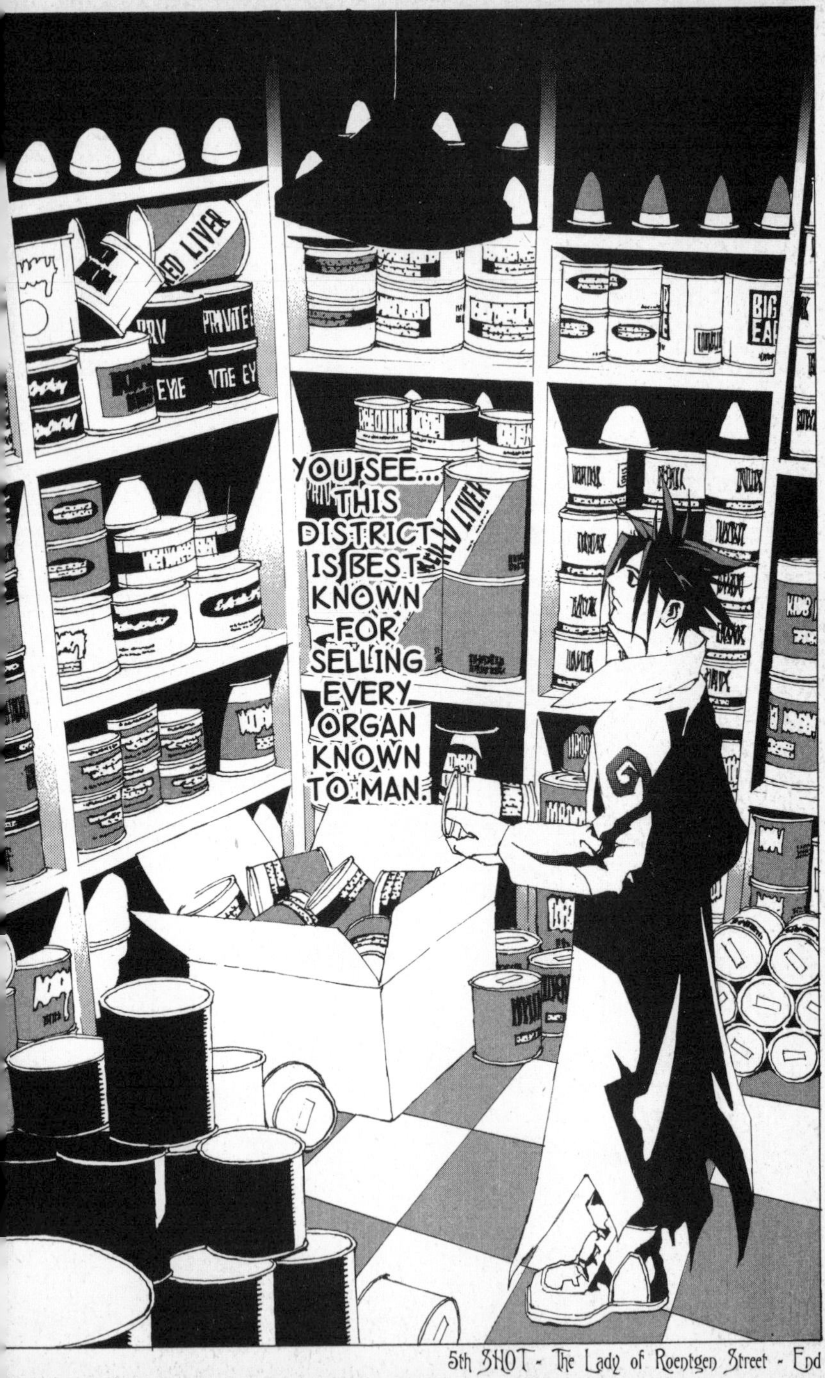
YOU SEE... THIS DISTRICT IS BEST KNOWN FOR SELLING EVERY ORGAN KNOWN TO MAN.

5th SHOT - The Lady of Roentgen Street - End

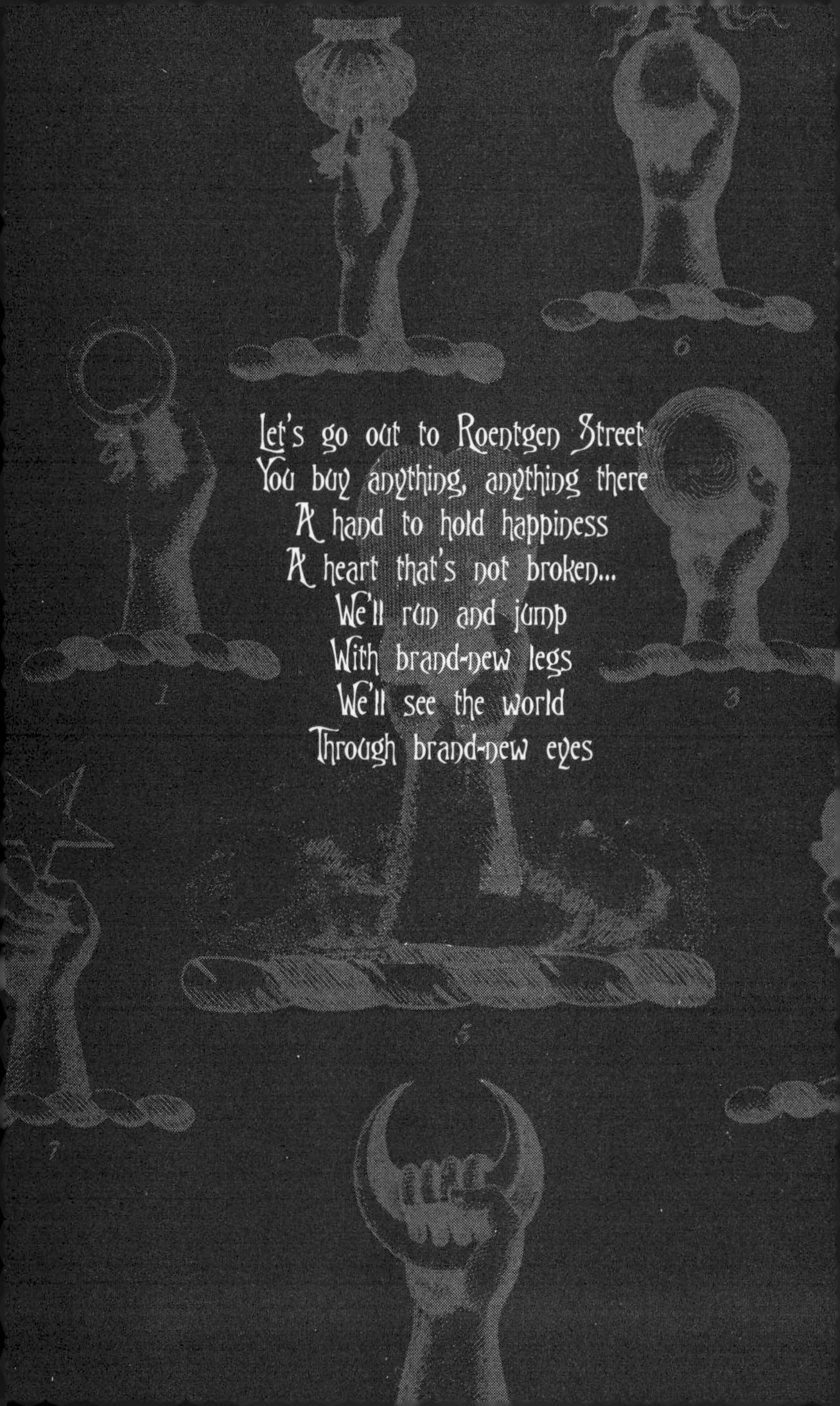

Let's go out to Roentgen Street
You buy anything, anything there
A hand to hold happiness
A heart that's not broken...
We'll run and jump
With brand-new legs
We'll see the world
Through brand-new eyes

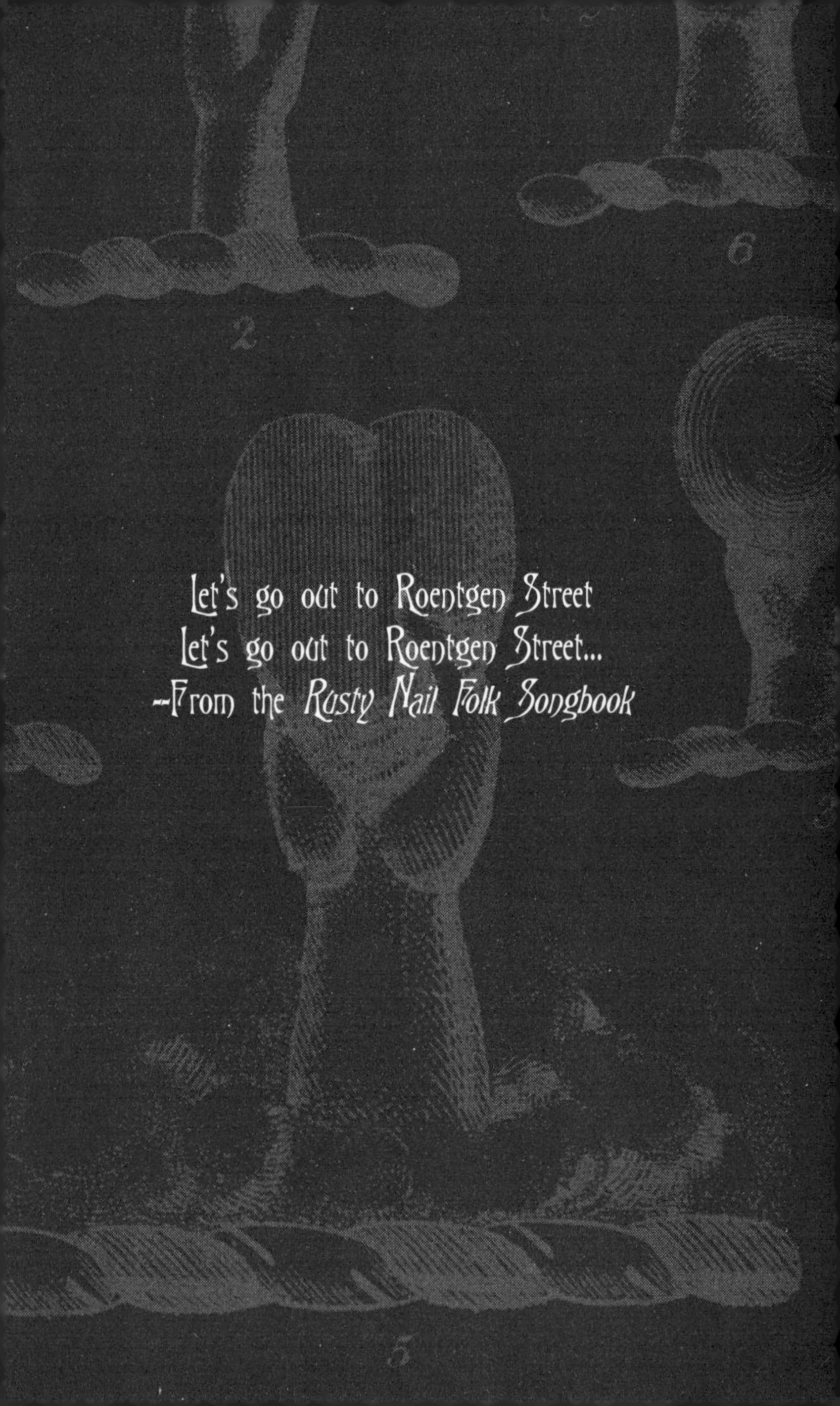
6
2
5

Let's go out to Roentgen Street
Let's go out to Roentgen Street...
--From the *Rusty Nail Folk Songbook*

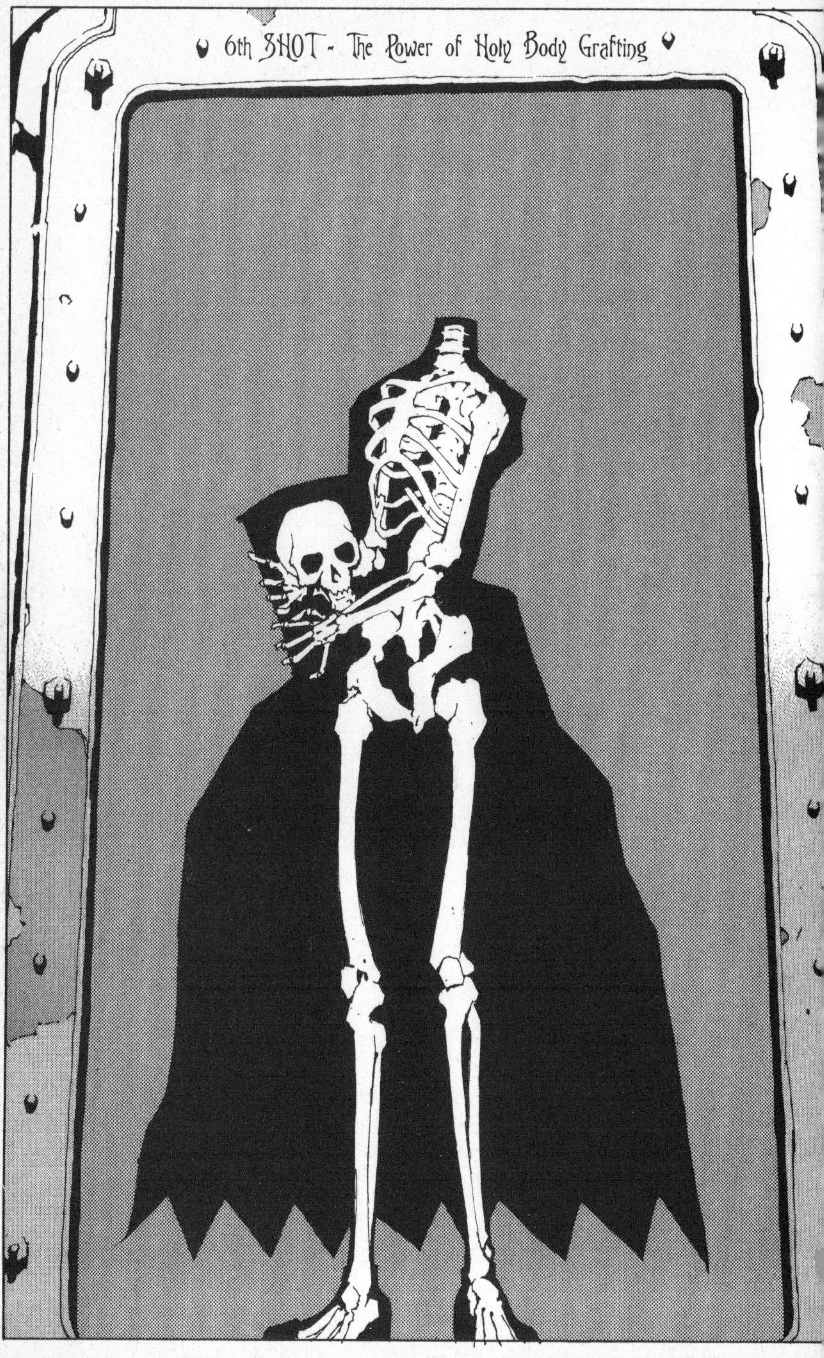
6th SHOT - The Power of Holy Body Grafting

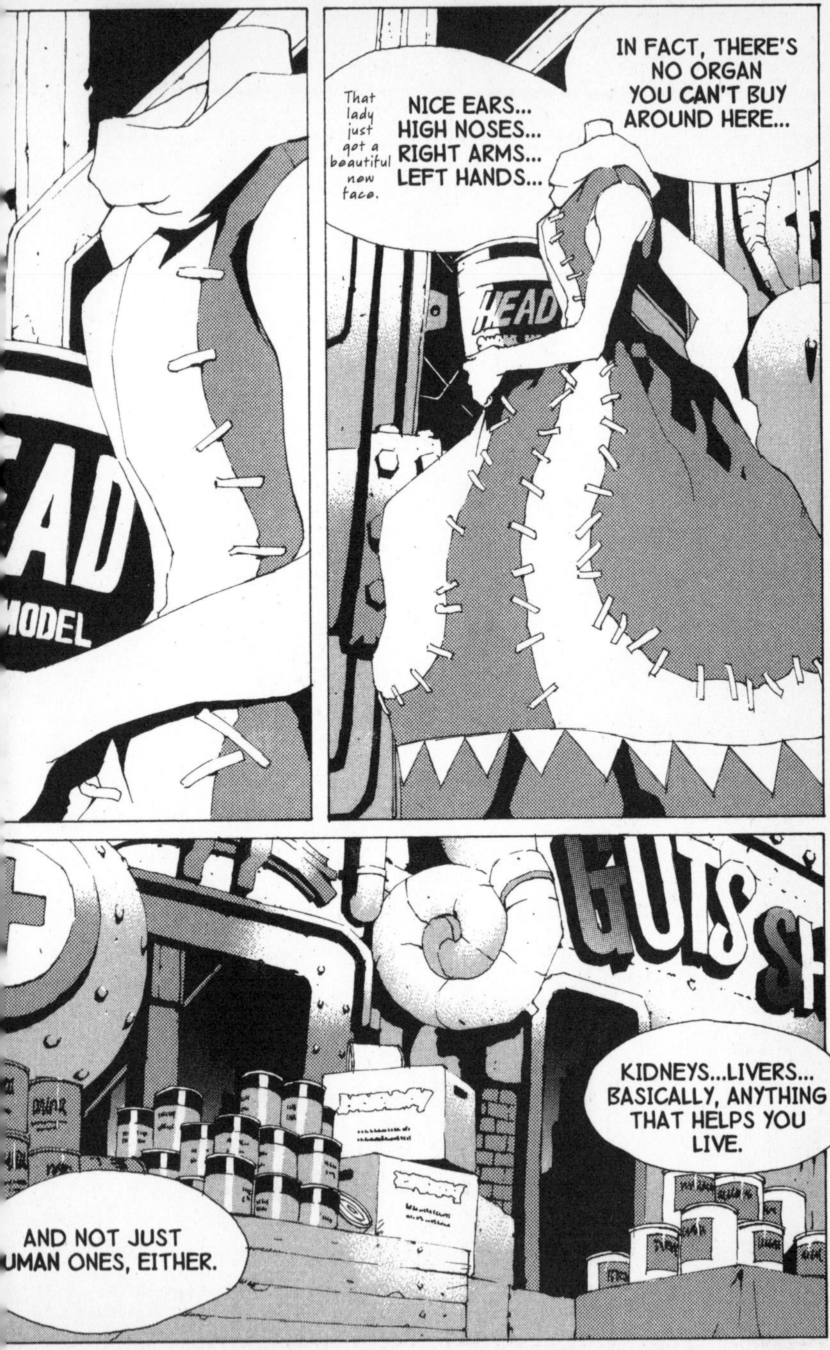
IN FACT, THERE'S NO ORGAN YOU CAN'T BUY AROUND HERE...
NICE EARS... HIGH NOSES... RIGHT ARMS... LEFT HANDS...
That lady just got a beautiful new face.
HEAD
GUTS
KIDNEYS...LIVERS... BASICALLY, ANYTHING THAT HELPS YOU LIVE.
AND NOT JUST UMAN ONES, EITHER.

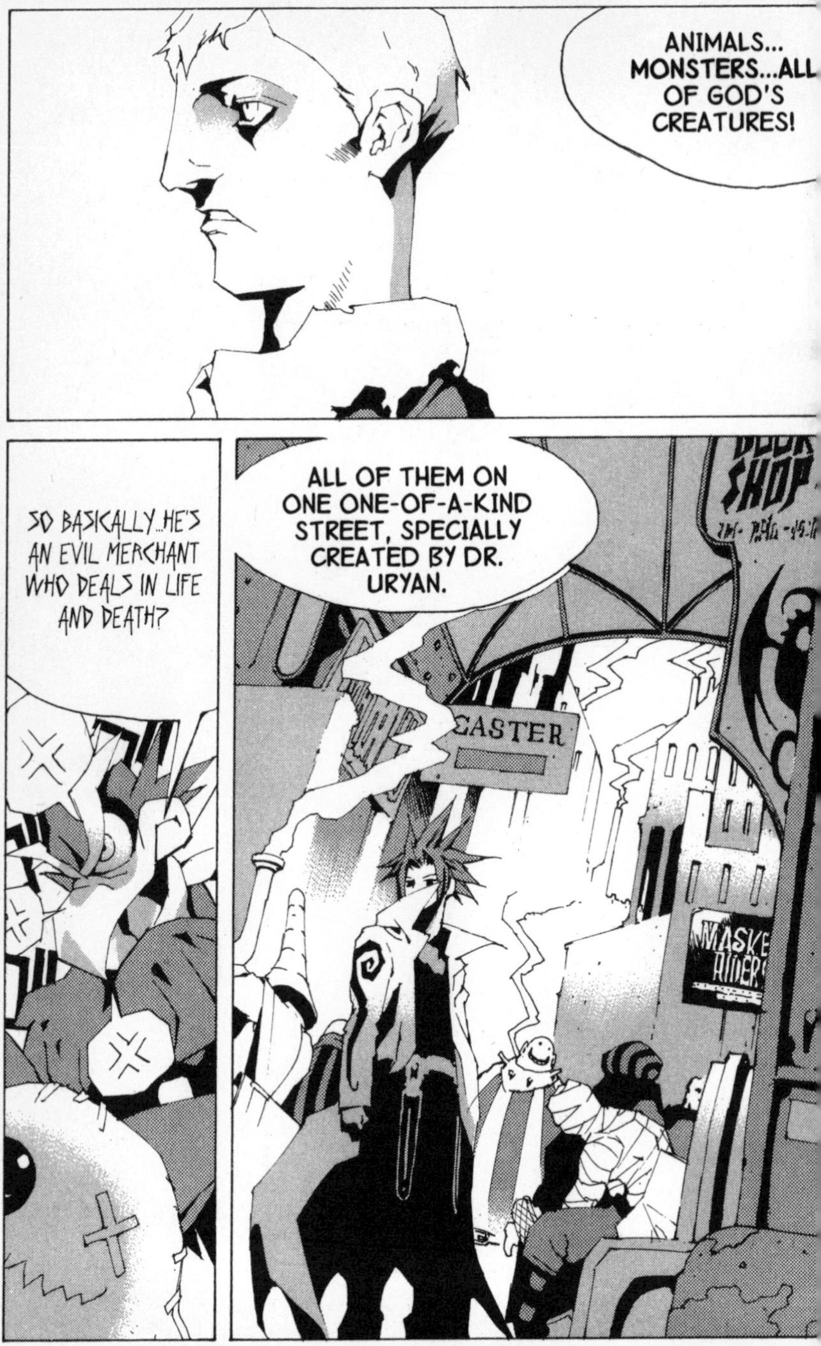
ANIMALS... MONSTERS...ALL OF GOD'S CREATURES!
ALL OF THEM ON ONE ONE-OF-A-KIND STREET, SPECIALLY CREATED BY DR. URYAN.
CASTER
SO BASICALLY...HE'S AN EVIL MERCHANT WHO DEALS IN LIFE AND DEATH?

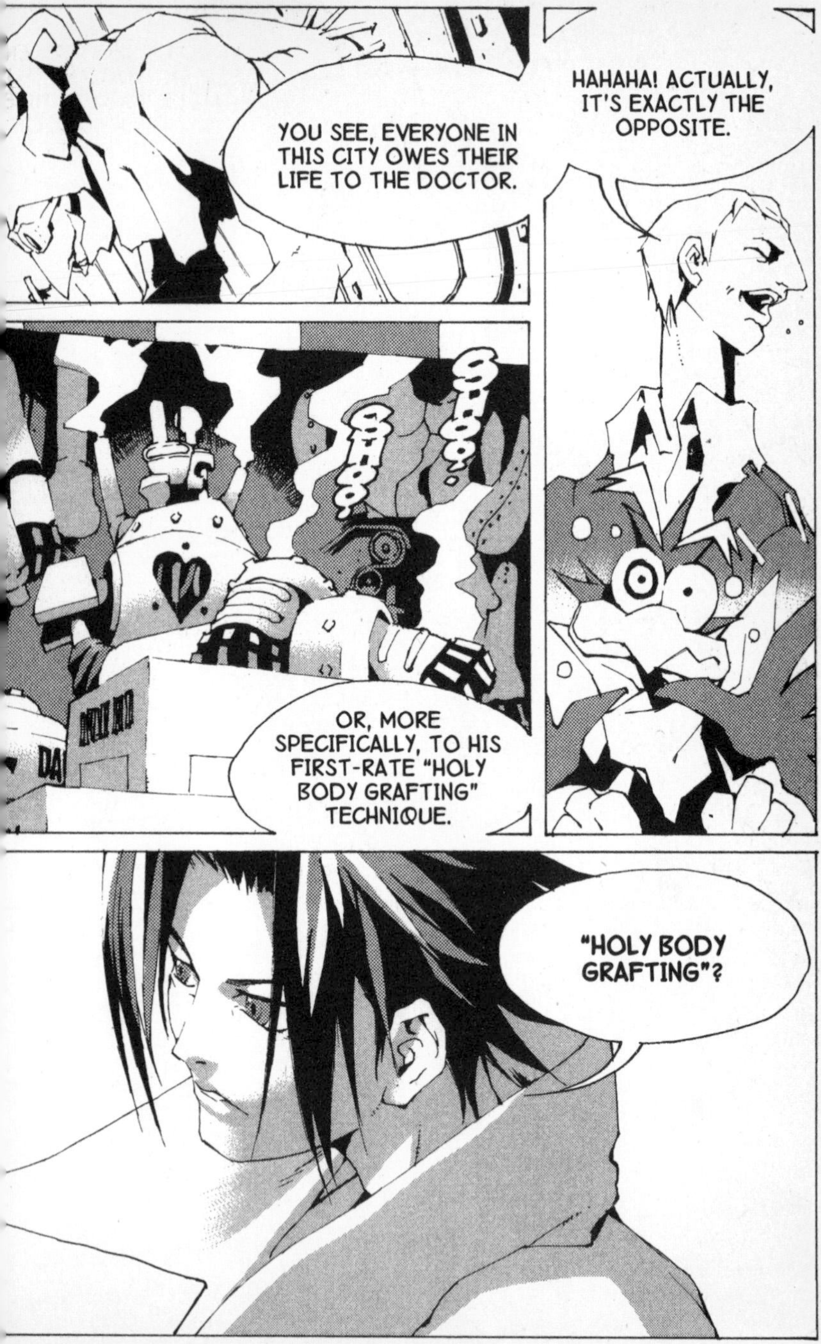
HAHAHA! ACTUALLY, IT'S EXACTLY THE OPPOSITE.
YOU SEE, EVERYONE IN THIS CITY OWES THEIR LIFE TO THE DOCTOR.
OR, MORE SPECIFICALLY, TO HIS FIRST-RATE "HOLY BODY GRAFTING" TECHNIQUE.
"HOLY BODY GRAFTING"?

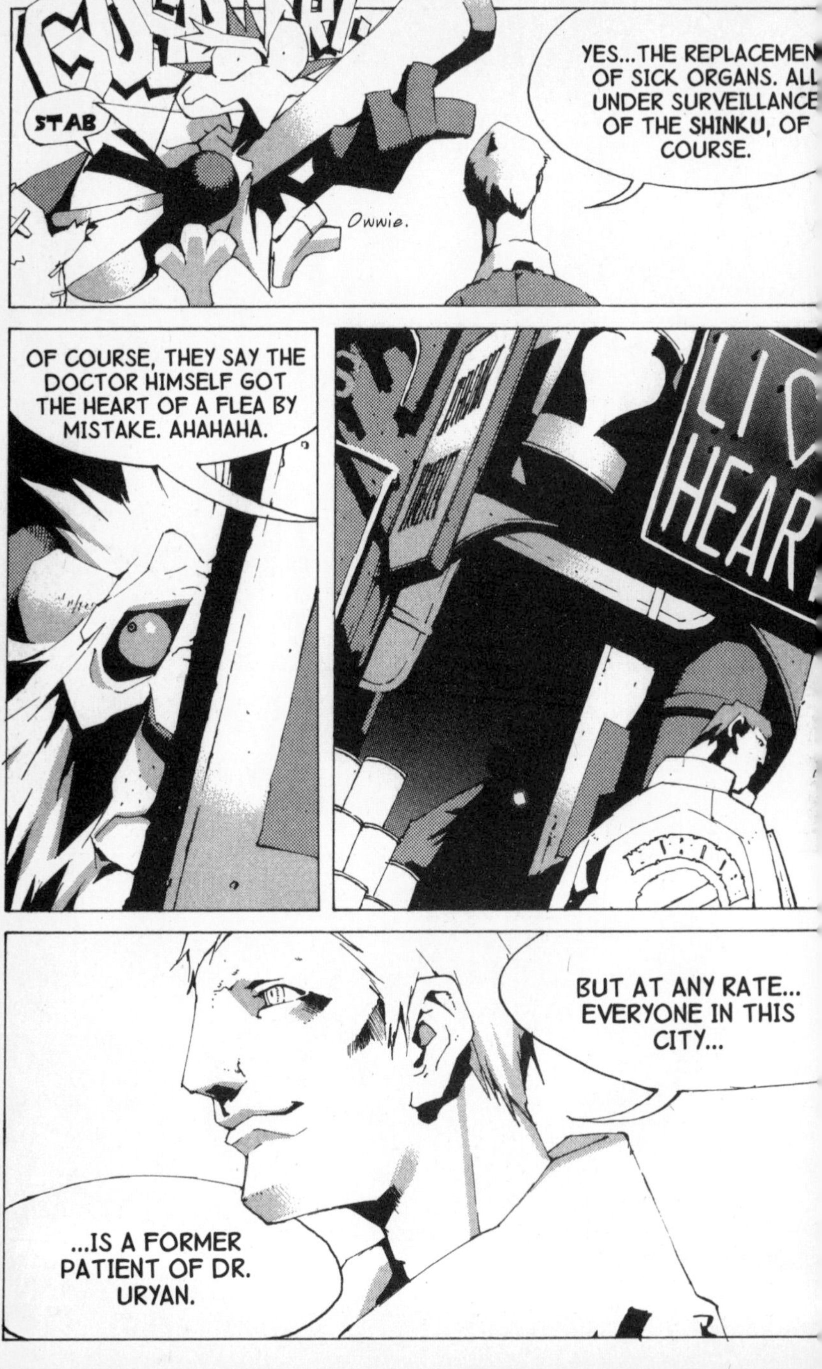
YES...THE REPLACEMEN OF SICK ORGANS. ALL UNDER SURVEILLANCE OF THE SHINKU, OF COURSE.
STAB
Owwie.
OF COURSE, THEY SAY THE DOCTOR HIMSELF GOT THE HEART OF A FLEA BY MISTAKE. AHAHAHA.
BUT AT ANY RATE... EVERYONE IN THIS CITY...
...IS A FORMER PATIENT OF DR. URYAN.

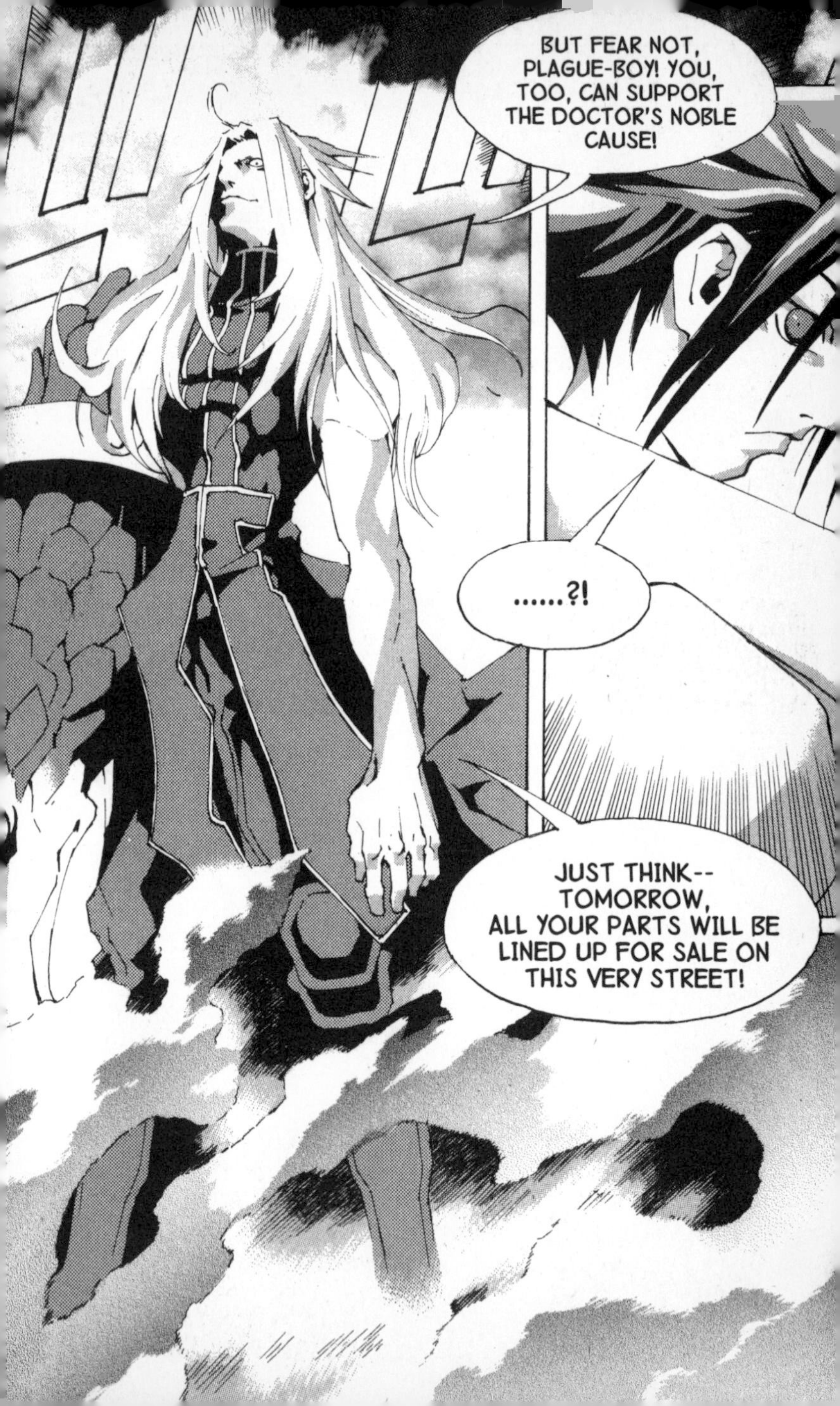
BUT FEAR NOT, PLAGUE-BOY! YOU, TOO, CAN SUPPORT THE DOCTOR'S NOBLE CAUSE!
......?!
JUST THINK-- TOMORROW, ALL YOUR PARTS WILL BE LINED UP FOR SALE ON THIS VERY STREET!

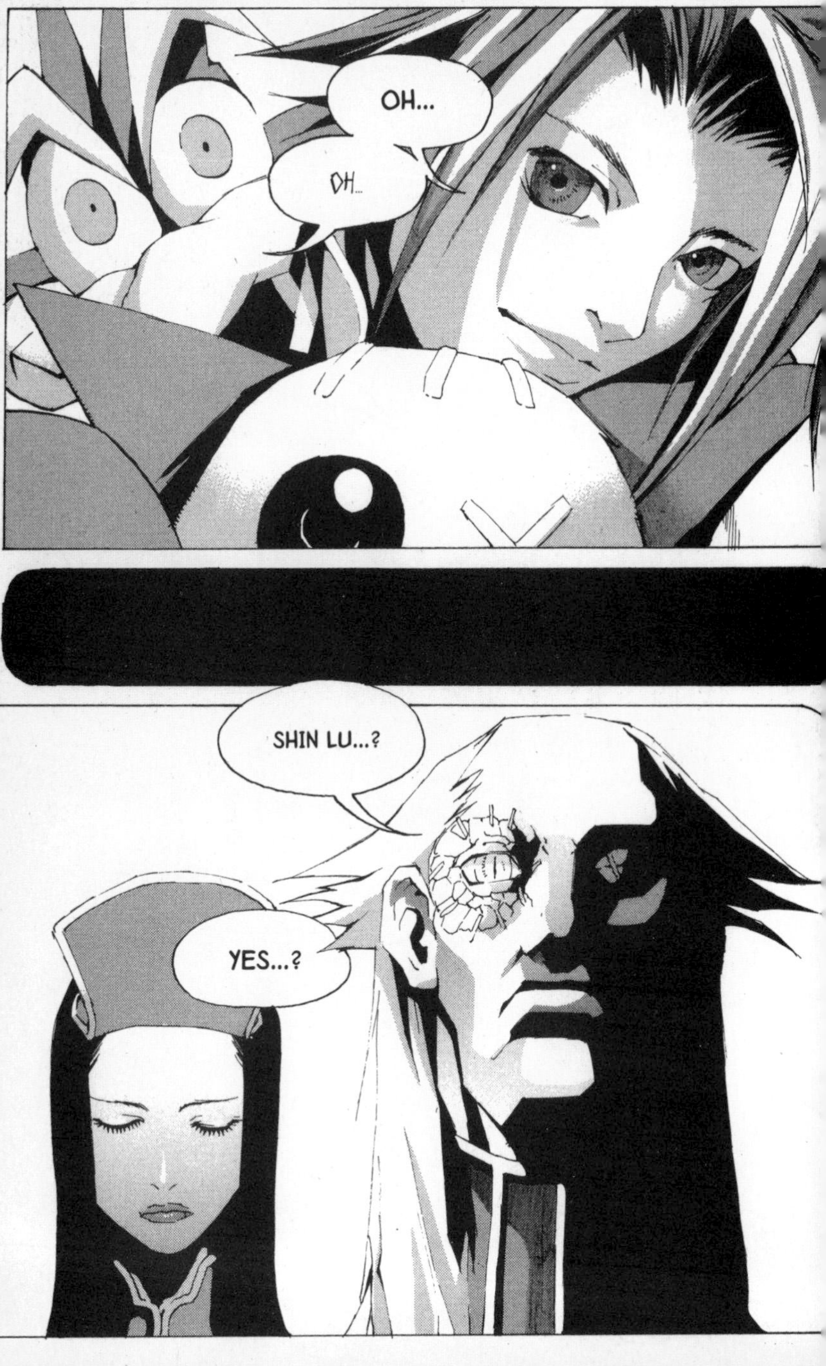
OH...
OH...
SHIN LU...?
YES...?

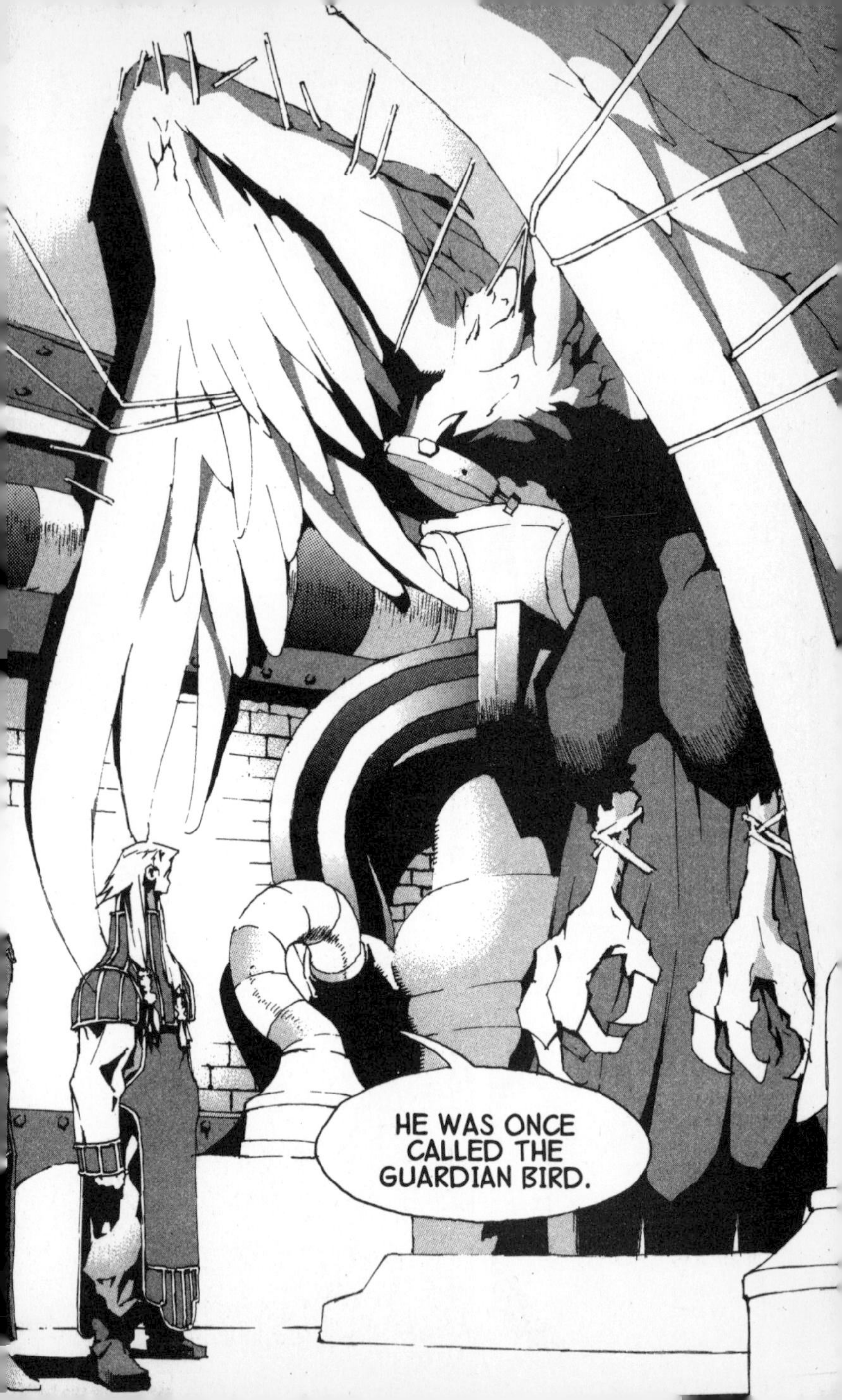
HE WAS ONCE CALLED THE GUARDIAN BIRD.

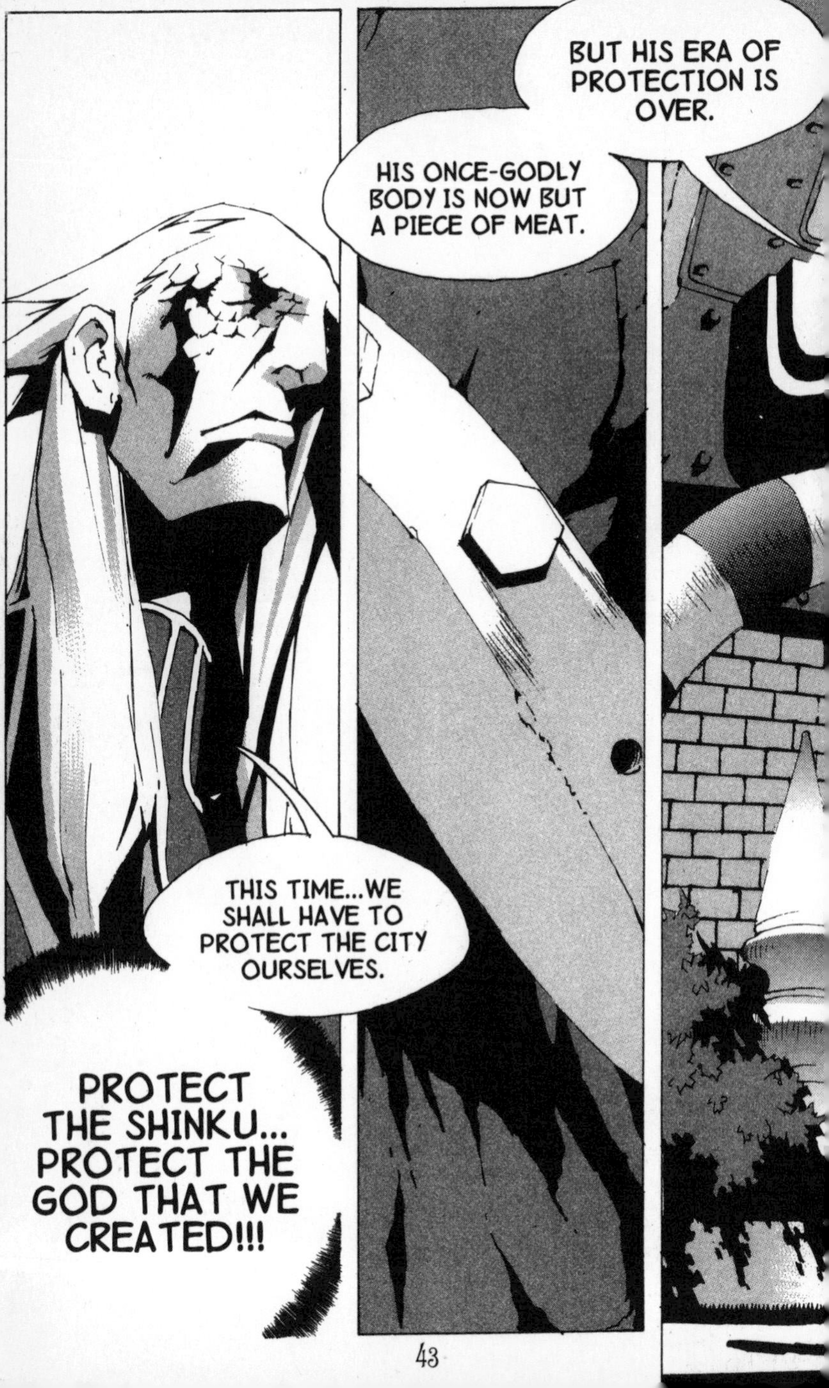
BUT HIS ERA OF PROTECTION IS OVER.
HIS ONCE-GODLY BODY IS NOW BUT A PIECE OF MEAT.
THIS TIME...WE SHALL HAVE TO PROTECT THE CITY OURSELVES.
PROTECT THE SHINKU... PROTECT THE GOD THAT WE CREATED!!!

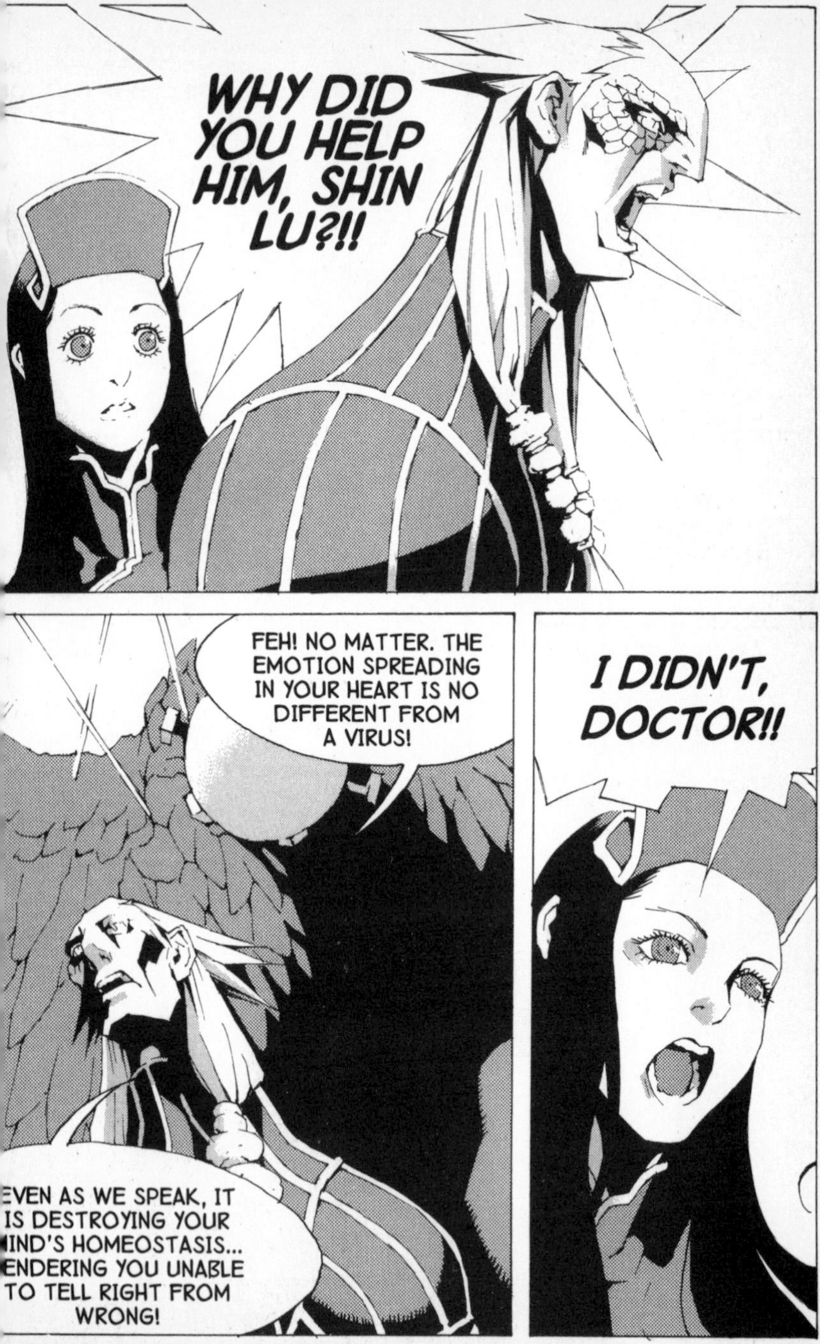
WHY DID YOU HELP HIM, SHIN LU?!!
I DIDN'T, DOCTOR!!
FEH! NO MATTER. THE EMOTION SPREADING IN YOUR HEART IS NO DIFFERENT FROM A VIRUS!
EVEN AS WE SPEAK, IT IS DESTROYING YOUR IND'S HOMEOSTASIS... ENDERING YOU UNABLE TO TELL RIGHT FROM WRONG!

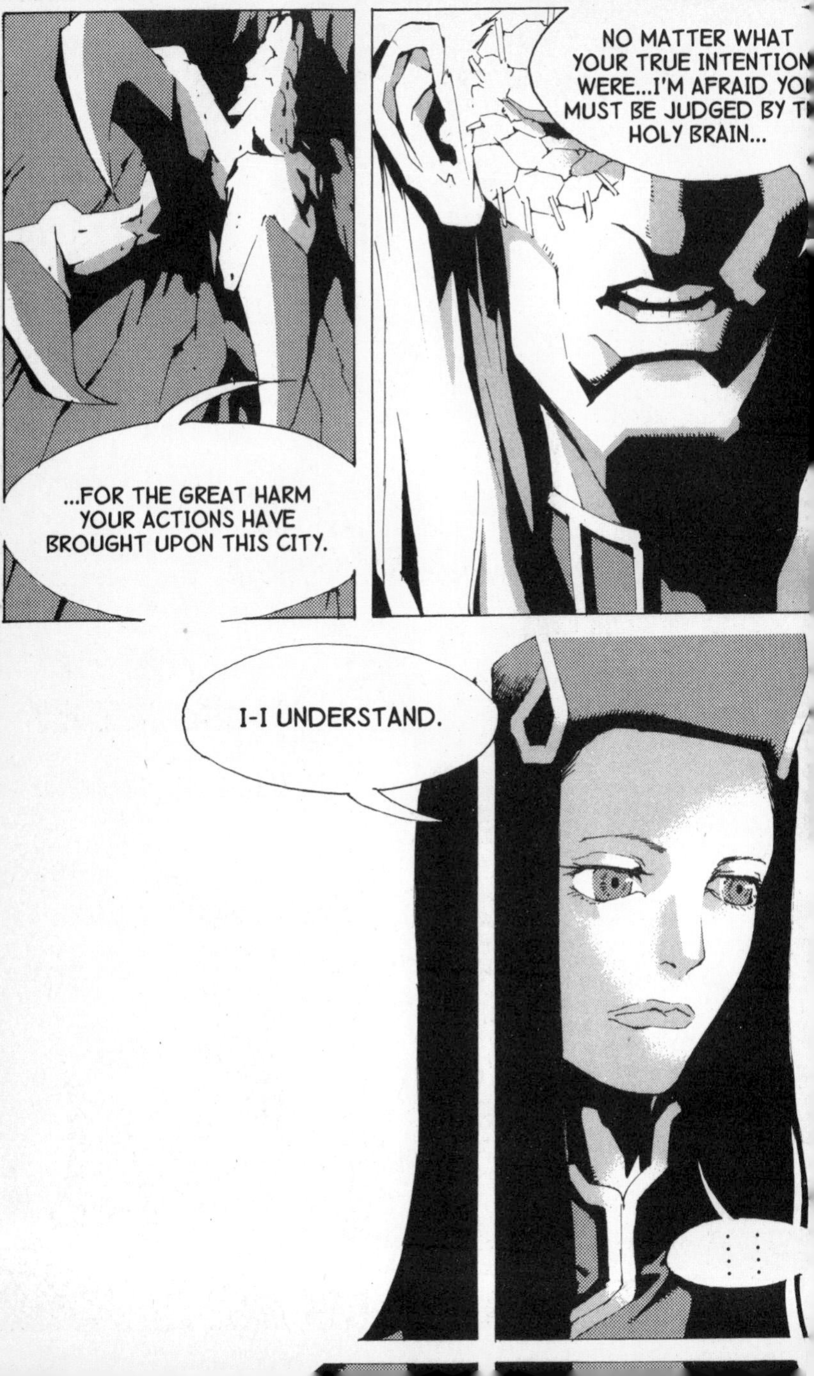
NO MATTER WHAT YOUR TRUE INTENTION WERE...I'M AFRAID YO MUST BE JUDGED BY T HOLY BRAIN...
...FOR THE GREAT HARM YOUR ACTIONS HAVE BROUGHT UPON THIS CITY.
I-I UNDERSTAND.

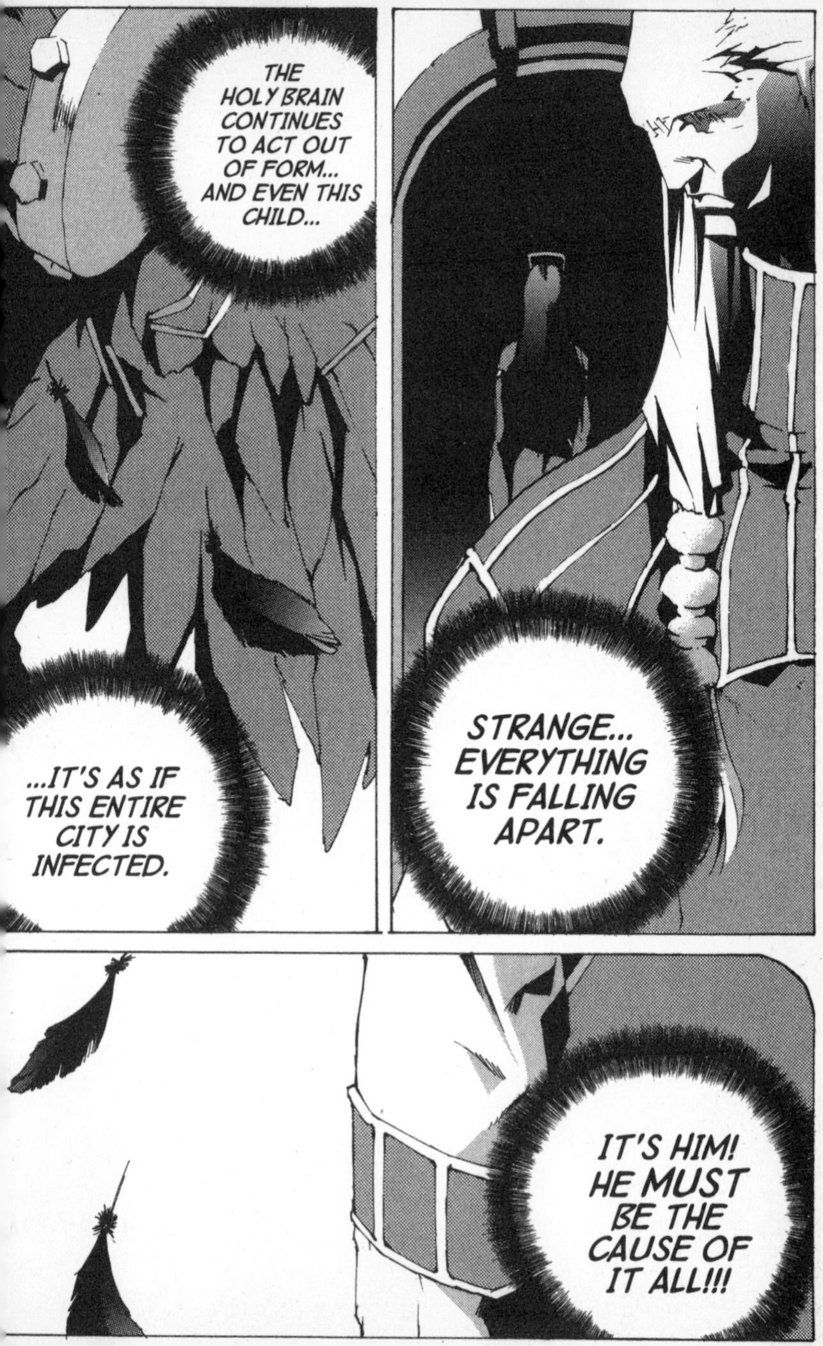
STRANGE... EVERYTHING IS FALLING APART.
THE HOLY BRAIN CONTINUES TO ACT OUT OF FORM... AND EVEN THIS CHILD...
...IT'S AS IF THIS ENTIRE CITY IS INFECTED.
IT'S HIM! HE MUST BE THE CAUSE OF IT ALL!!!

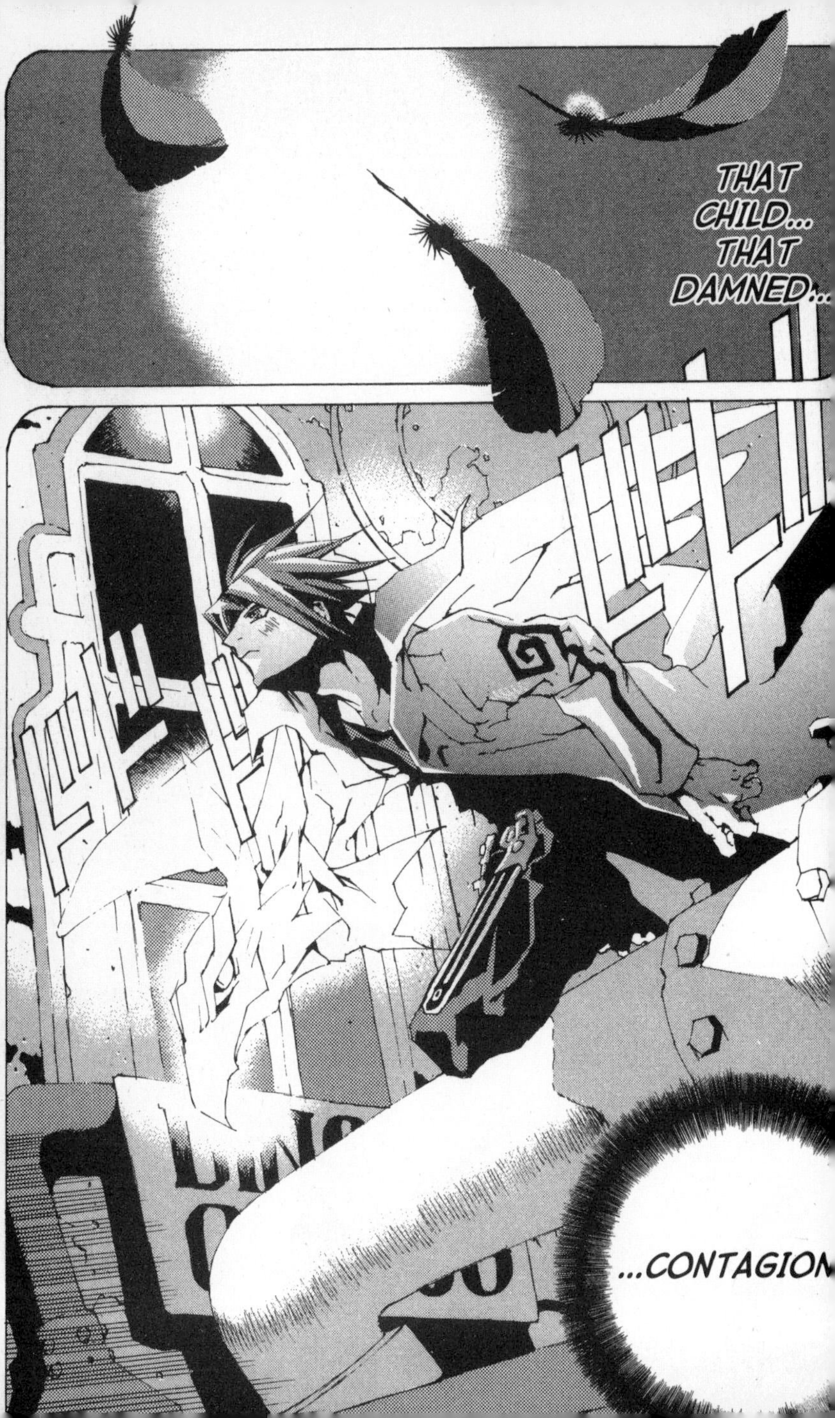
THAT CHILD... THAT DAMNED...
...CONTAGION

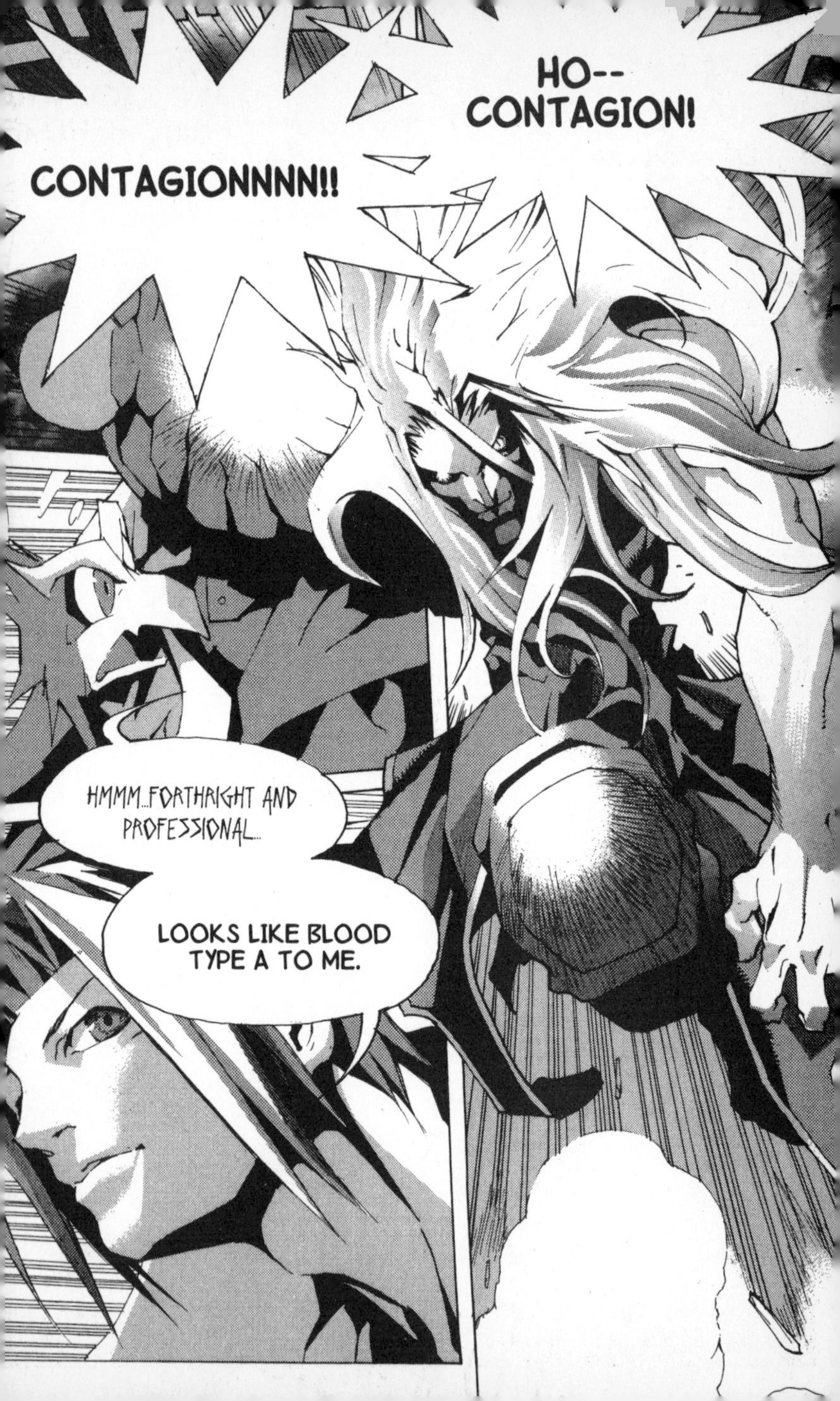
HO-- CONTAGION!
CONTAGIONNNN!!
HMMM...FORTHRIGHT AND PROFESSIONAL...
LOOKS LIKE BLOOD TYPE A TO ME.

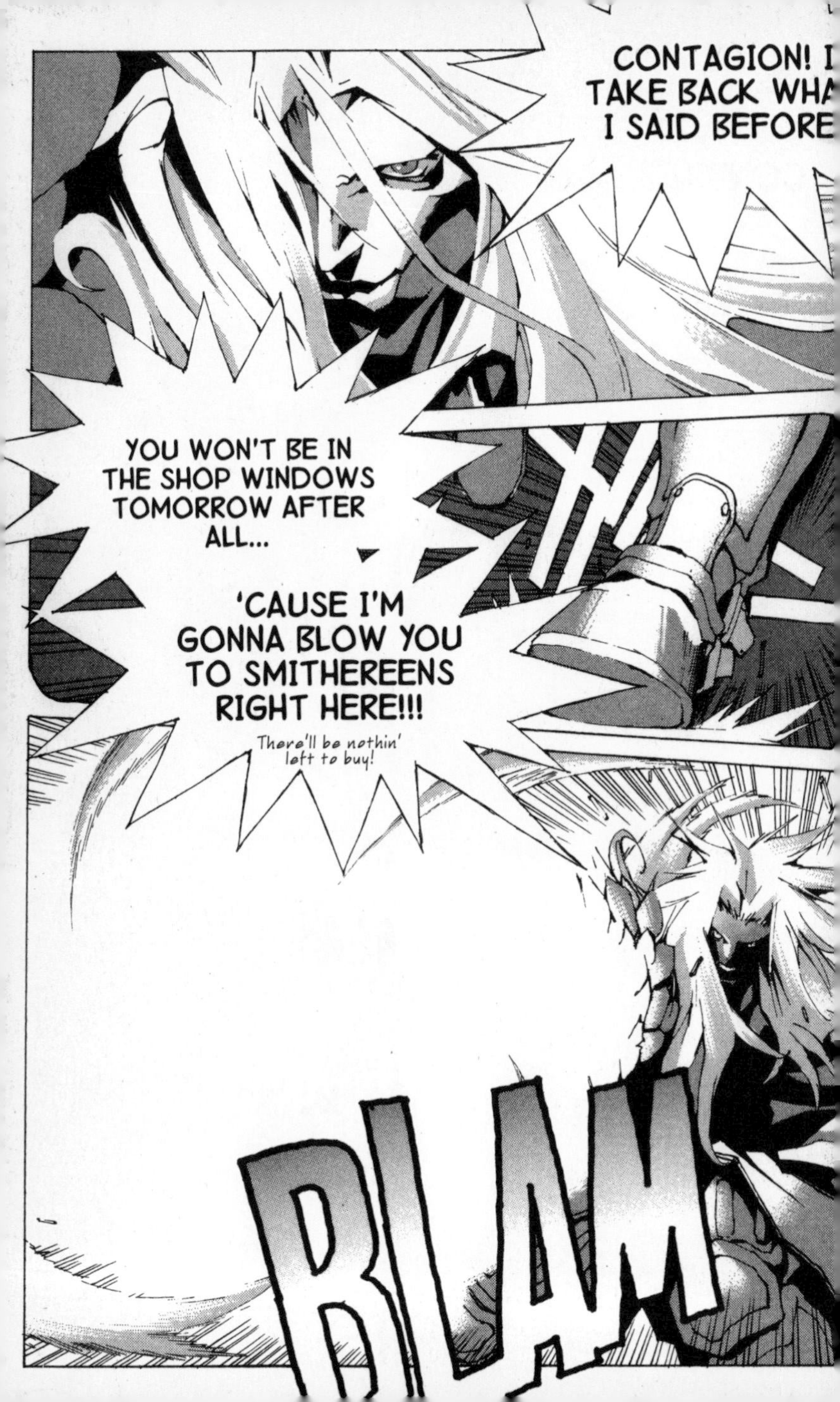
CONTAGION! I TAKE BACK WHA I SAID BEFORE
YOU WON'T BE IN THE SHOP WINDOWS TOMORROW AFTER ALL...
'CAUSE I'M GONNA BLOW YOU TO SMITHEREENS RIGHT HERE!!!
There'll be nothin' left to buy!
BLAM

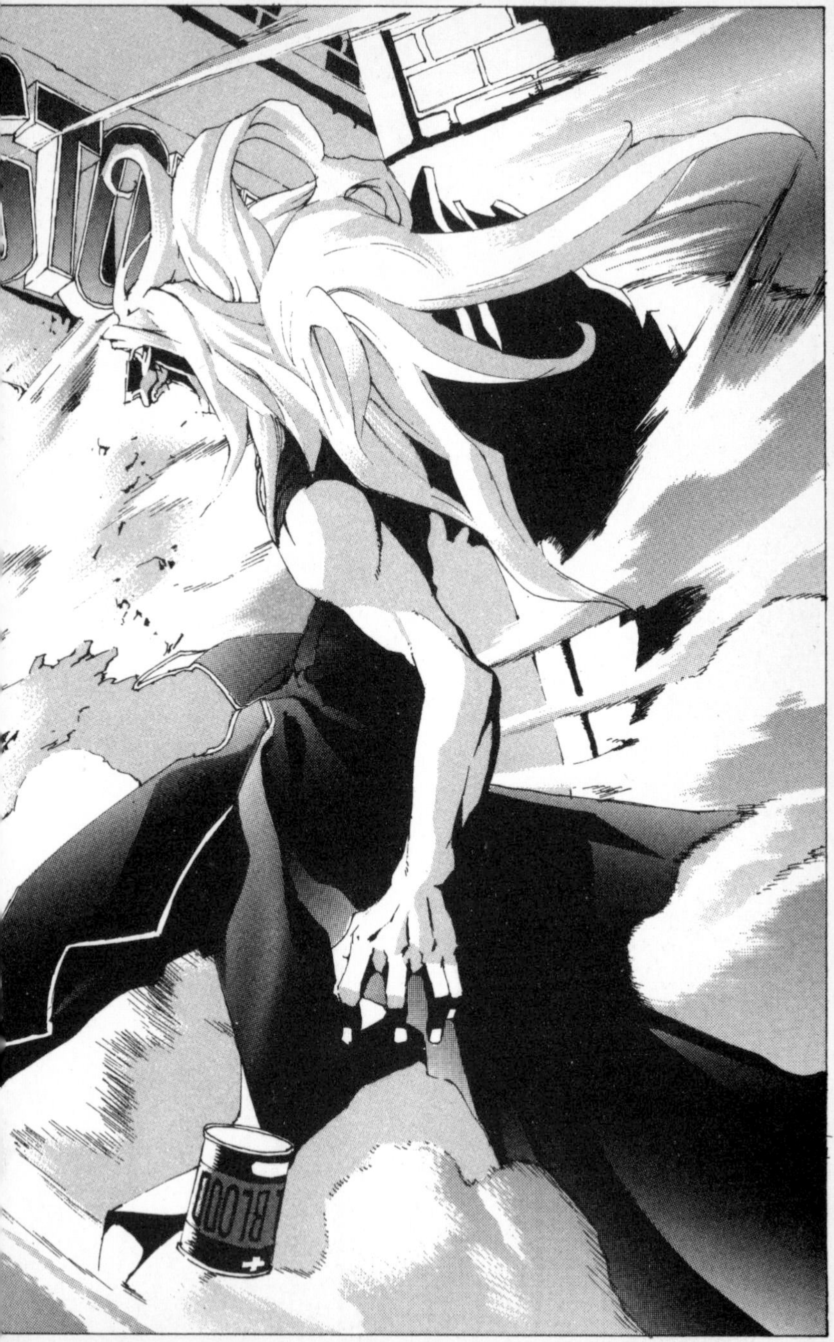
BLOOD

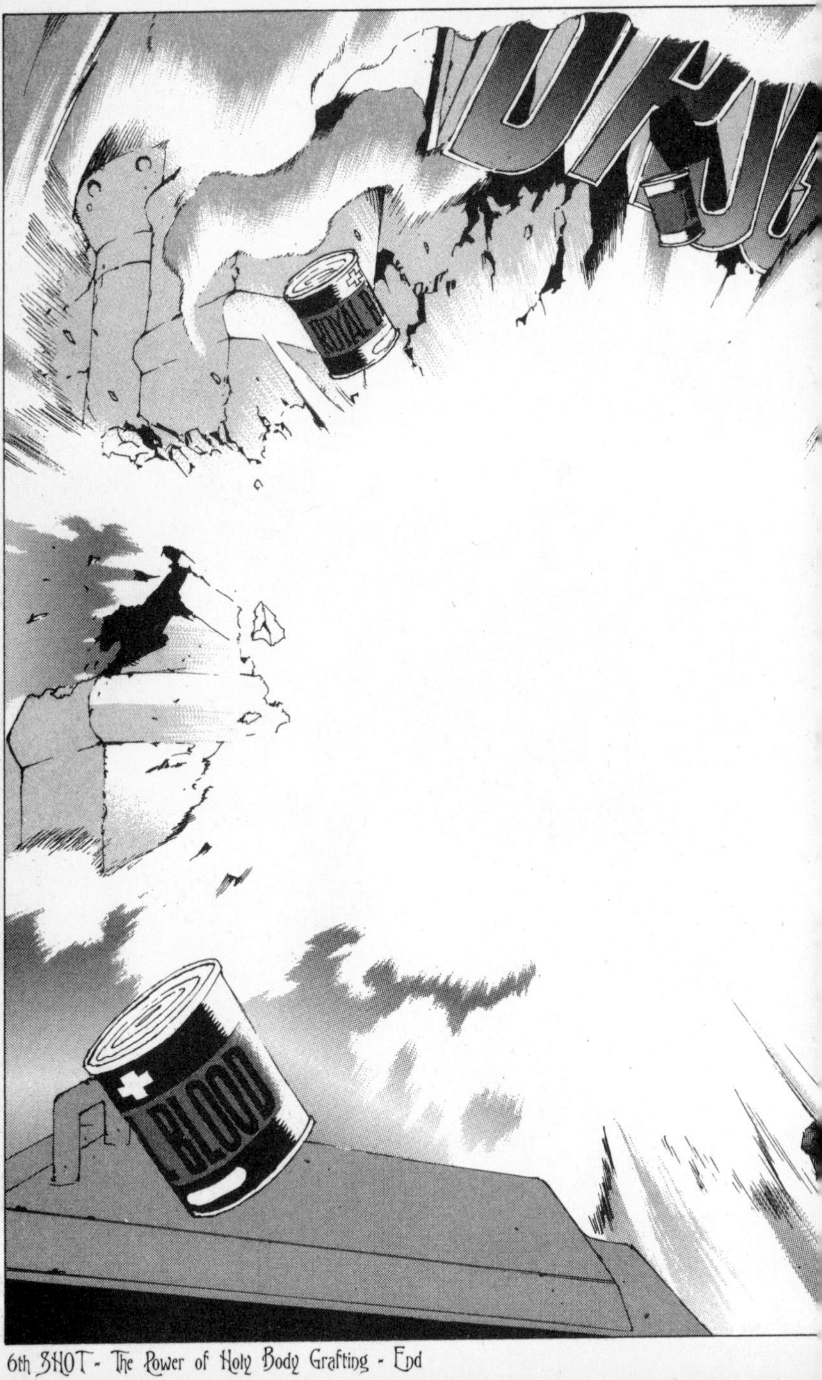
BLOOD

6th SHOT - The Power of Holy Body Grafting - End

7th SHOT - Thirty-four Pursuers

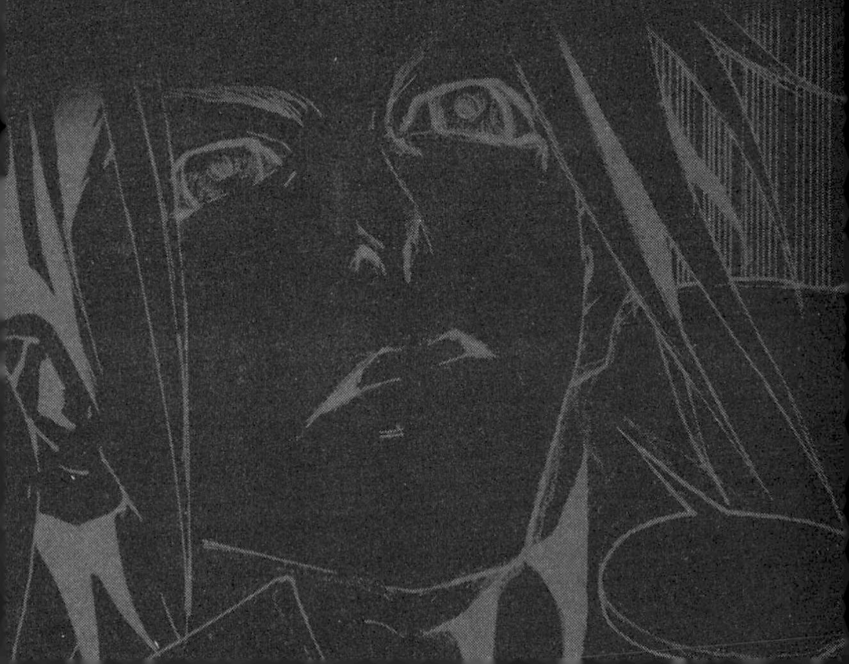

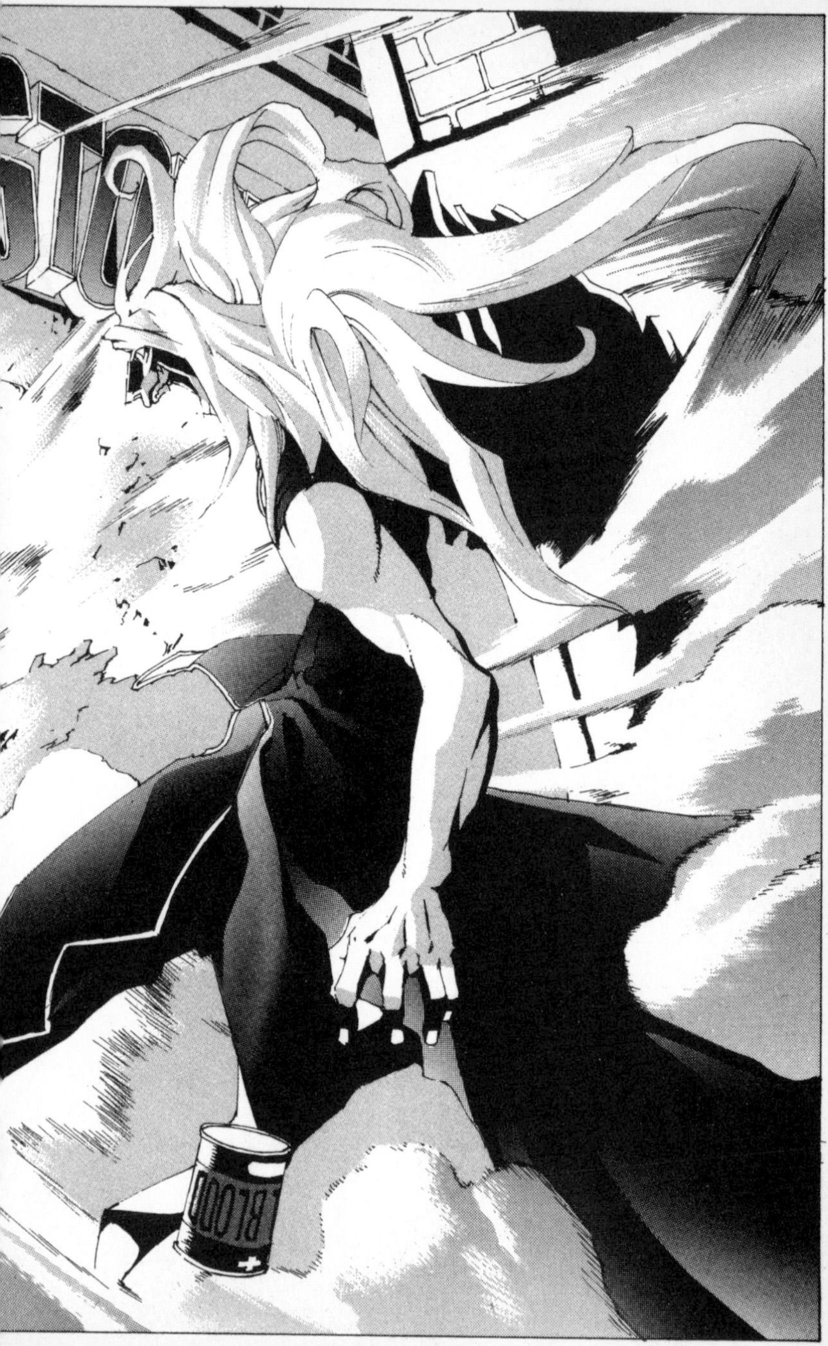
BLOOD

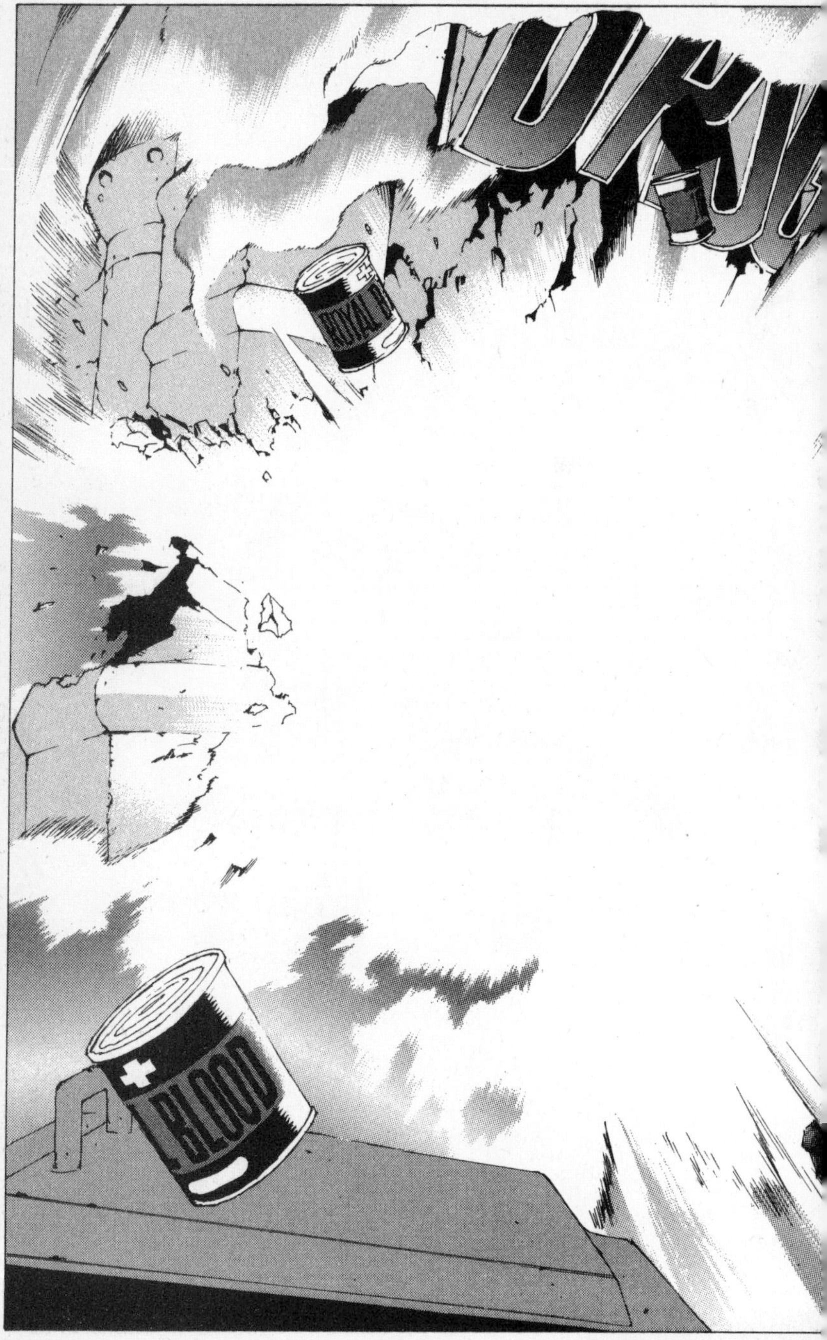
ROYAL
BLOOD

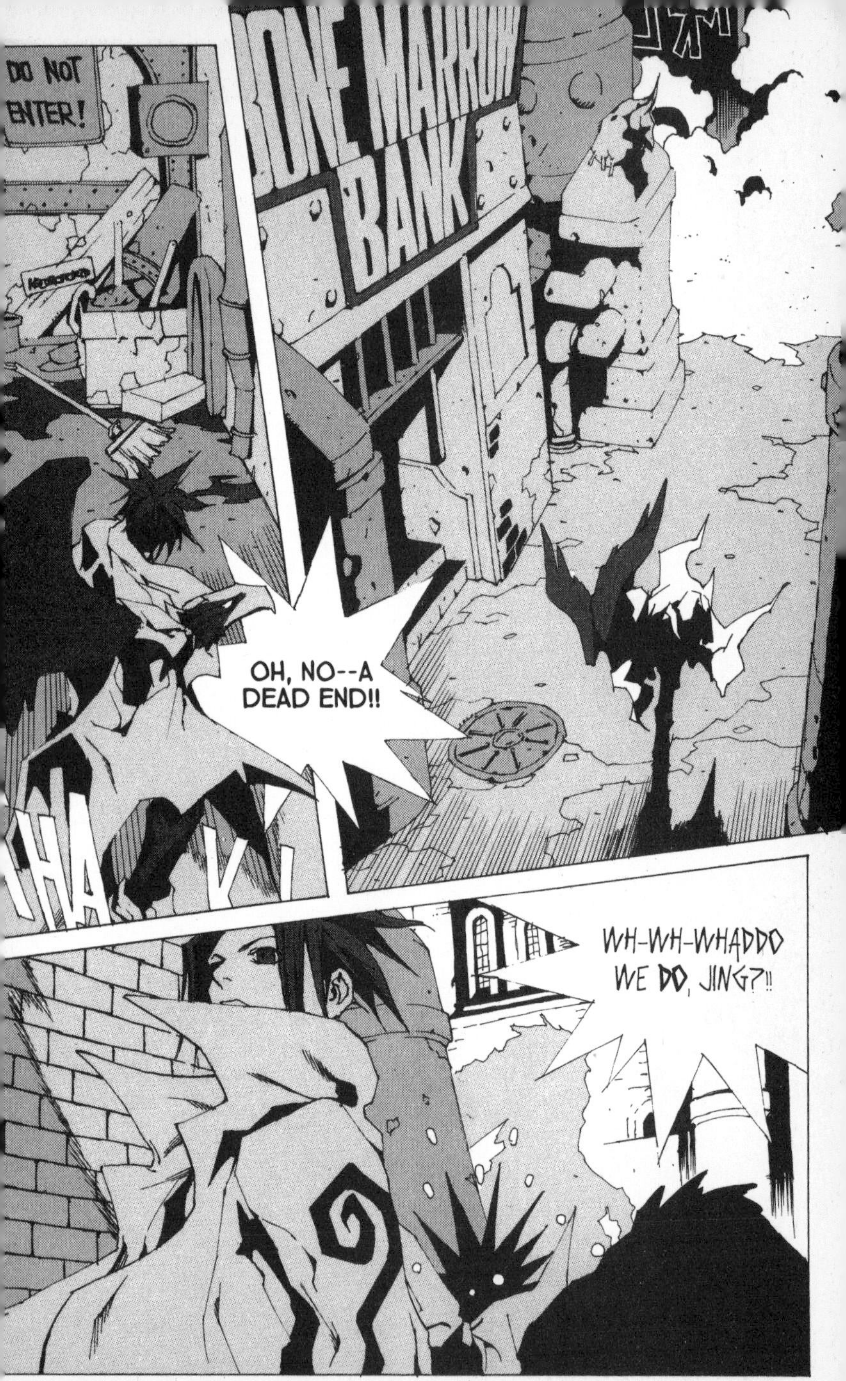
DO NOT ENTER!
BONE MARROW BANK
OH, NO--A DEAD END!!
CHA KI
WH-WH-WHADDO WE DO, JING?!!

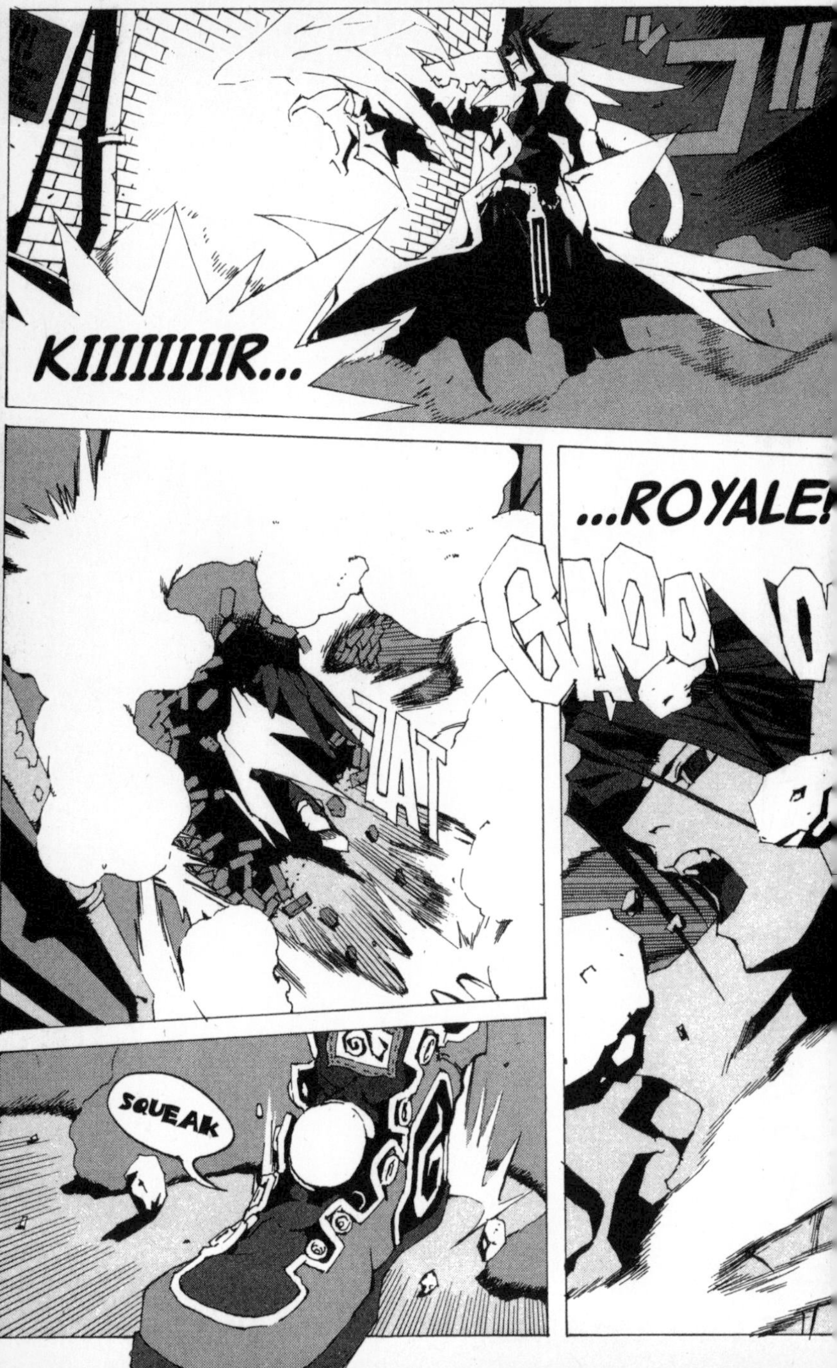
KIIIIIIIR...
...ROYALE!
ZAT
SQUEAK

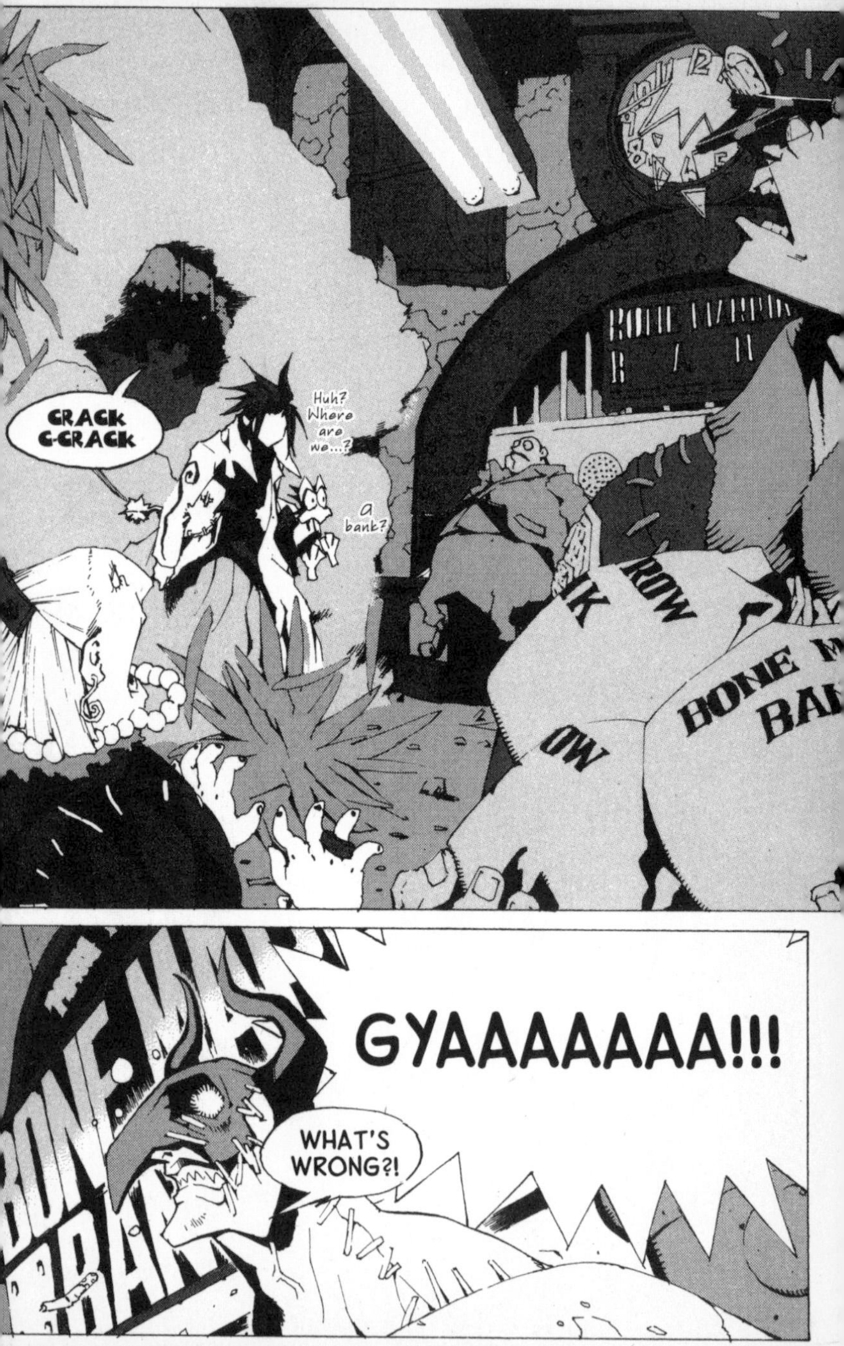
Huh? Where are we...?
CRACK C-CRACK
a bank?
GYAAAAAAAA!!!
WHAT'S WRONG?!

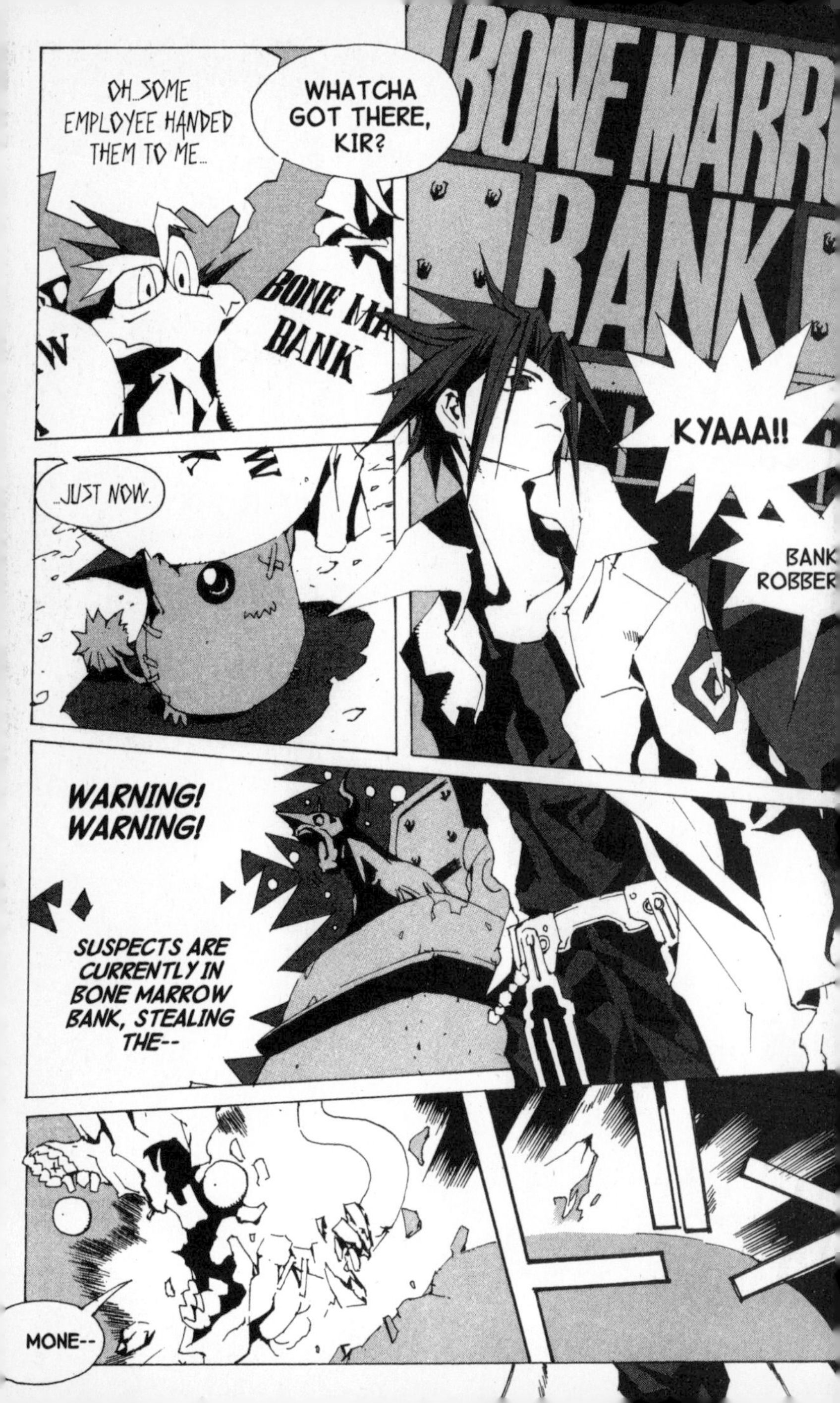
BONE MARR
BANK
KYAAA!!
BANK ROBBER
WHATCHA GOT THERE, KIR?
OH...SOME EMPLOYEE HANDED THEM TO ME...
BONE MA
BANK
...JUST NOW.
WARNING! WARNING!
SUSPECTS ARE CURRENTLY IN BONE MARROW BANK, STEALING THE--
MONE--

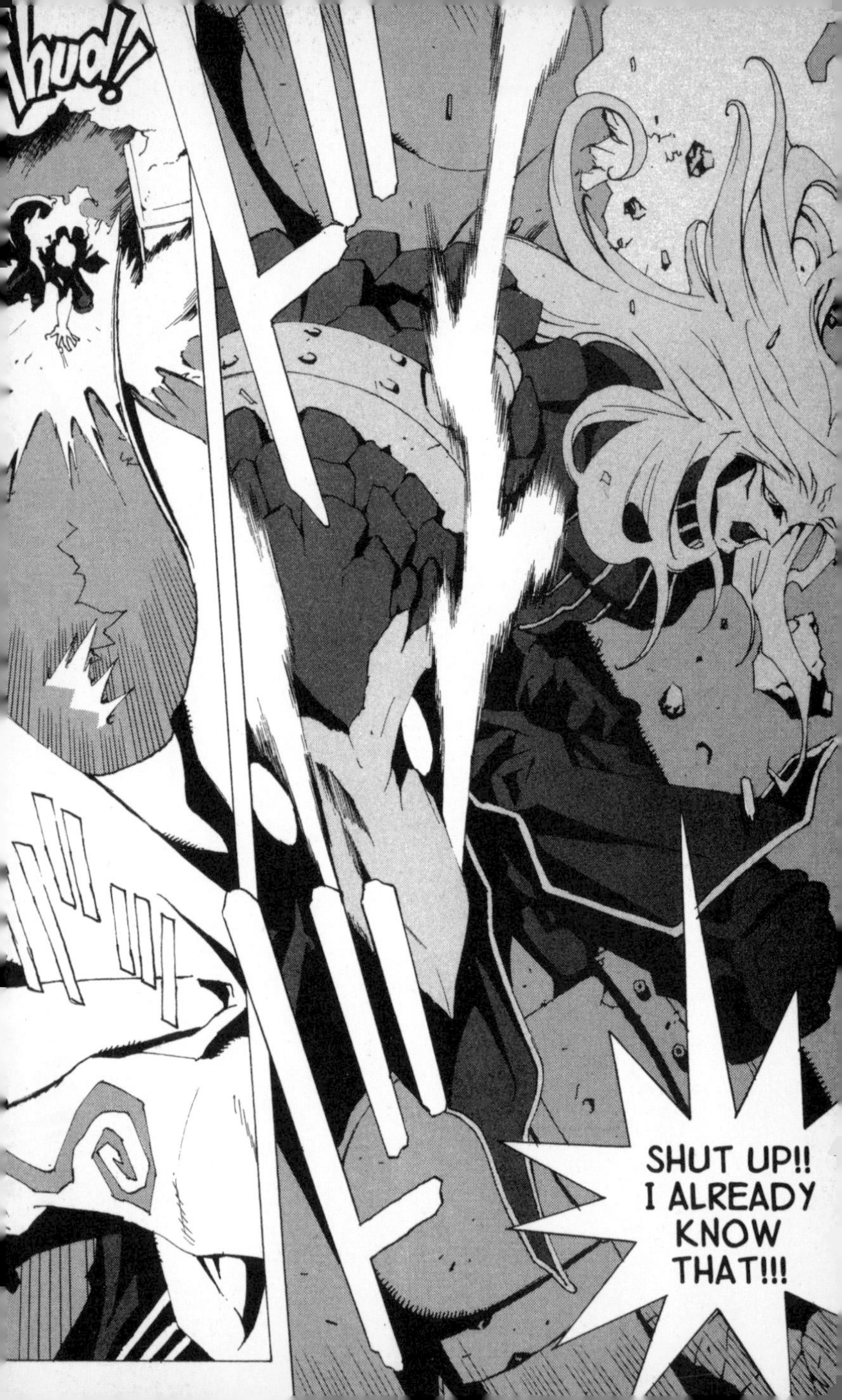
SHUT UP!!
I ALREADY
KNOW
THAT!!!

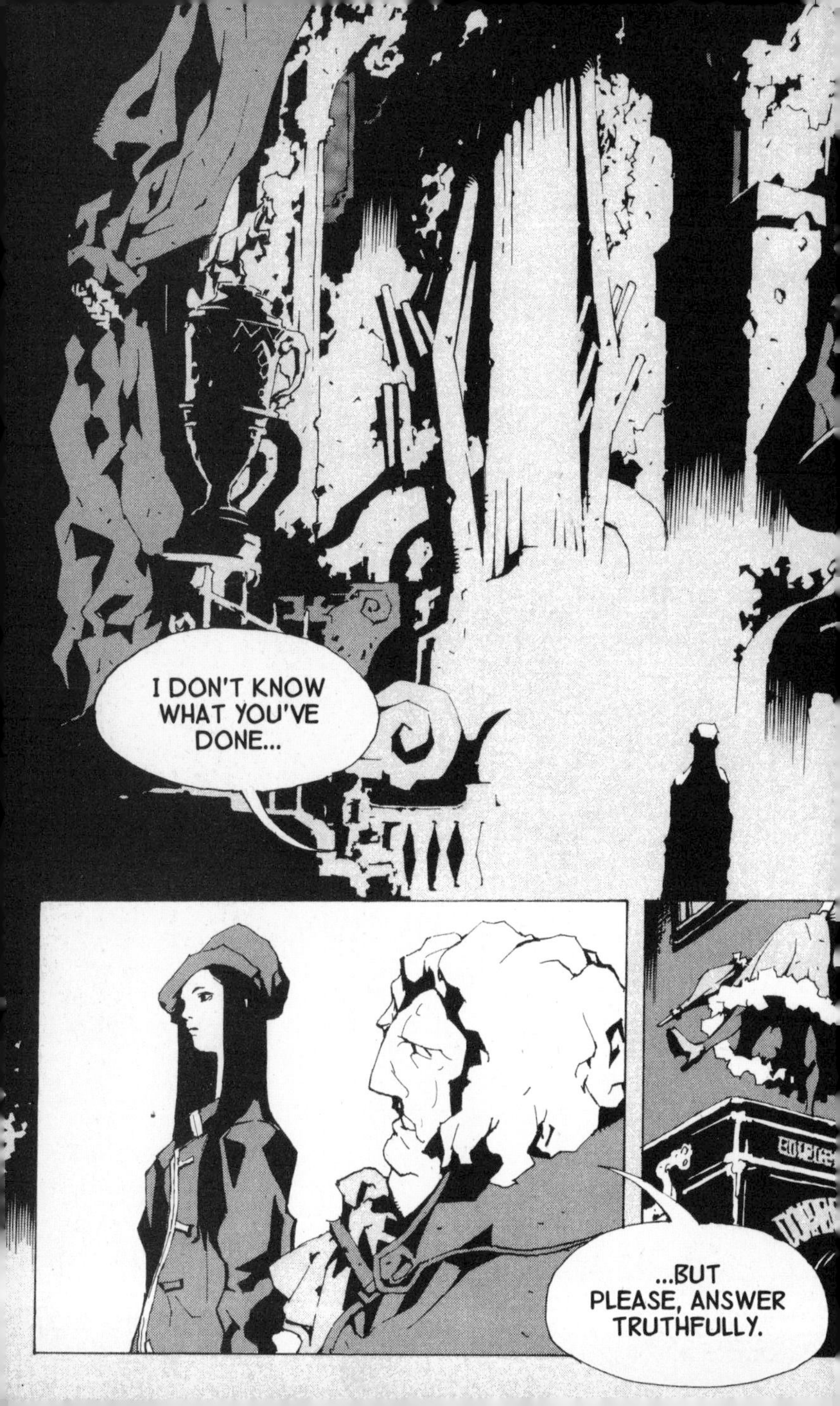
I DON'T KNOW WHAT YOU'VE DONE...
...BUT PLEASE, ANSWER TRUTHFULLY.

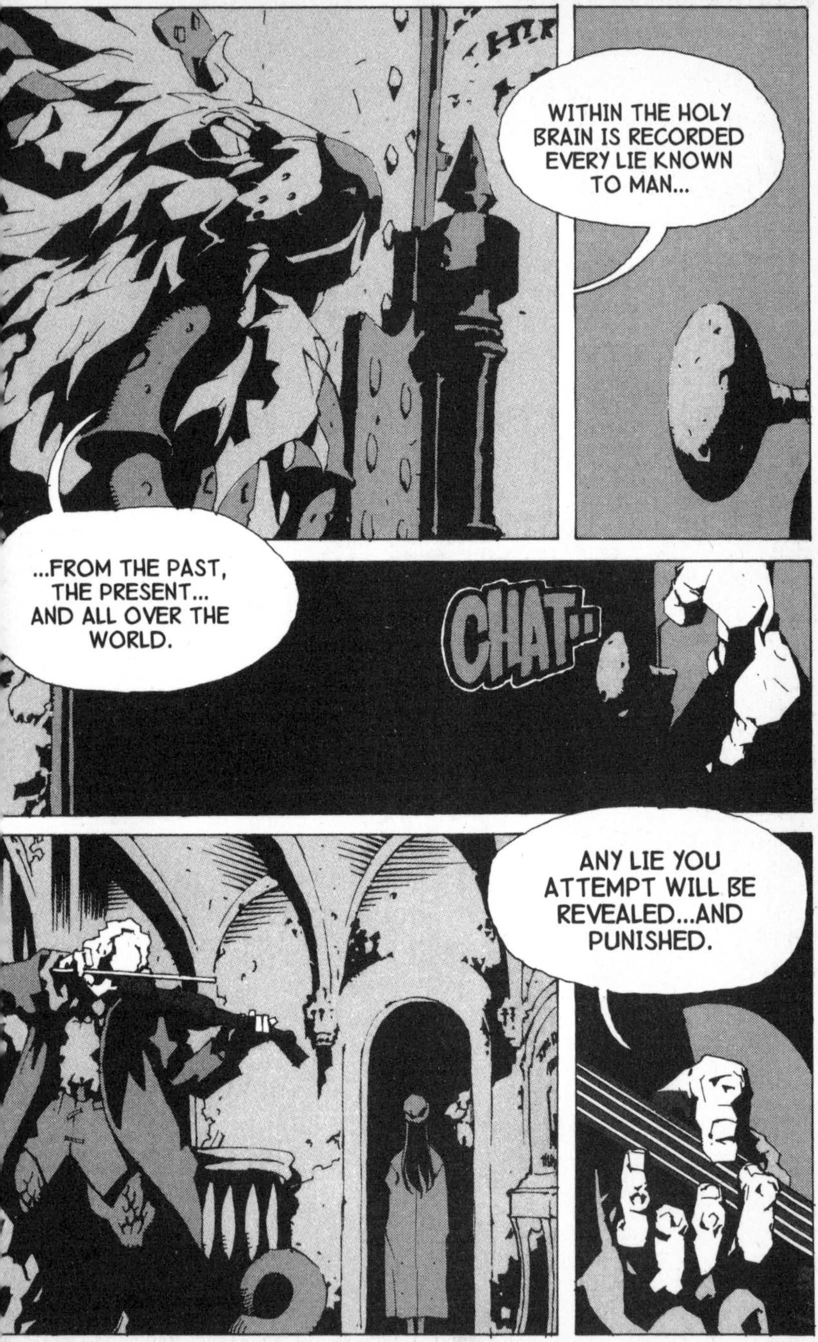
WITHIN THE HOLY BRAIN IS RECORDED EVERY LIE KNOWN TO MAN...
...FROM THE PAST, THE PRESENT... AND ALL OVER THE WORLD.
CHAT..
ANY LIE YOU ATTEMPT WILL BE REVEALED...AND PUNISHED.

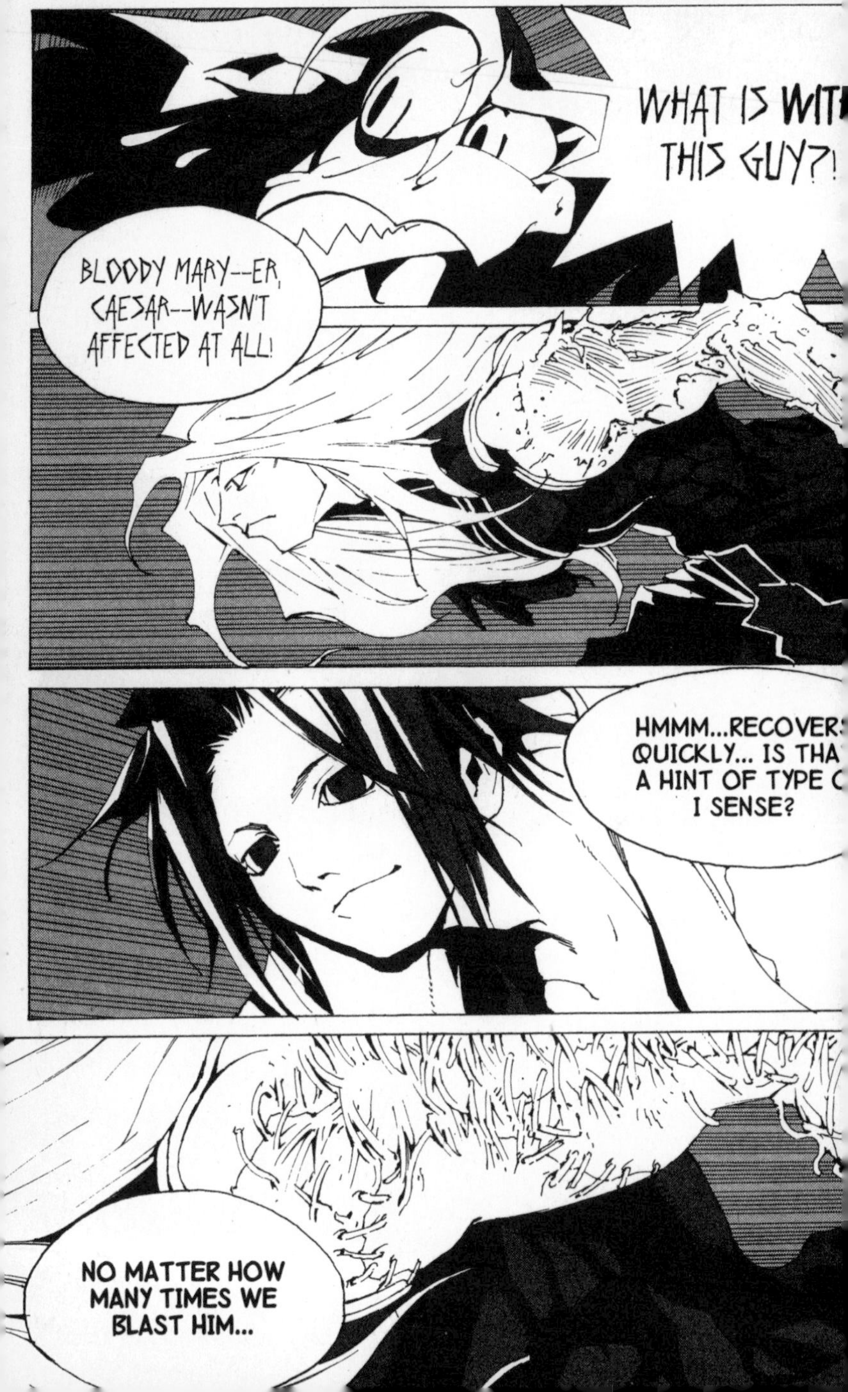
WHAT IS WIT THIS GUY?!
BLOODY MARY--ER, CAESAR--WASN'T AFFECTED AT ALL!
HMMM...RECOVER QUICKLY... IS THA A HINT OF TYPE I SENSE?
NO MATTER HOW MANY TIMES WE BLAST HIM...

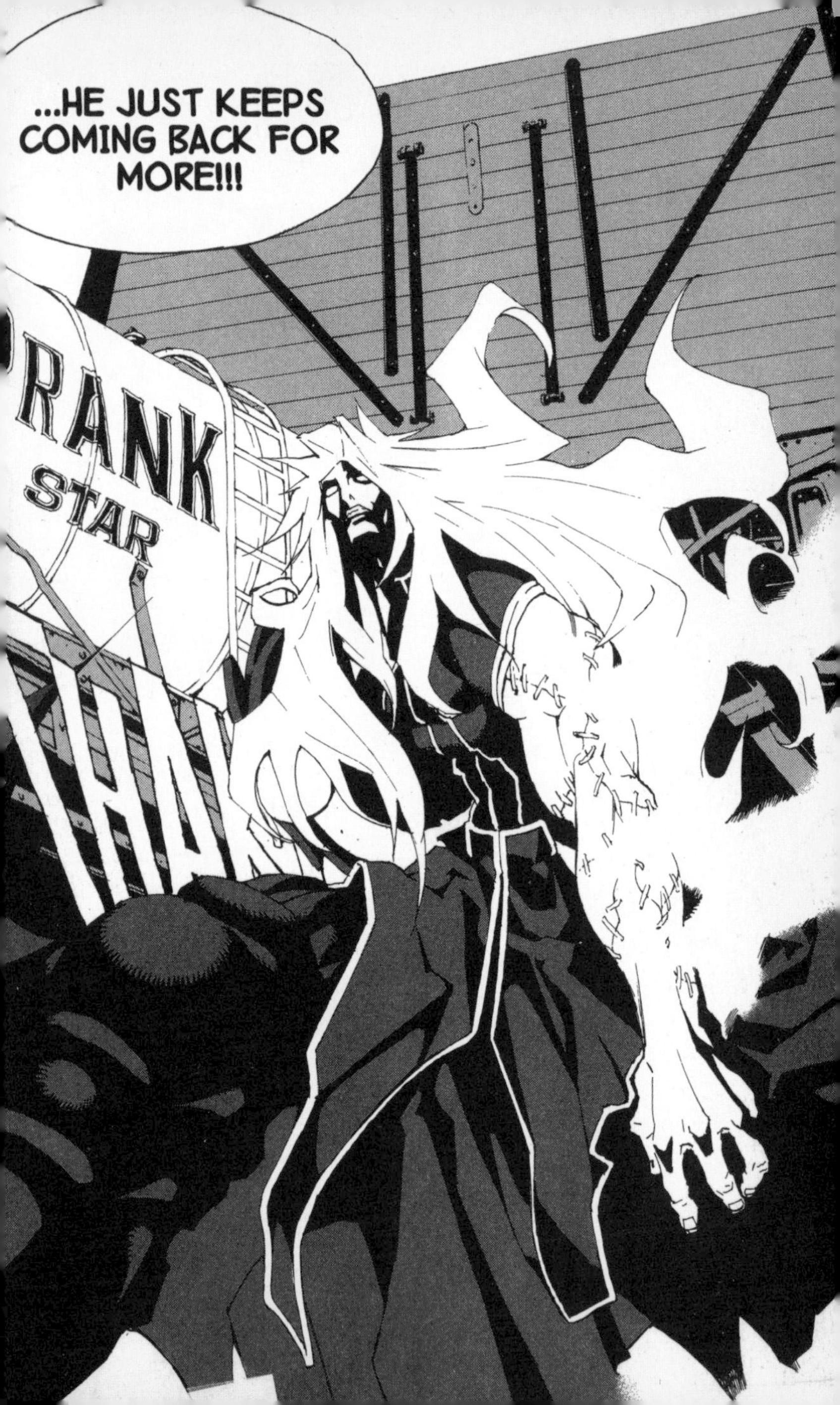
...HE JUST KEEPS COMING BACK FOR MORE!!!
PRANK
STAR

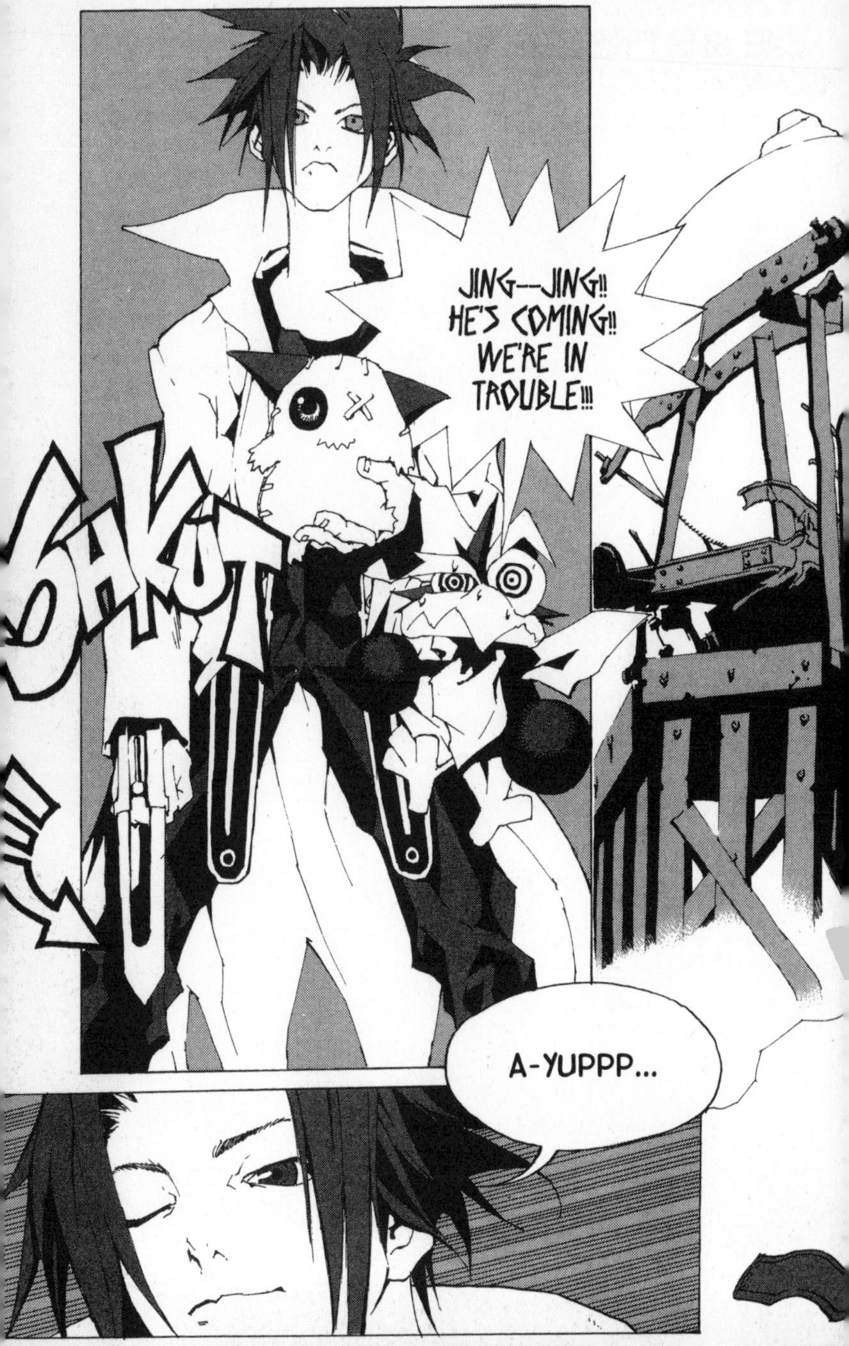
JING--JING!! HE'S COMING!! WE'RE IN TROUBLE!!!
SHAKUT!!!
A-YUPPP...

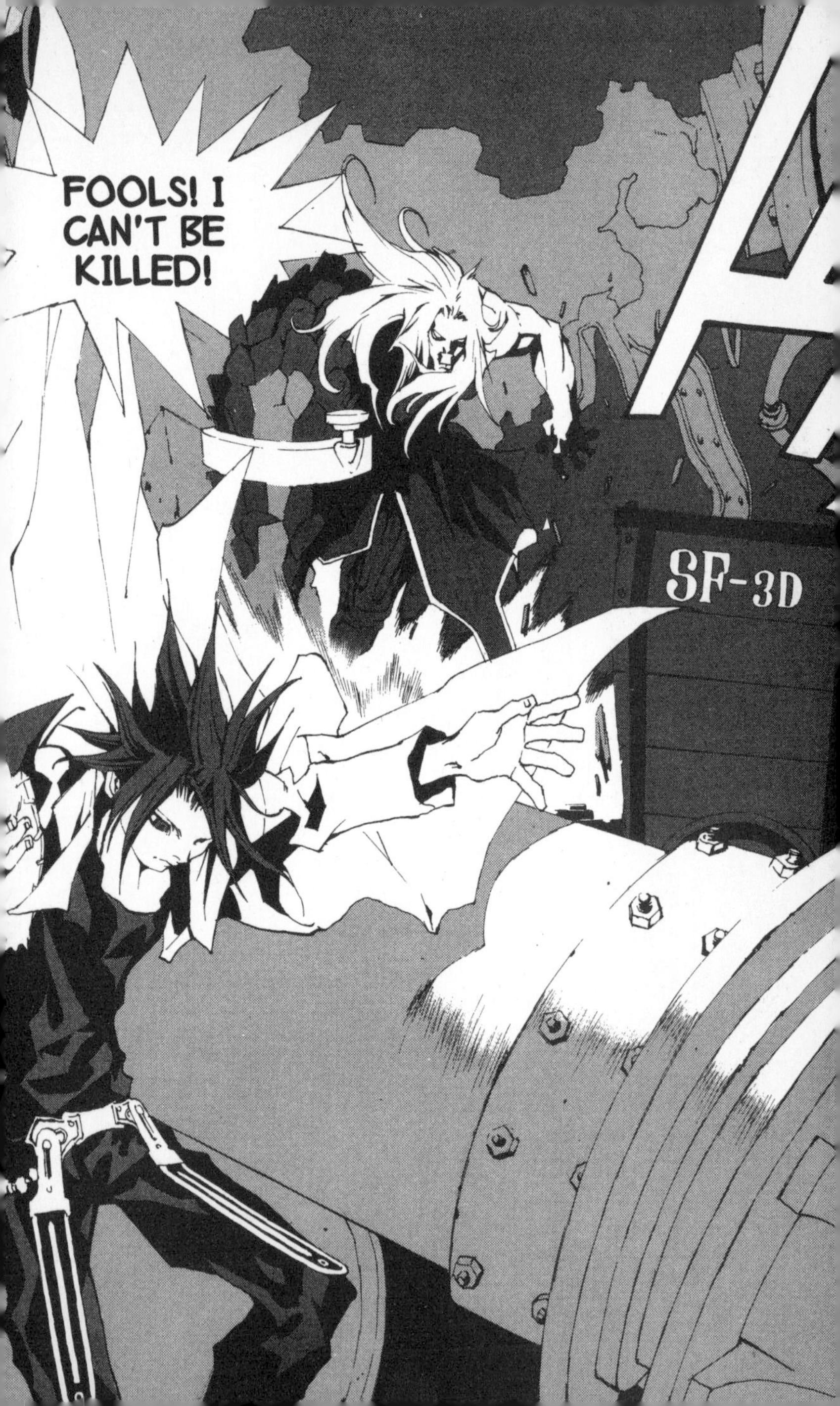
FOOLS! I CAN'T BE KILLED!
SF-3D

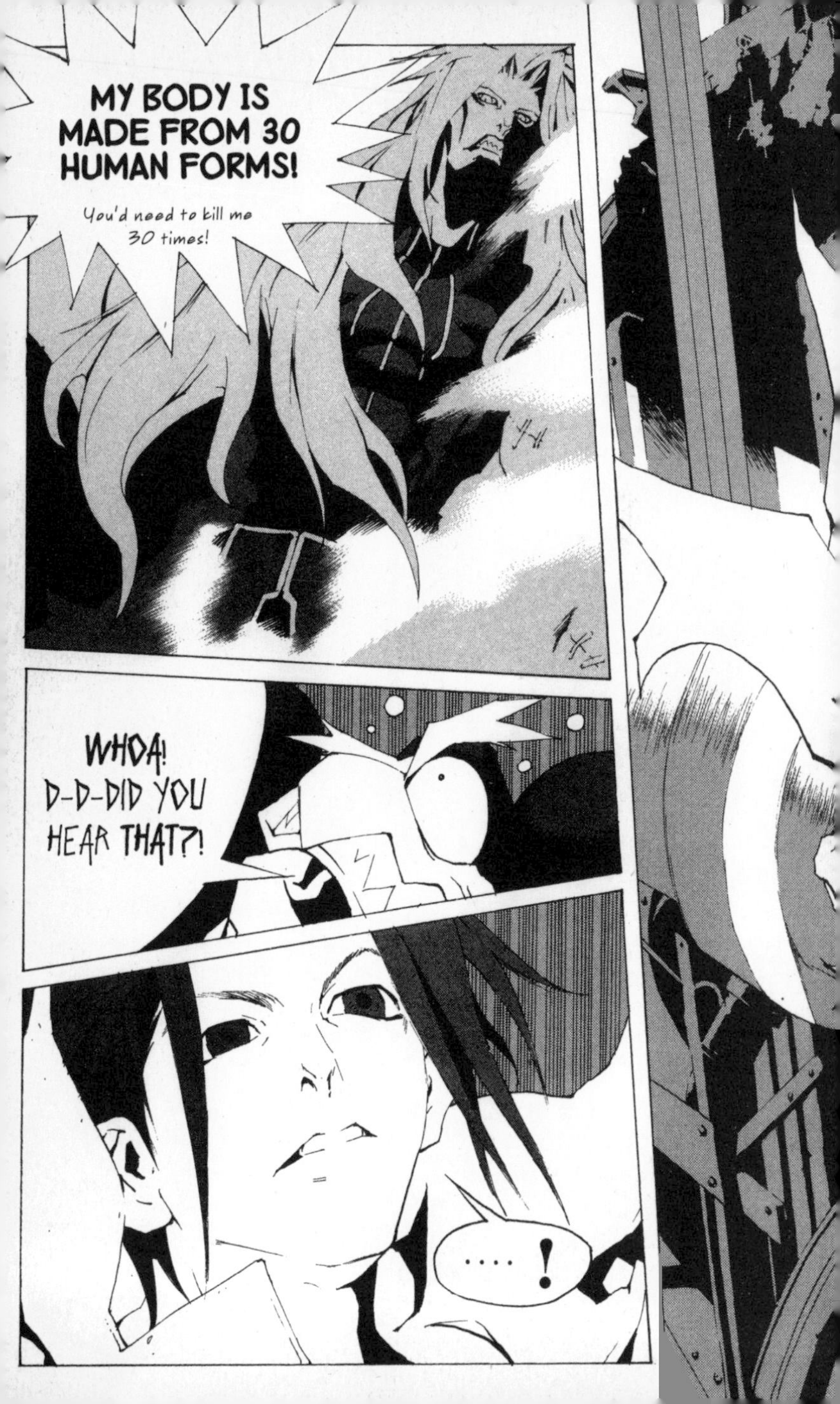
MY BODY IS MADE FROM 30 HUMAN FORMS!
You'd need to kill me 30 times!
WHOA! D-D-DID YOU HEAR THAT?!
.... !

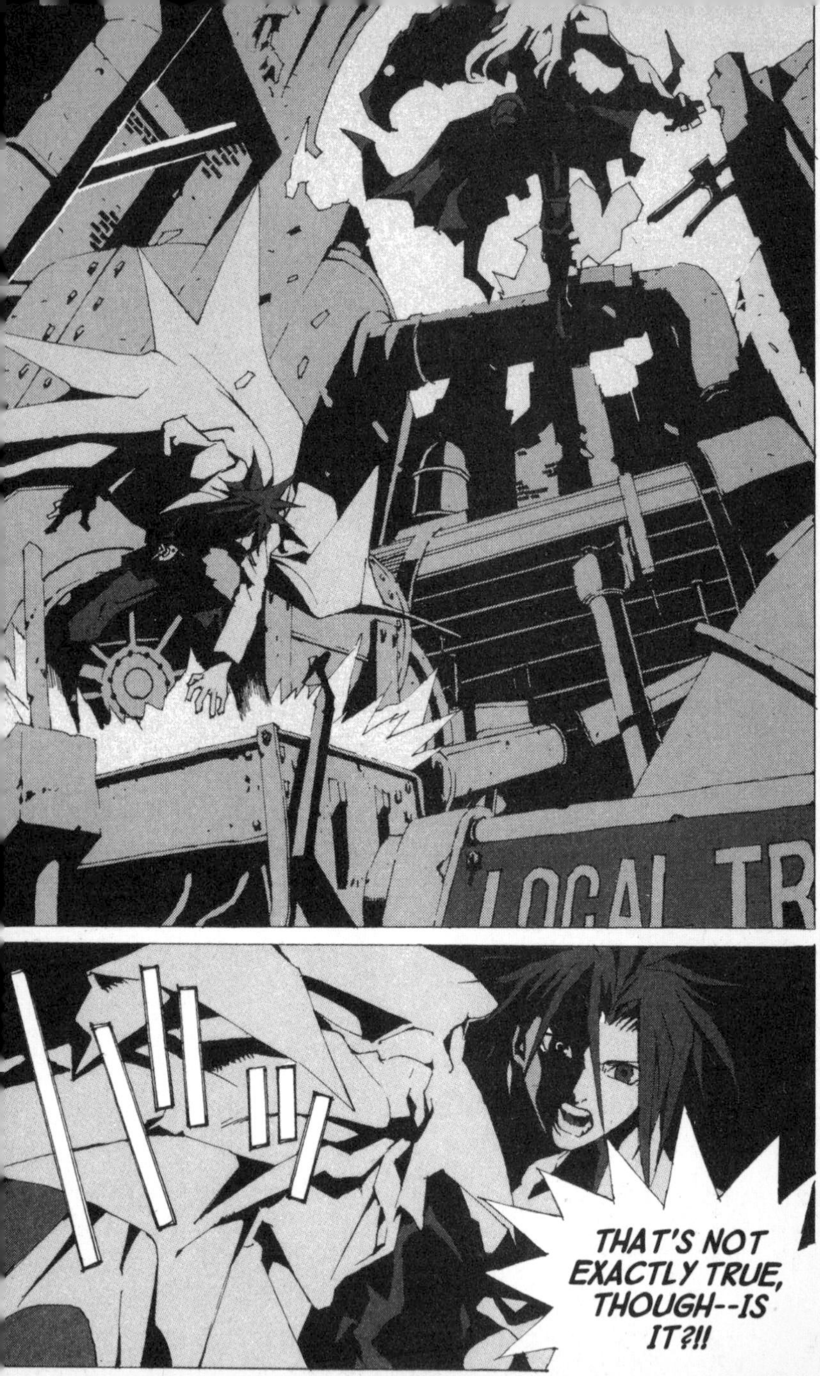
THAT'S NOT EXACTLY TRUE, THOUGH--IS IT?!!

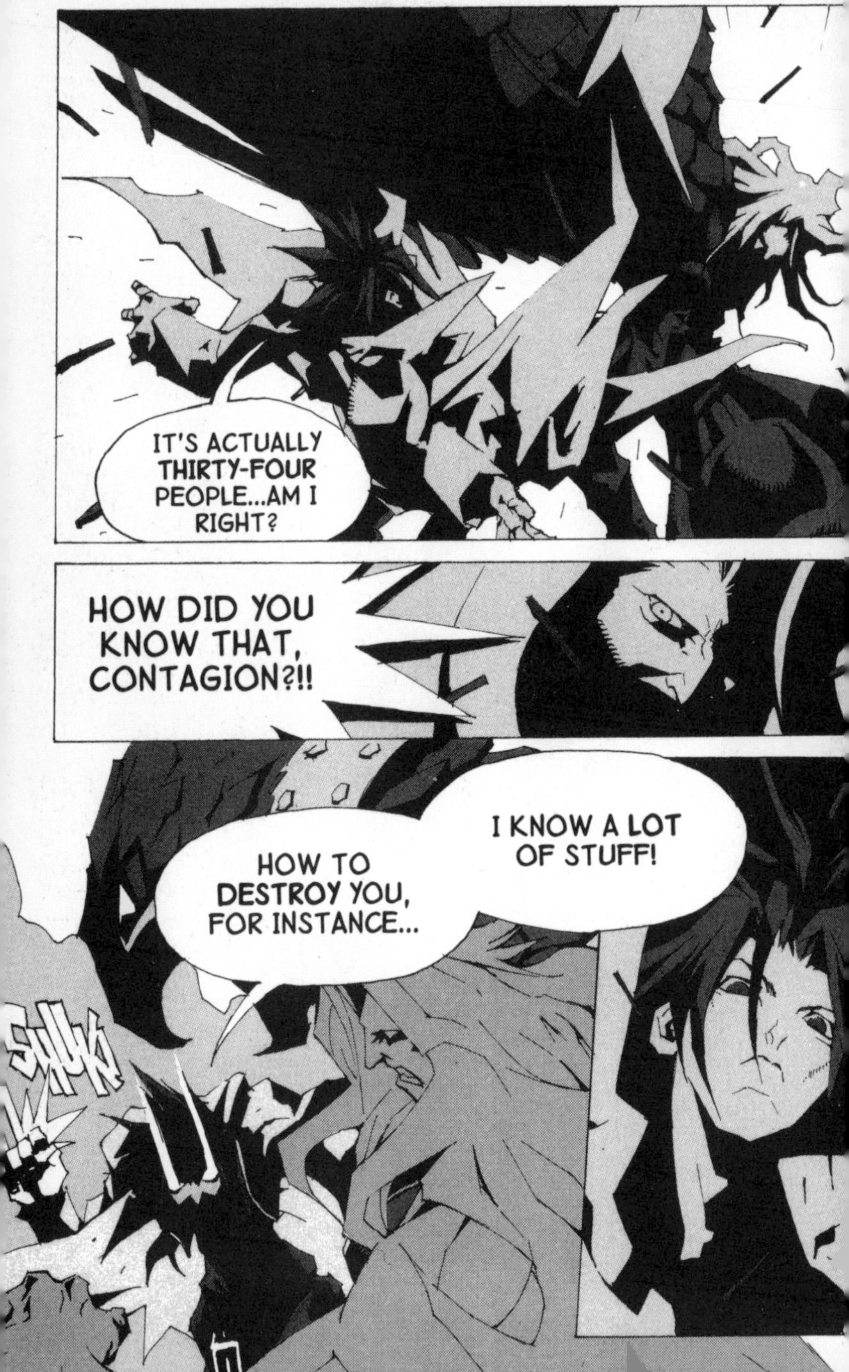
IT'S ACTUALLY THIRTY-FOUR PEOPLE...AM I RIGHT?
HOW DID YOU KNOW THAT, CONTAGION?!!
I KNOW A LOT OF STUFF!
HOW TO DESTROY YOU, FOR INSTANCE...

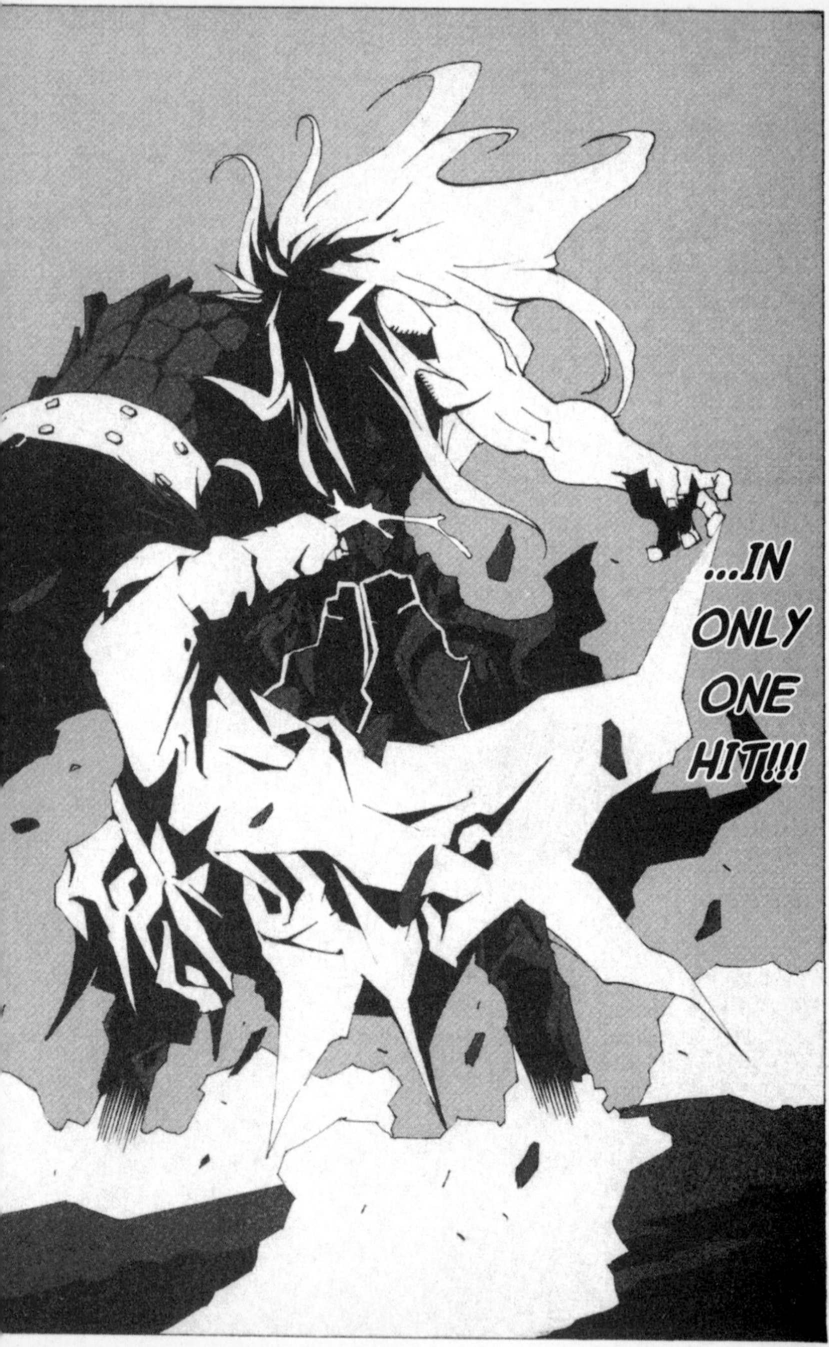
...IN ONLY ONE HIT!!!

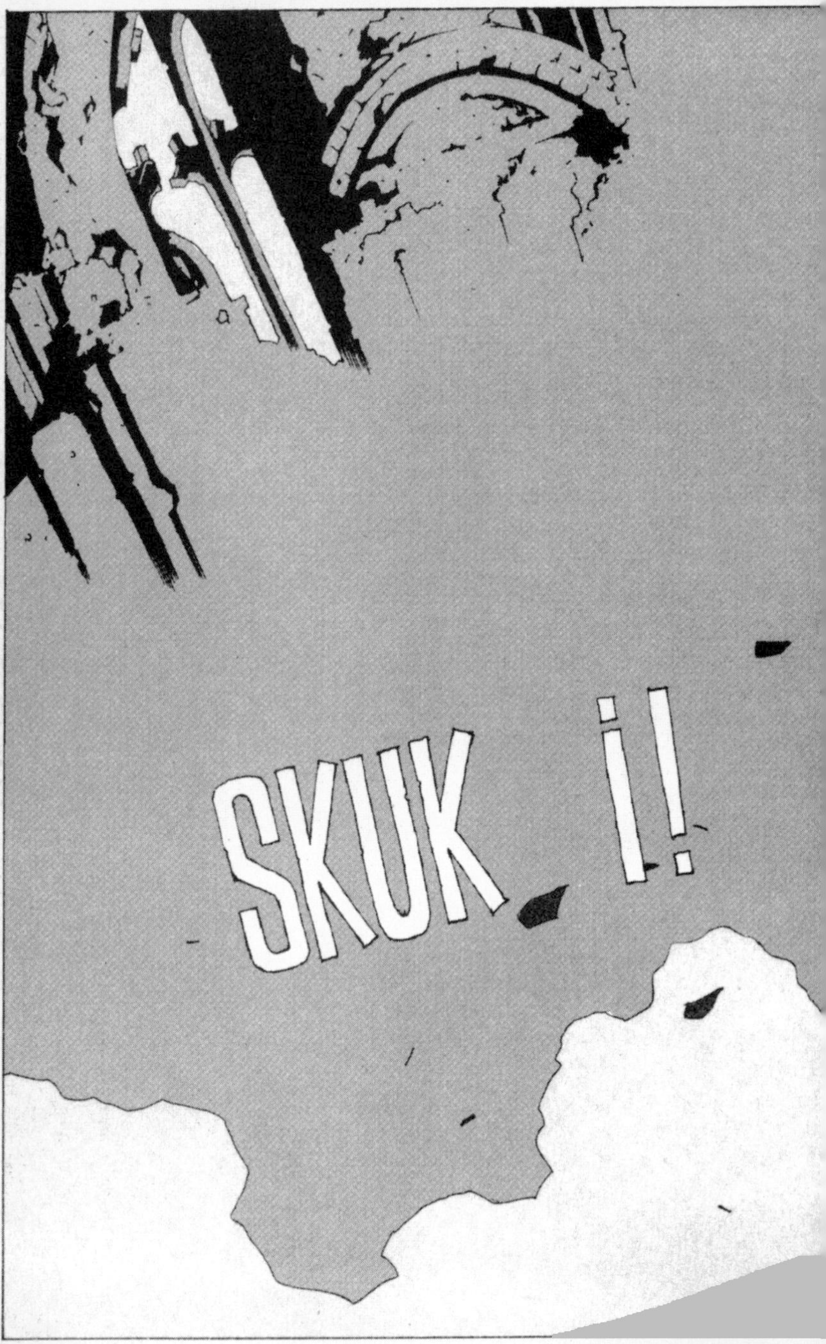
SKUK !!

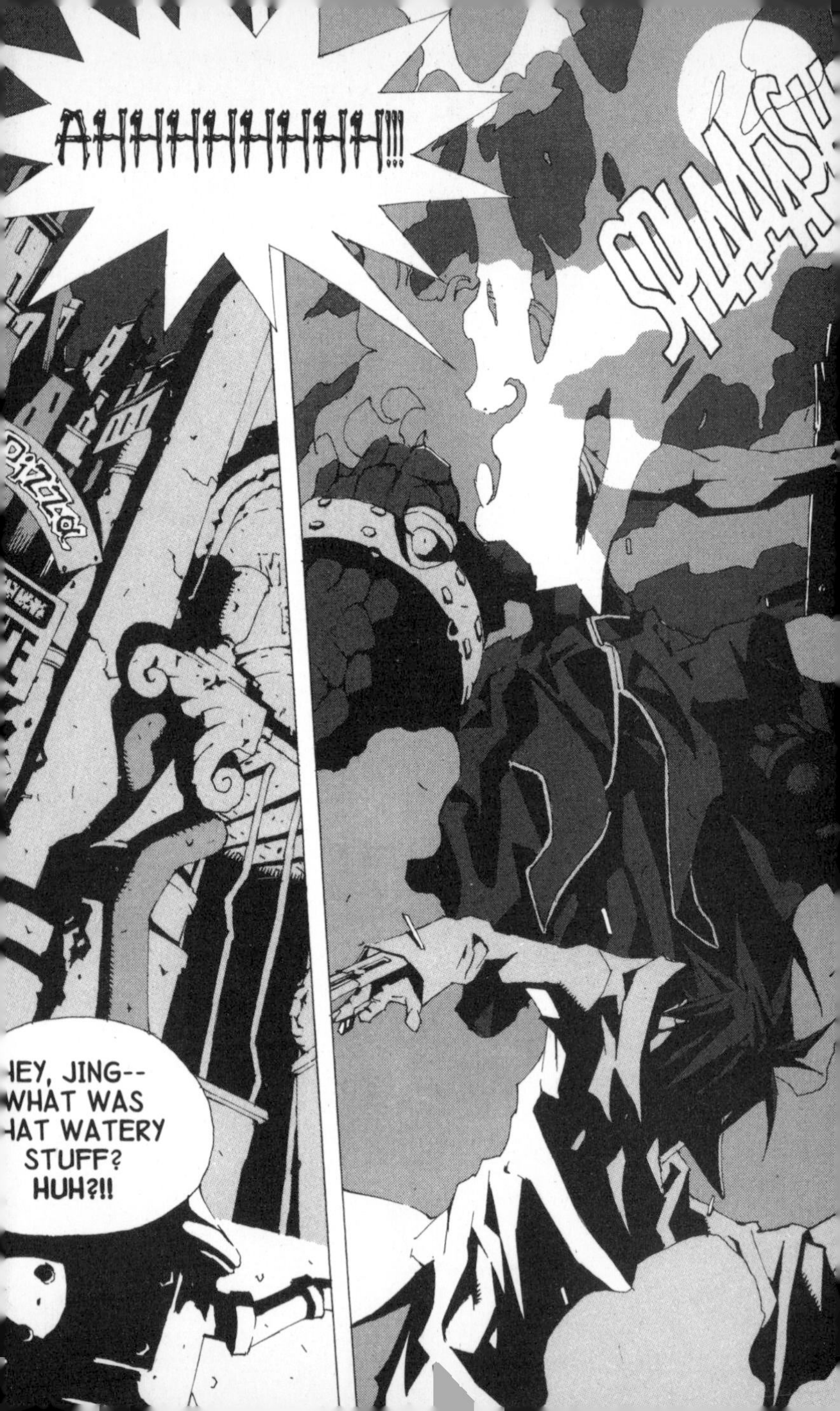
AHHHHHHHH!!!
SPLAASH!
HEY, JING-- WHAT WAS HAT WATERY STUFF? HUH?!!

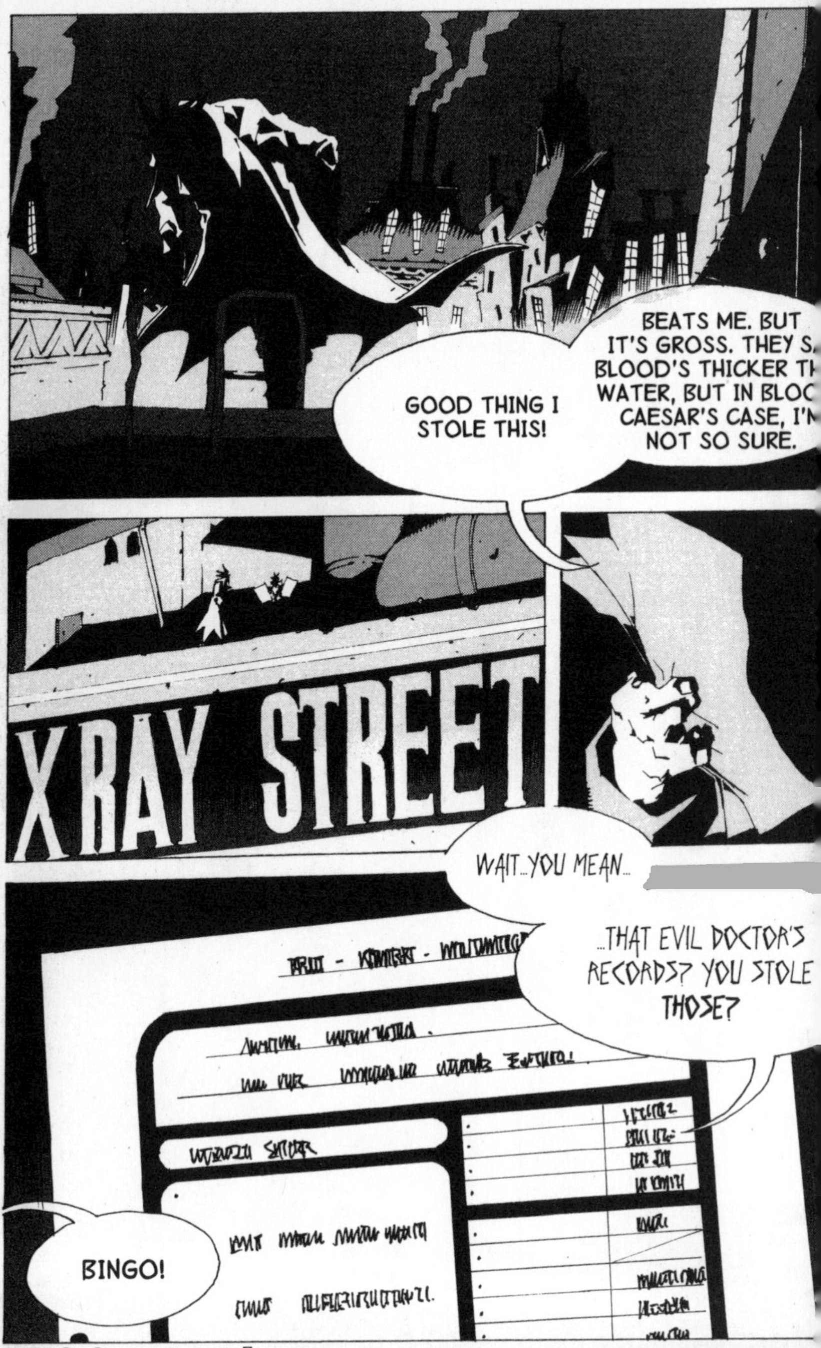
BEATS ME. BUT IT'S GROSS. THEY S BLOOD'S THICKER TH WATER, BUT IN BLOC CAESAR'S CASE, I'M NOT SO SURE.
GOOD THING I STOLE THIS!
XRAY STREET
WAIT...YOU MEAN...
...THAT EVIL DOCTOR'S RECORDS? YOU STOLE THOSE?
BINGO!

7th SHOT - Thirty-four Pursuers - End

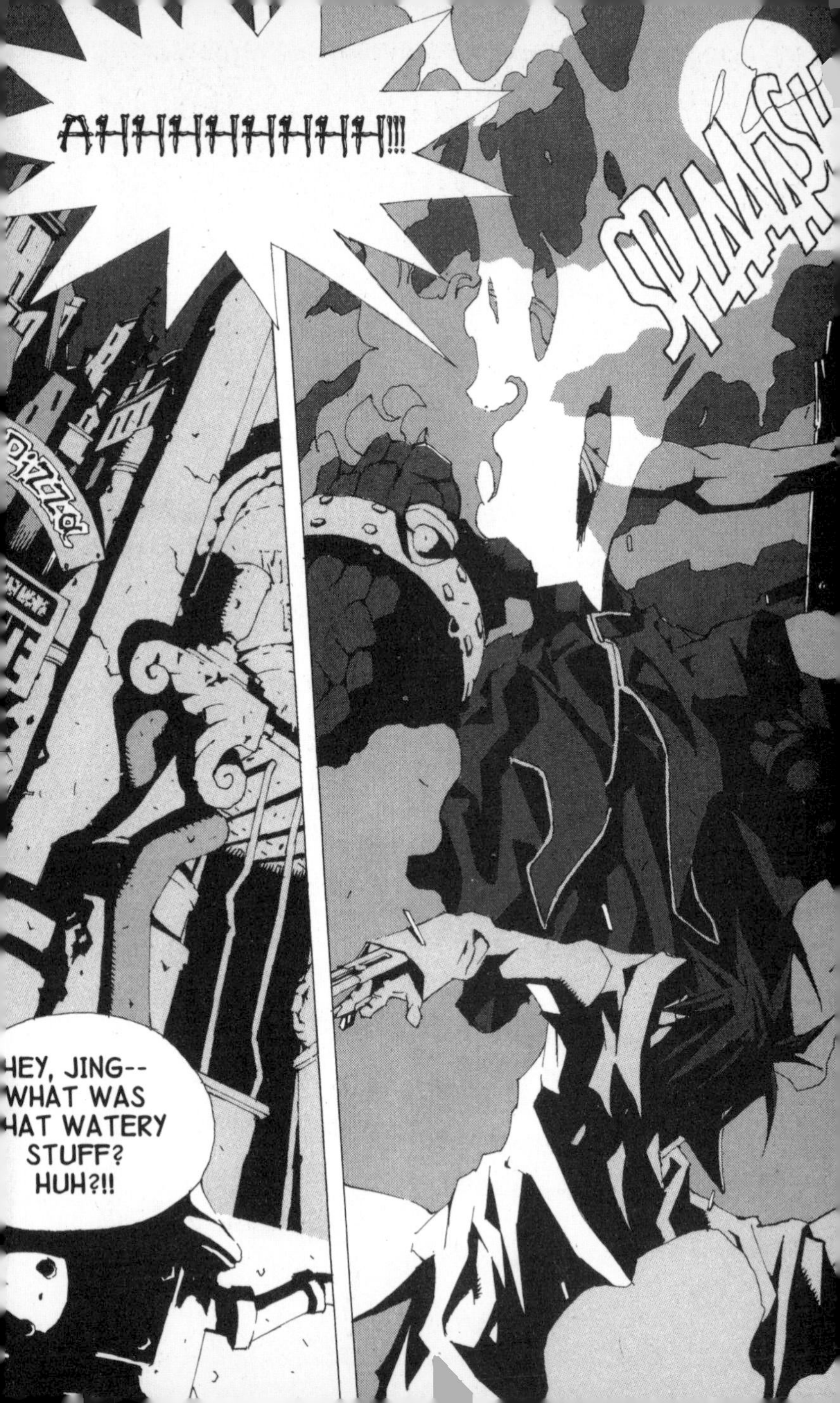

AHHHHHHHH!!!
SPLAAASH!
HEY, JING-- WHAT WAS HAT WATERY STUFF? HUH?!!

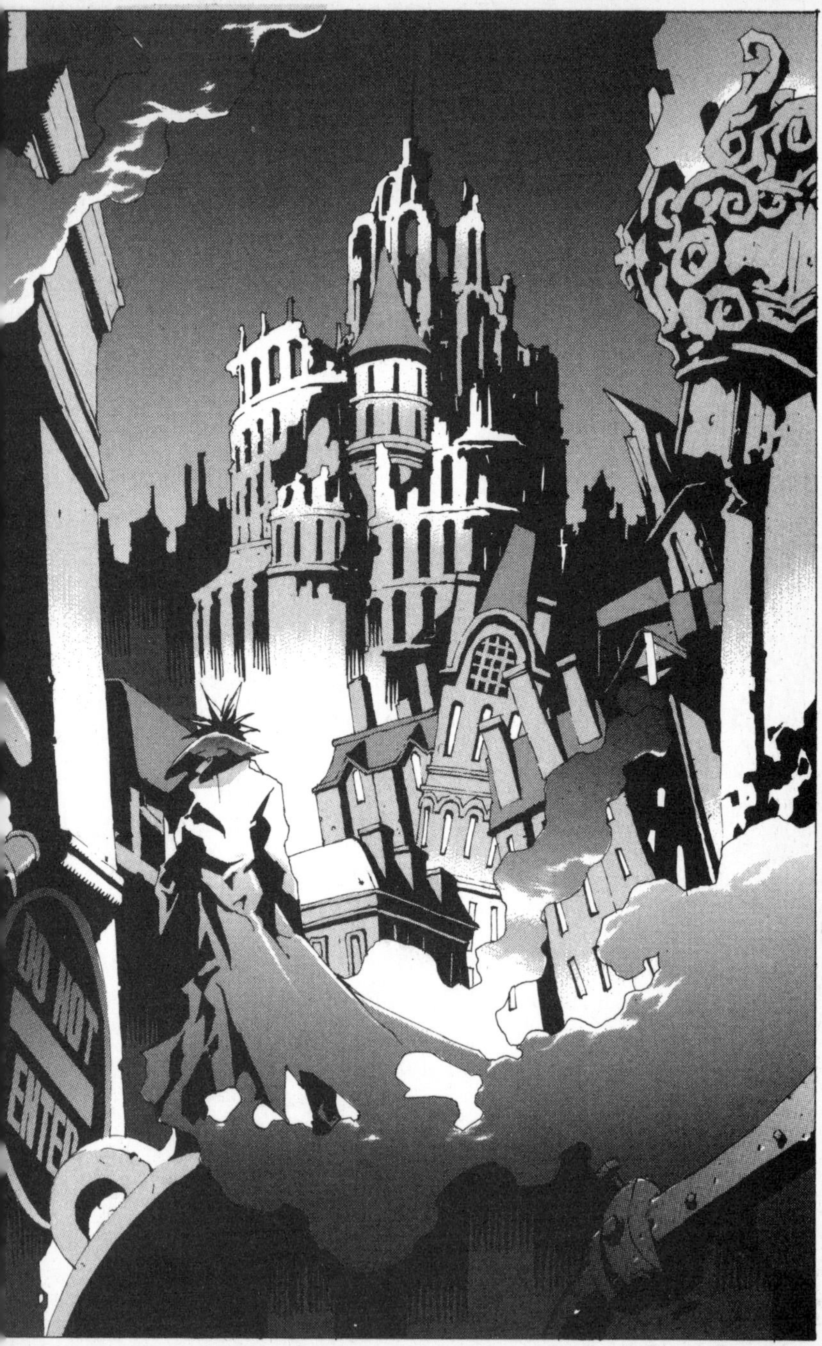
DO NOT ENTER

8th SHOT - A Medicine Called Freedom

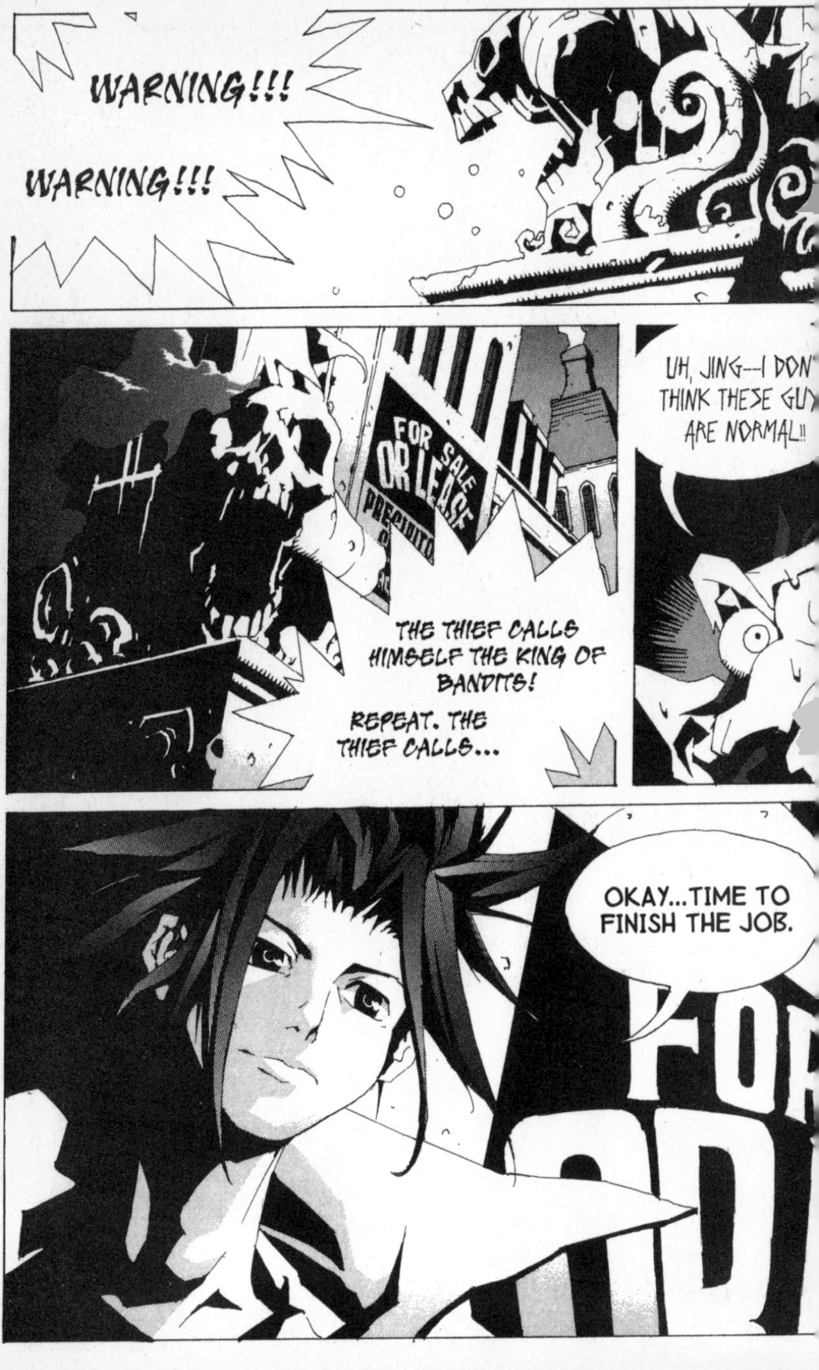
WARNING!!!
WARNING!!!
UH, JING--I DON THINK THESE GU ARE NORMAL!!
FOR SALE OR LEASE
THE THIEF CALLS HIMSELF THE KING OF BANDITS!
REPEAT. THE THIEF CALLS...
OKAY...TIME TO FINISH THE JOB.

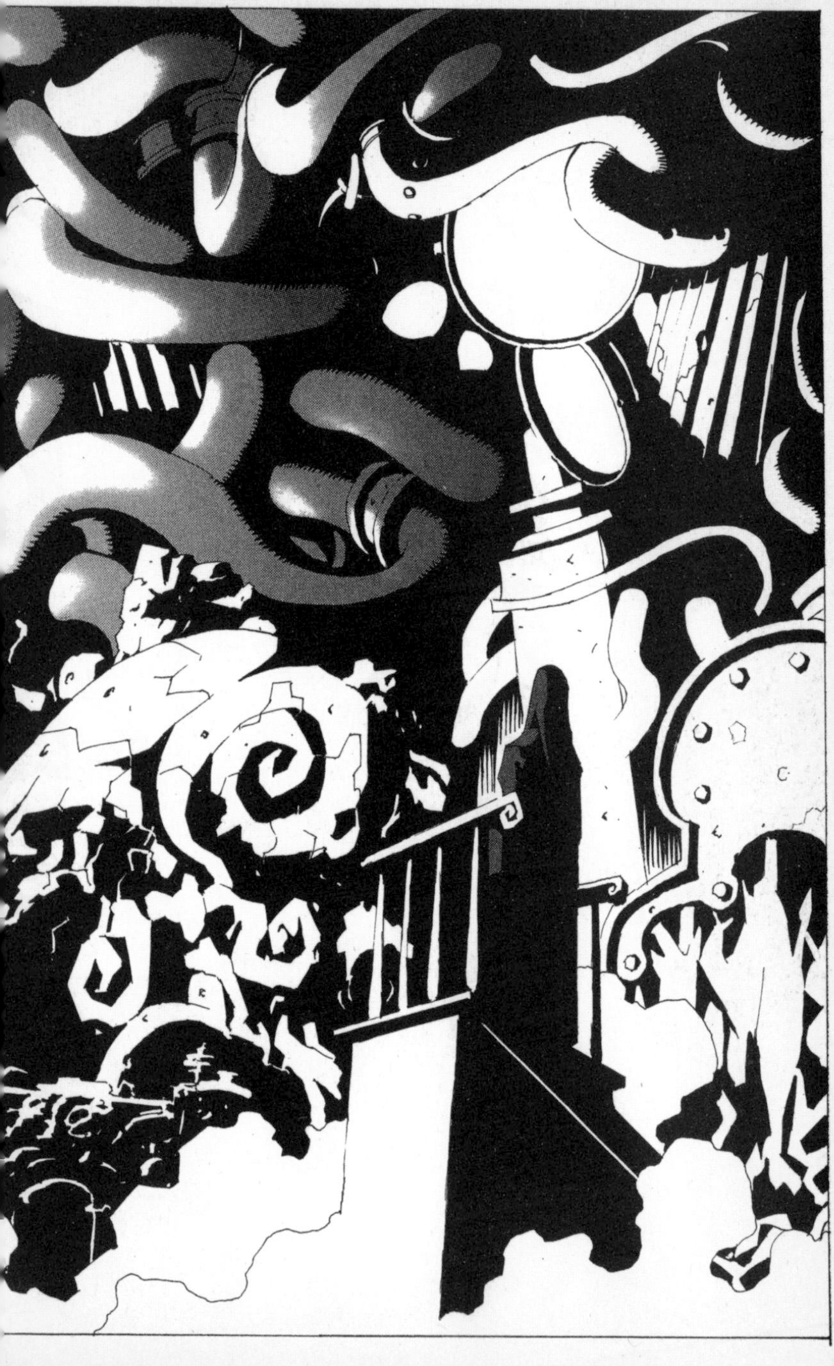

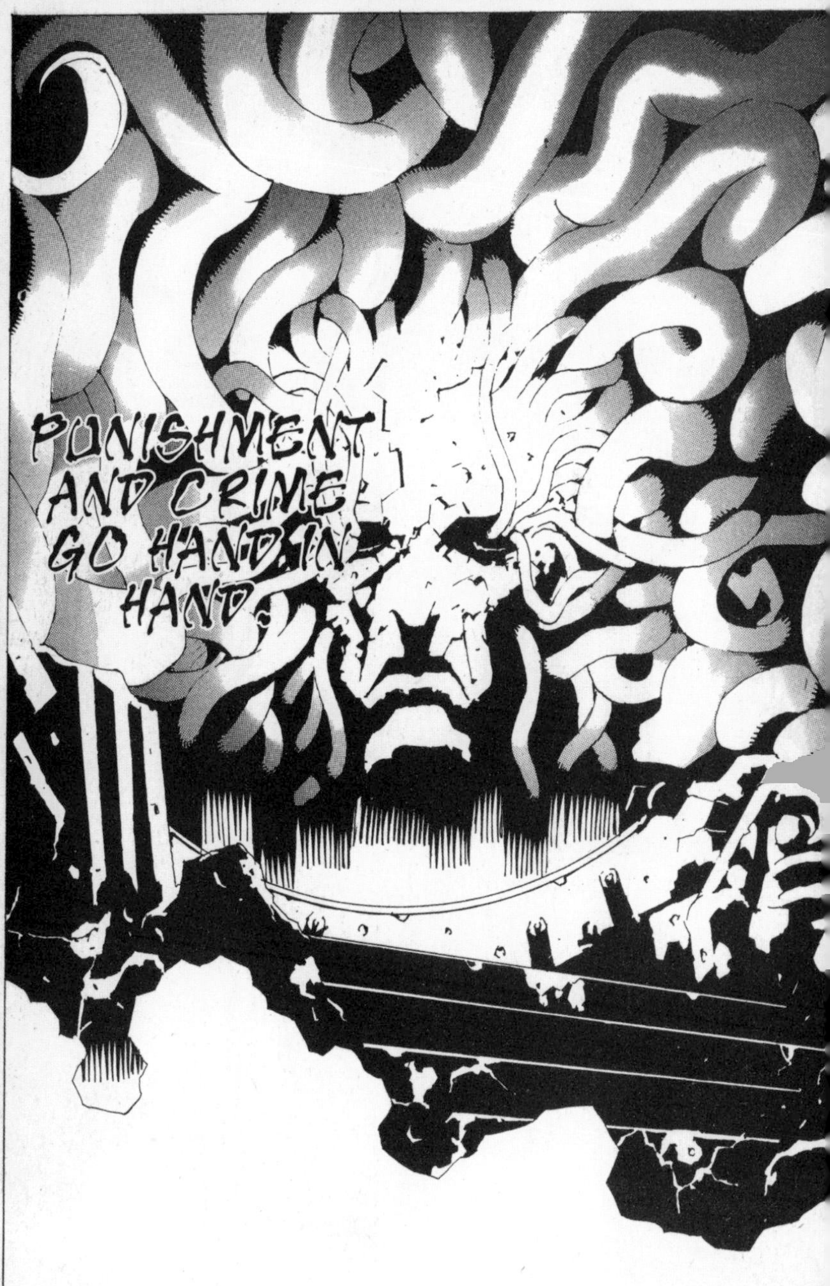
PUNISHMENT AND CRIME GO HAND-IN-HAND.

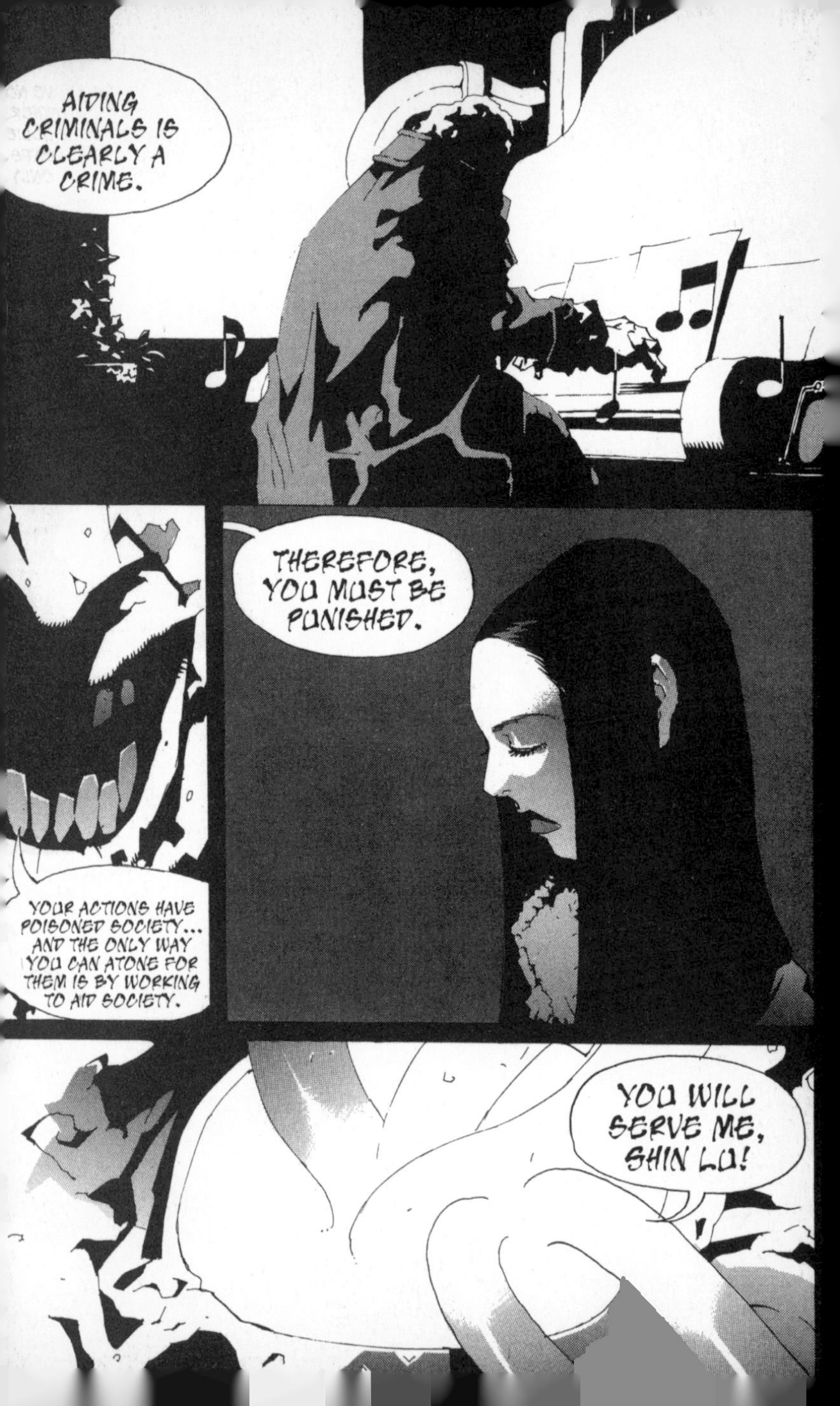
AIDING CRIMINALS IS CLEARLY A CRIME.
THEREFORE, YOU MUST BE PUNISHED.
YOUR ACTIONS HAVE POISONED SOCIETY... AND THE ONLY WAY YOU CAN ATONE FOR THEM IS BY WORKING TO AID SOCIETY.
YOU WILL SERVE ME, SHIN LU!

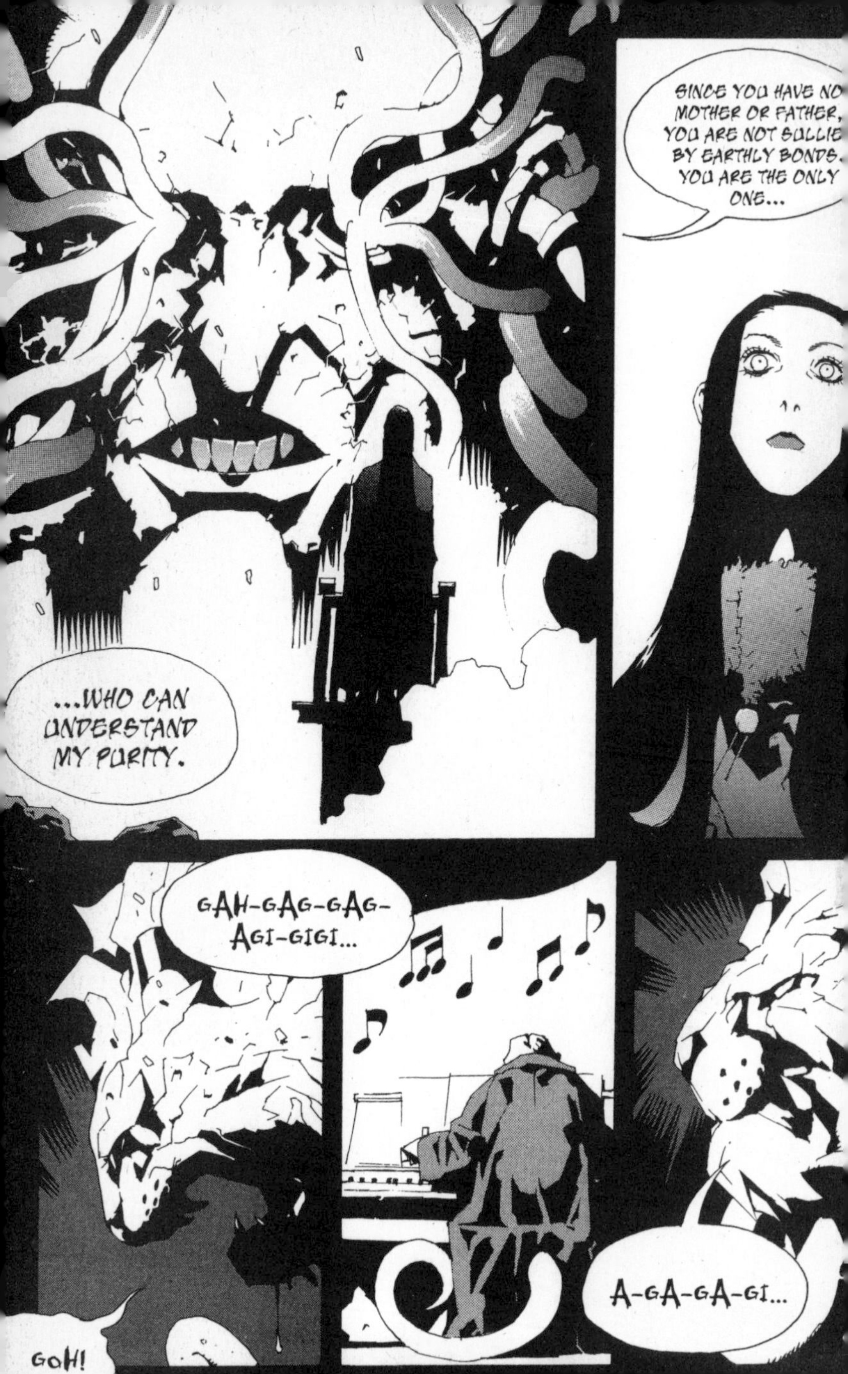
SINCE YOU HAVE NO MOTHER OR FATHER, YOU ARE NOT SULLIE BY EARTHLY BONDS. YOU ARE THE ONLY ONE...
...WHO CAN UNDERSTAND MY PURITY.
A-GA-GA-GI...
GAH-GAG-GAG-AGI-GIGI...
GOH!

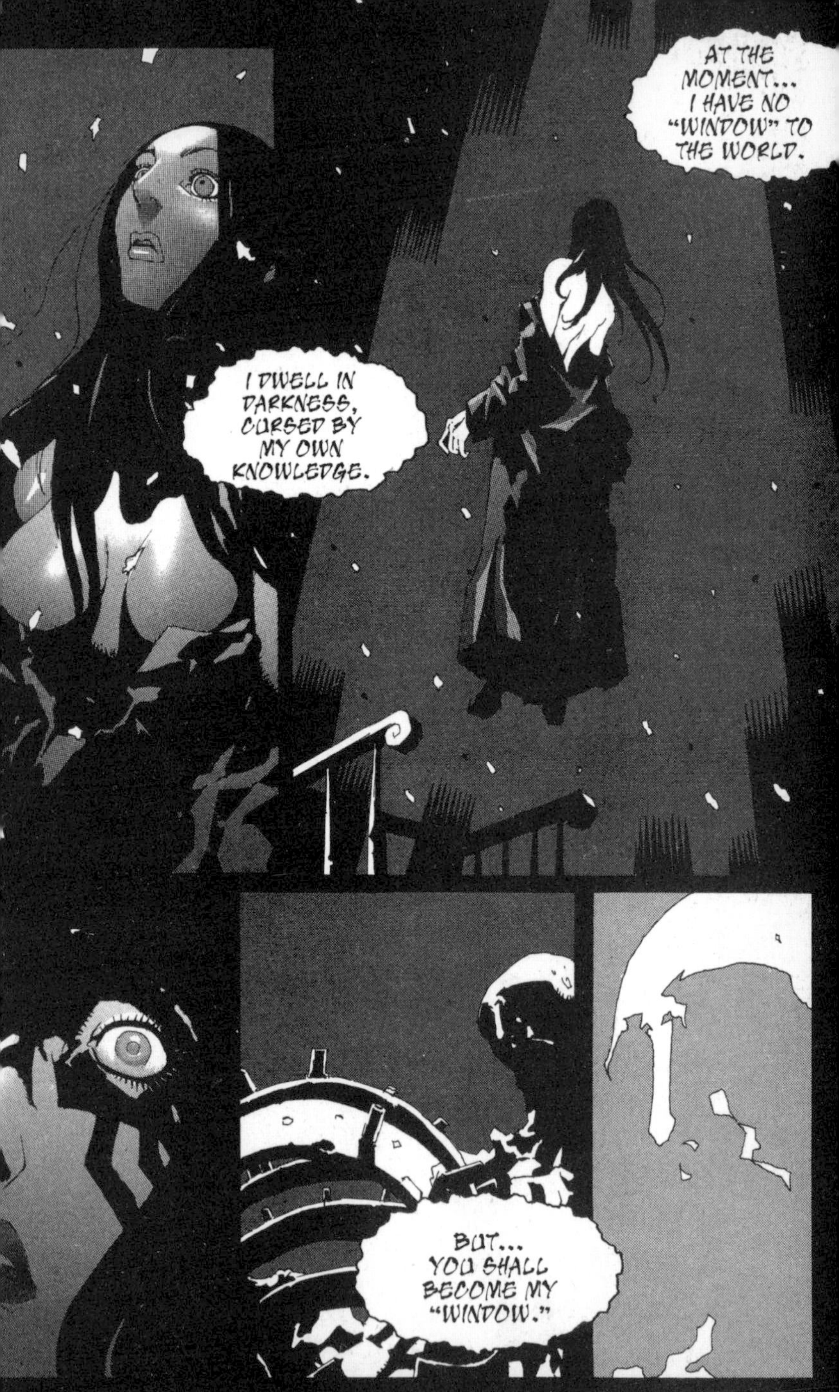
AT THE MOMENT... I HAVE NO "WINDOW" TO THE WORLD.
I DWELL IN DARKNESS, CURSED BY MY OWN KNOWLEDGE.
BUT... YOU SHALL BECOME MY "WINDOW."

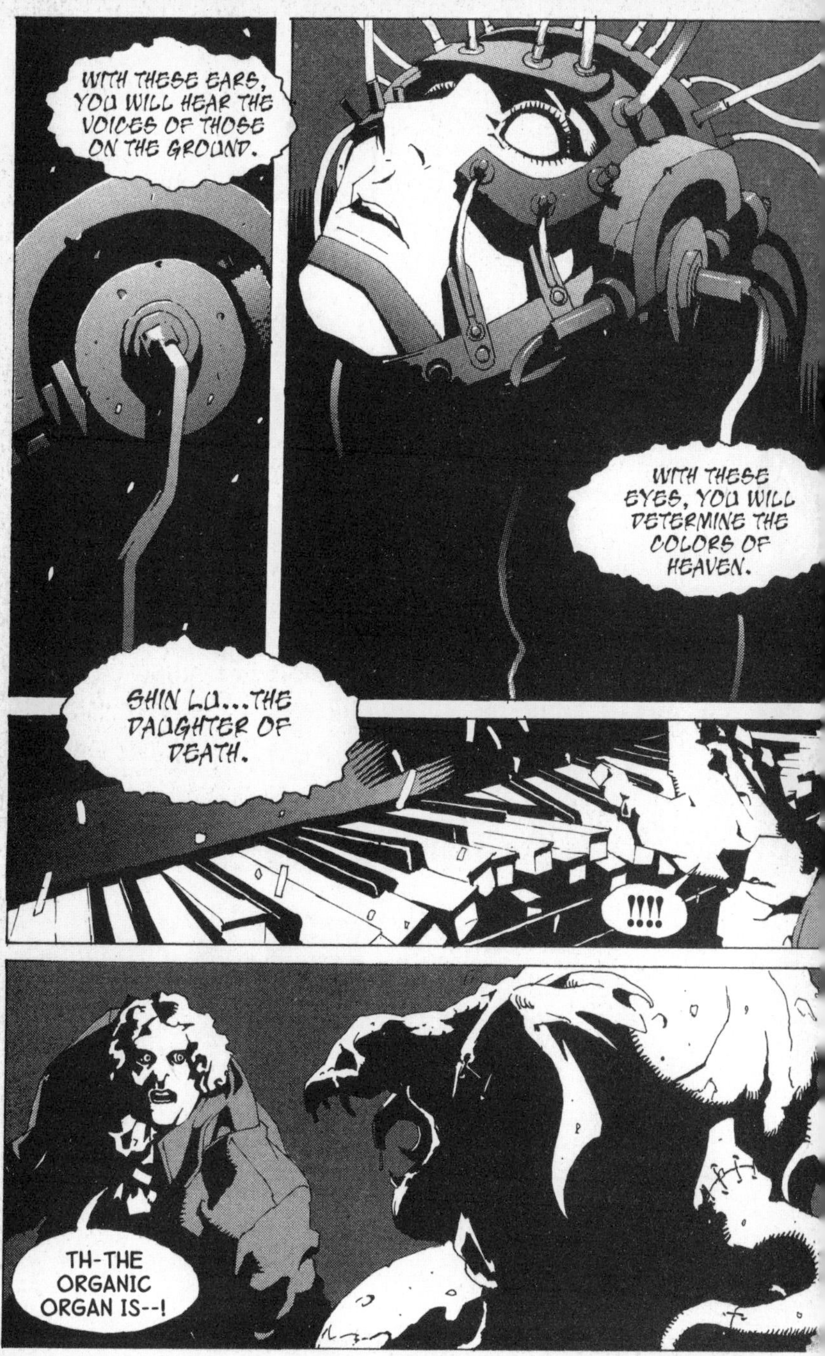
WITH THESE EYES, YOU WILL DETERMINE THE COLORS OF HEAVEN.
WITH THESE EARS, YOU WILL HEAR THE VOICES OF THOSE ON THE GROUND.
SHIN LU...THE DAUGHTER OF DEATH.
!!!!
TH-THE ORGANIC ORGAN IS--!

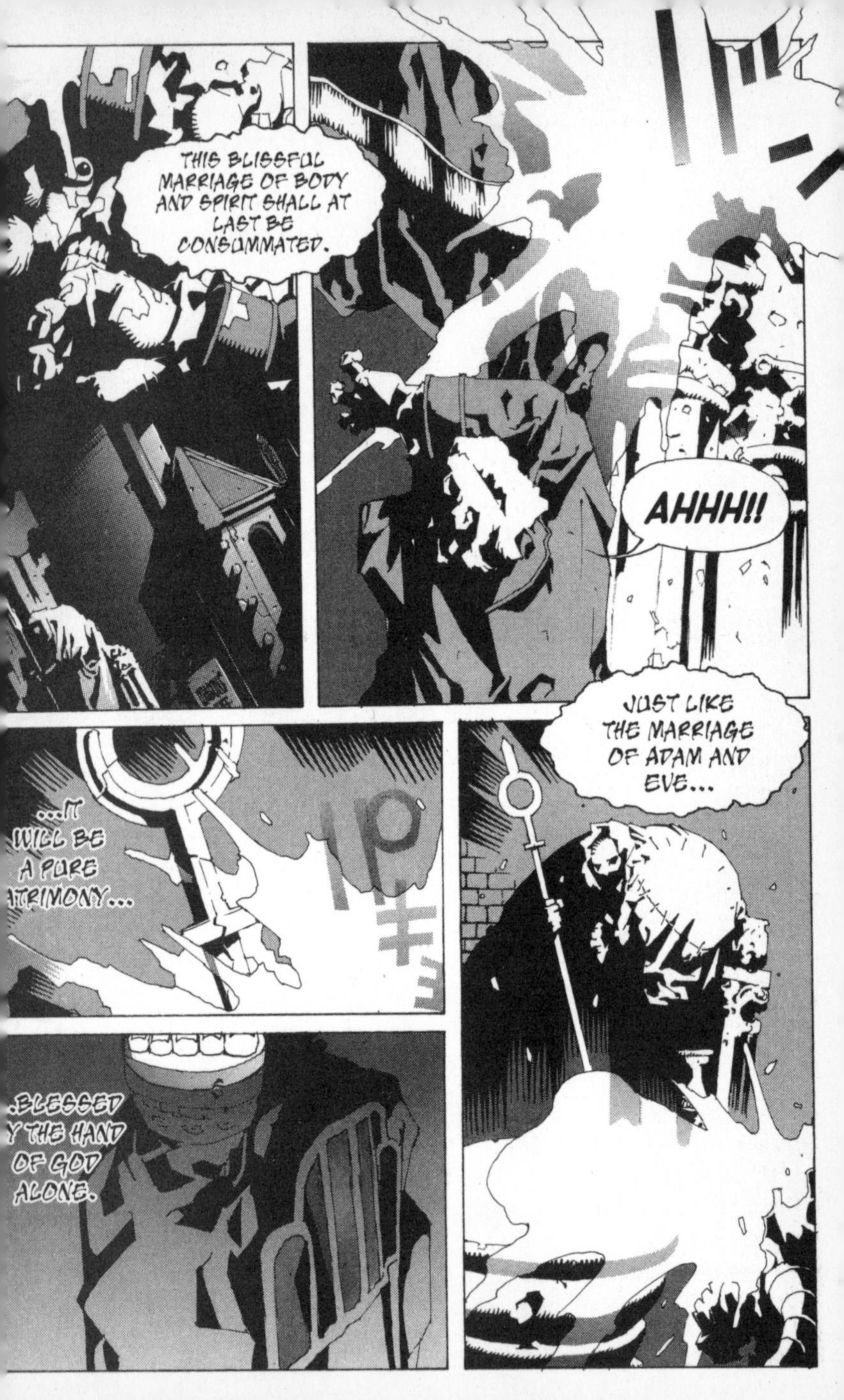
AHHH!!
THIS BLISSFUL MARRIAGE OF BODY AND SPIRIT SHALL AT LAST BE CONSUMMATED.
JUST LIKE THE MARRIAGE OF ADAM AND EVE...
...IT WILL BE A PURE ATRIMONY...
.BLESSED Y THE HAND OF GOD ALONE.

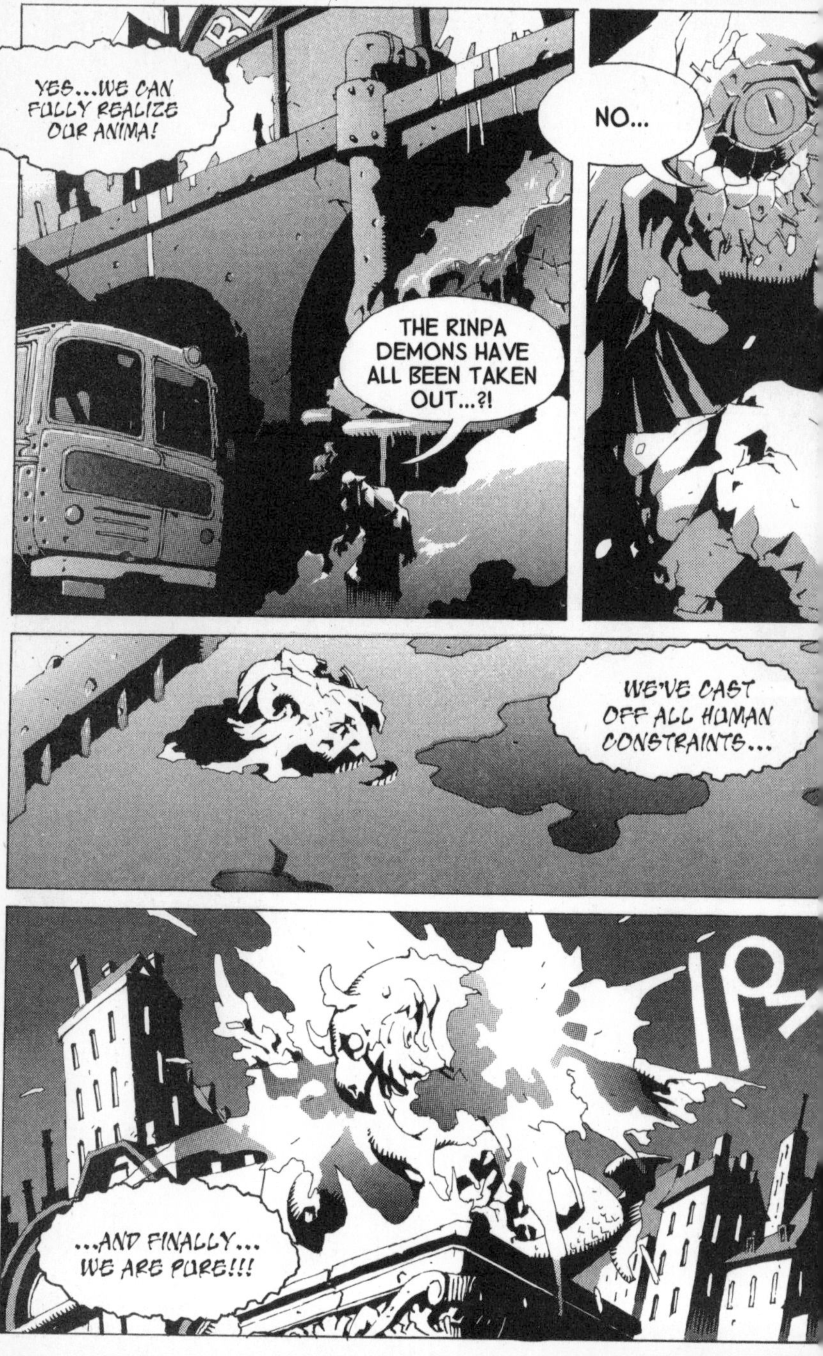
NO...
YES...WE CAN FULLY REALIZE OUR ANIMA!
THE RINPA DEMONS HAVE ALL BEEN TAKEN OUT...?!
WE'VE CAST OFF ALL HUMAN CONSTRAINTS...
...AND FINALLY... WE ARE PURE!!!

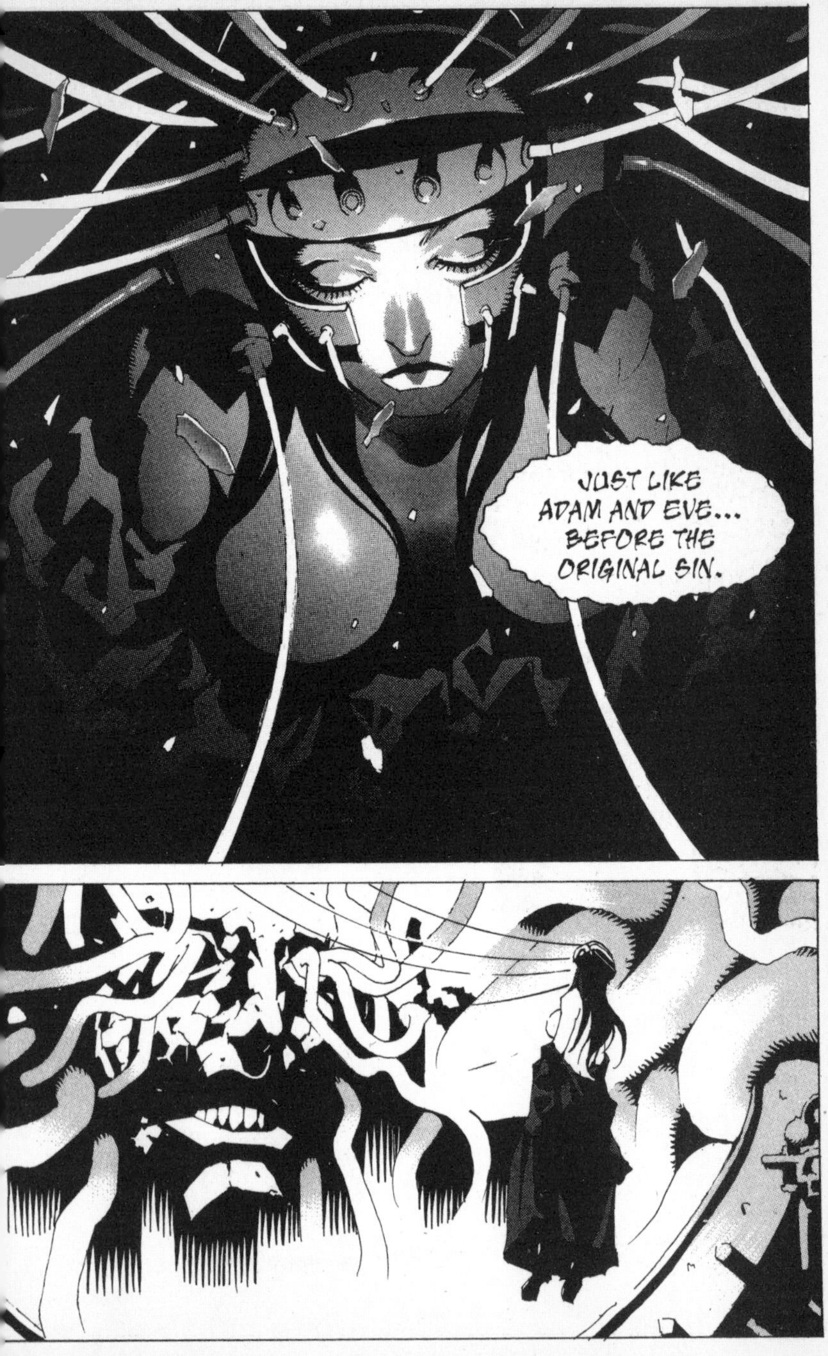
JUST LIKE ADAM AND EVE... BEFORE THE ORIGINAL SIN.

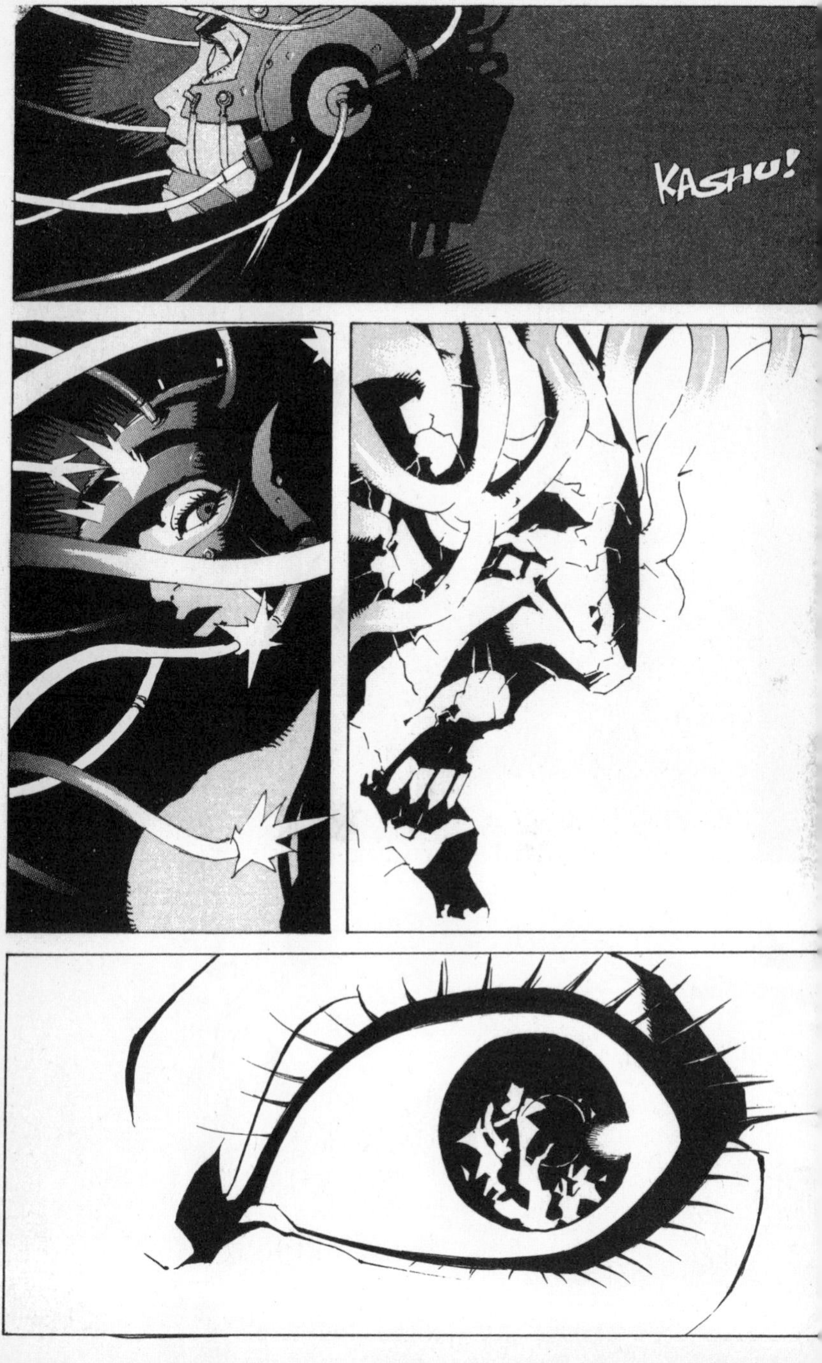
KASHU!

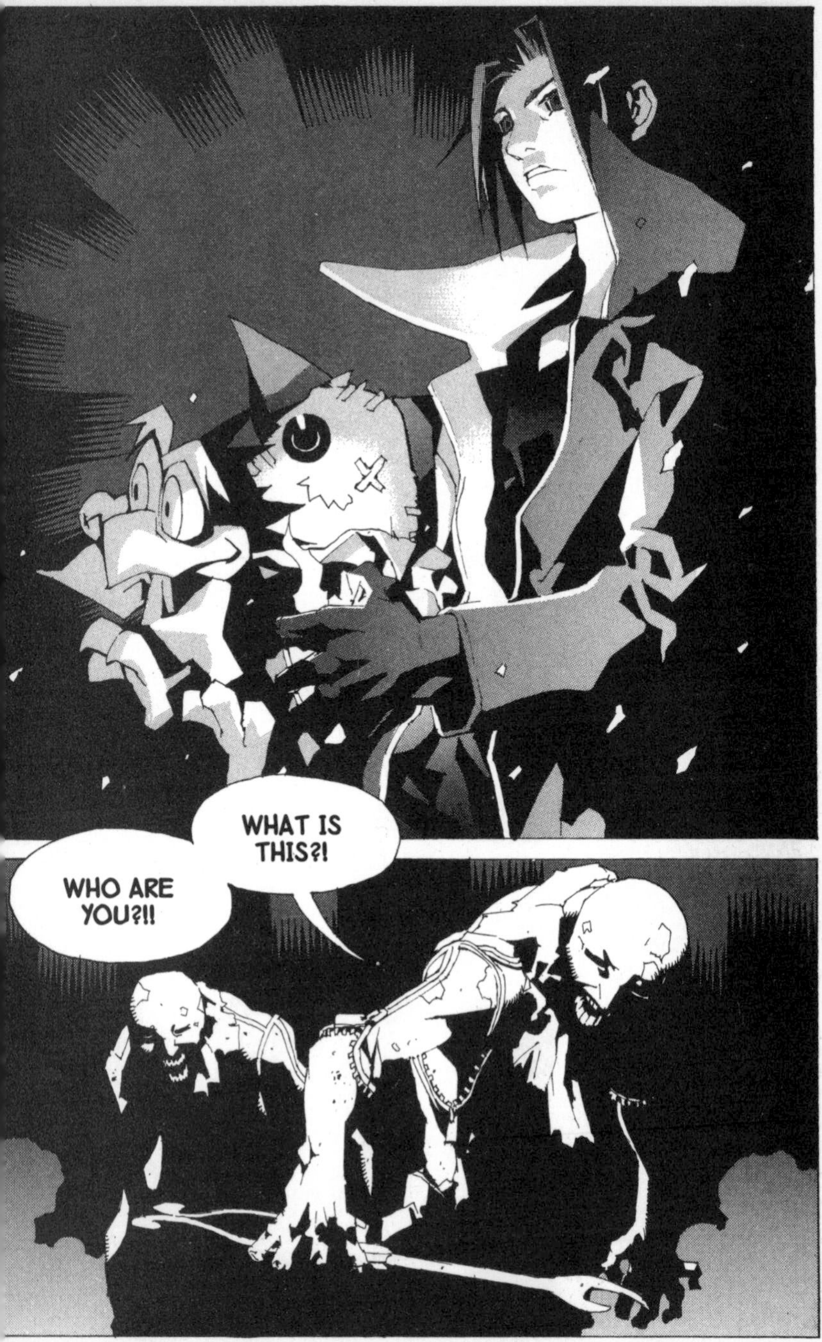
WHAT IS THIS?!
WHO ARE YOU?!!

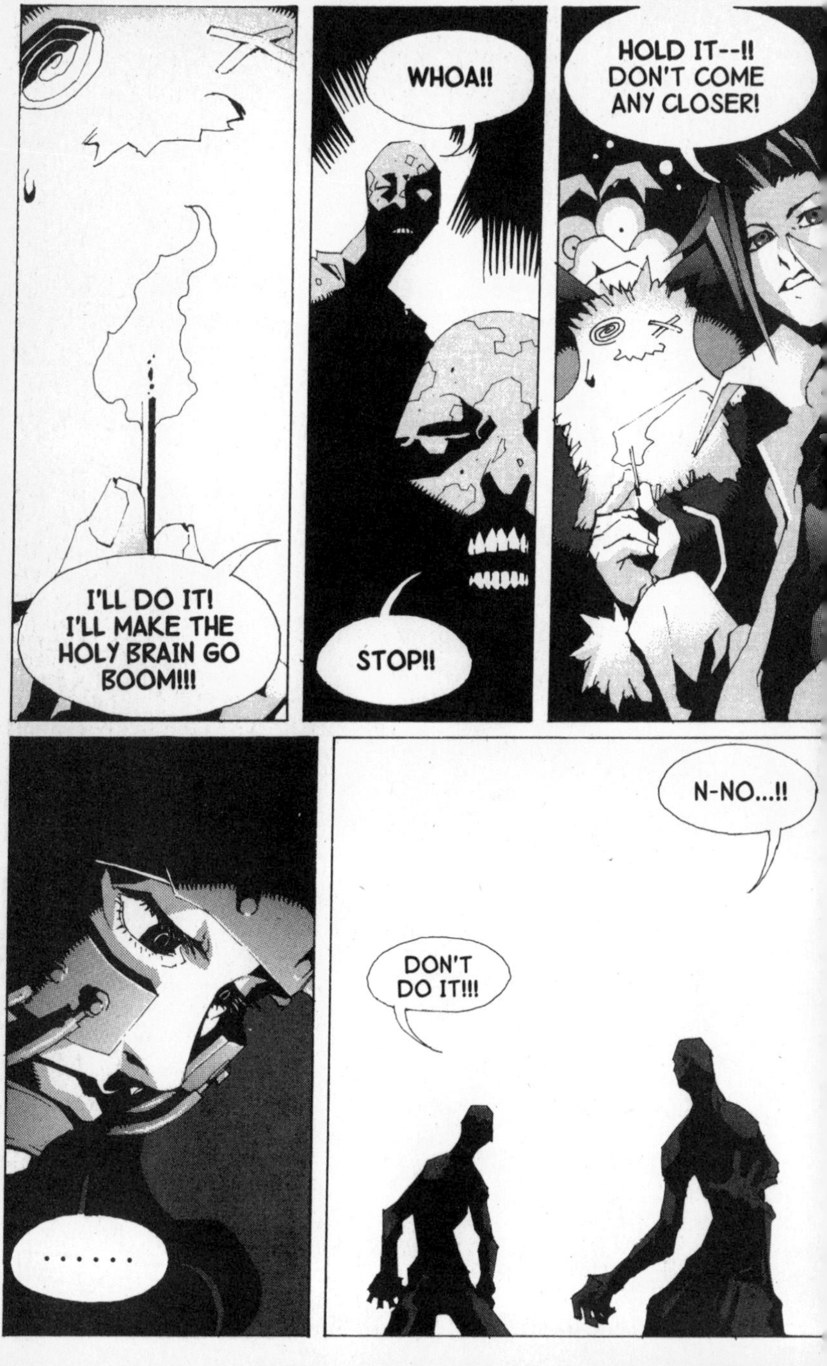
HOLD IT--!! DON'T COME ANY CLOSER!
WHOA!!
STOP!!
I'LL DO IT! I'LL MAKE THE HOLY BRAIN GO BOOM!!!
N-NO...!!
DON'T DO IT!!!
....

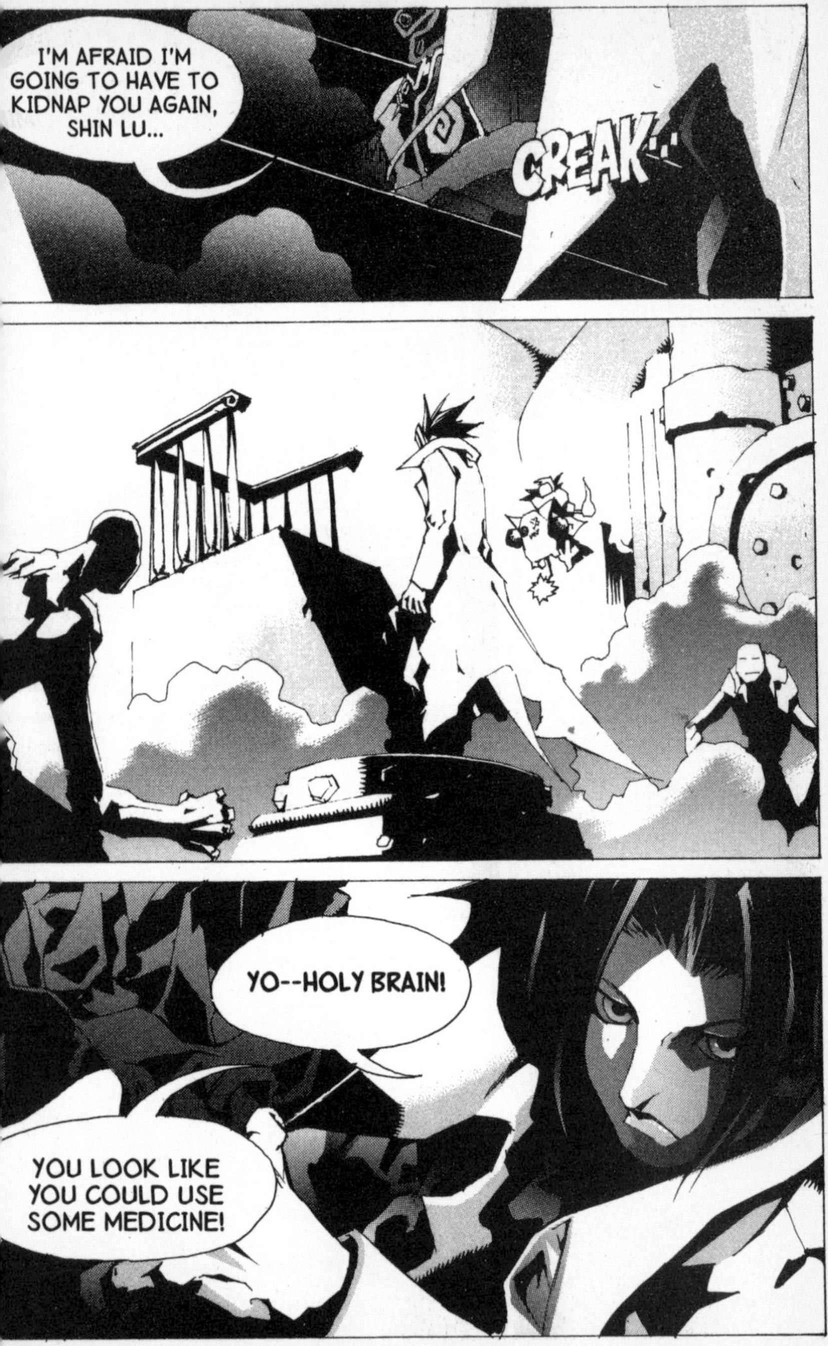
I'M AFRAID I'M GOING TO HAVE TO KIDNAP YOU AGAIN, SHIN LU...
CREAK..
YO--HOLY BRAIN!
YOU LOOK LIKE YOU COULD USE SOME MEDICINE!

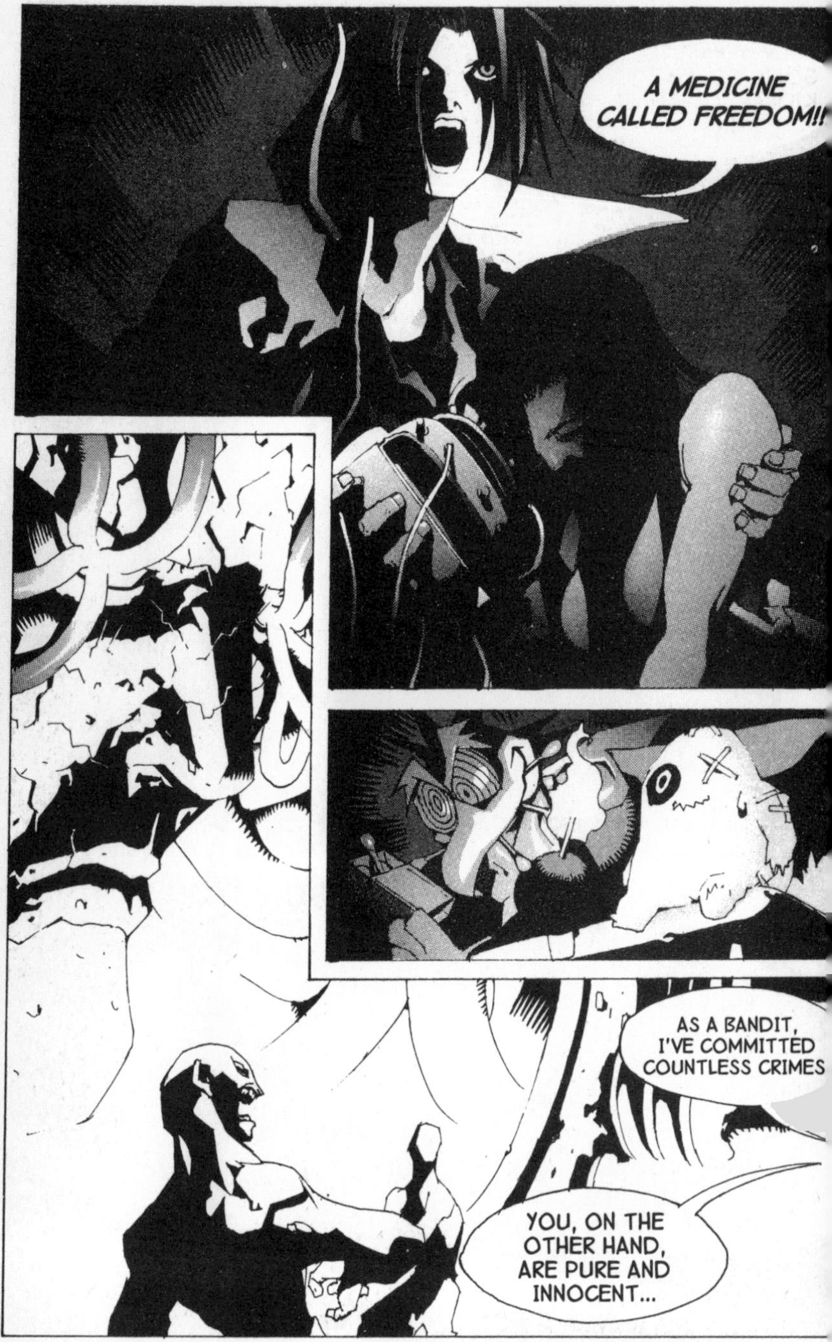
A MEDICINE CALLED FREEDOM!!
AS A BANDIT, I'VE COMMITTED COUNTLESS CRIMES
YOU, ON THE OTHER HAND, ARE PURE AND INNOCENT...

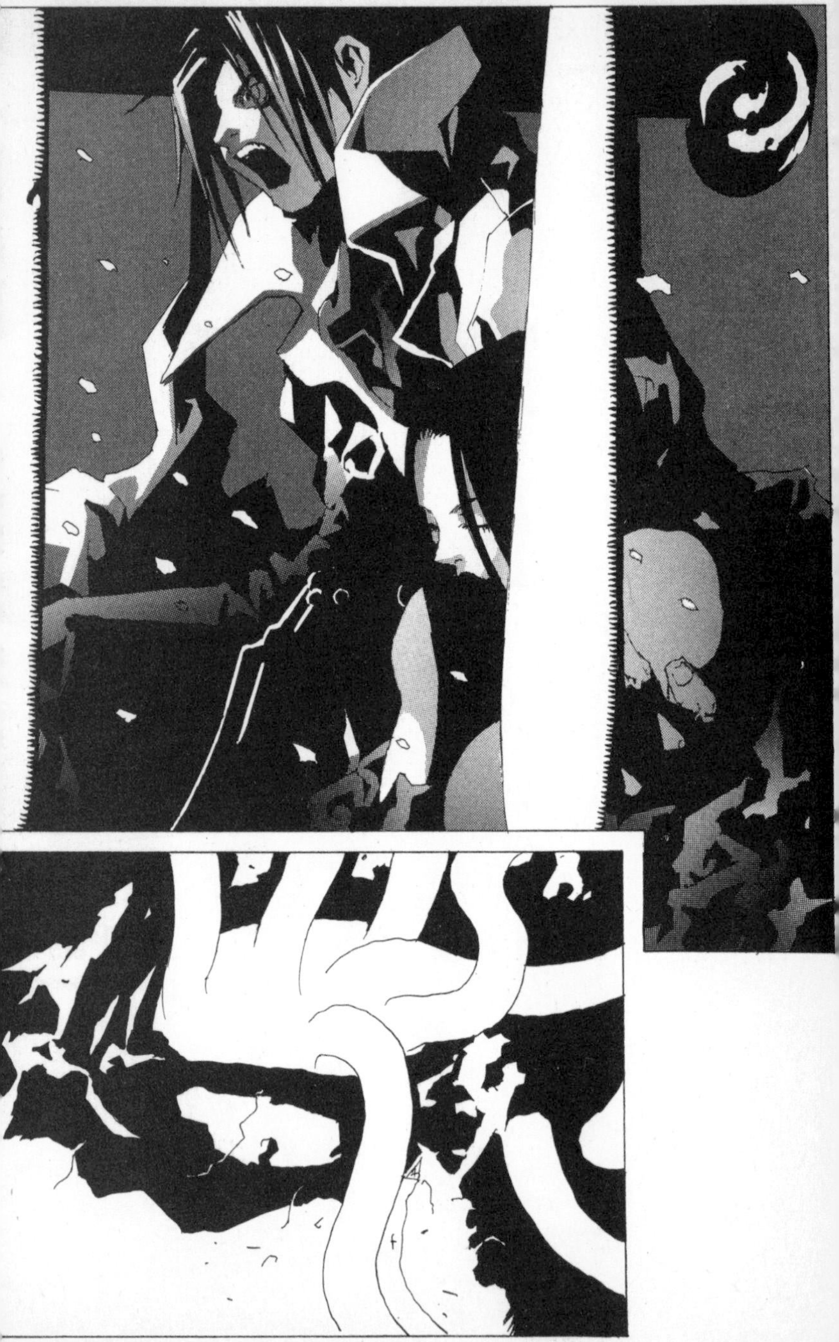

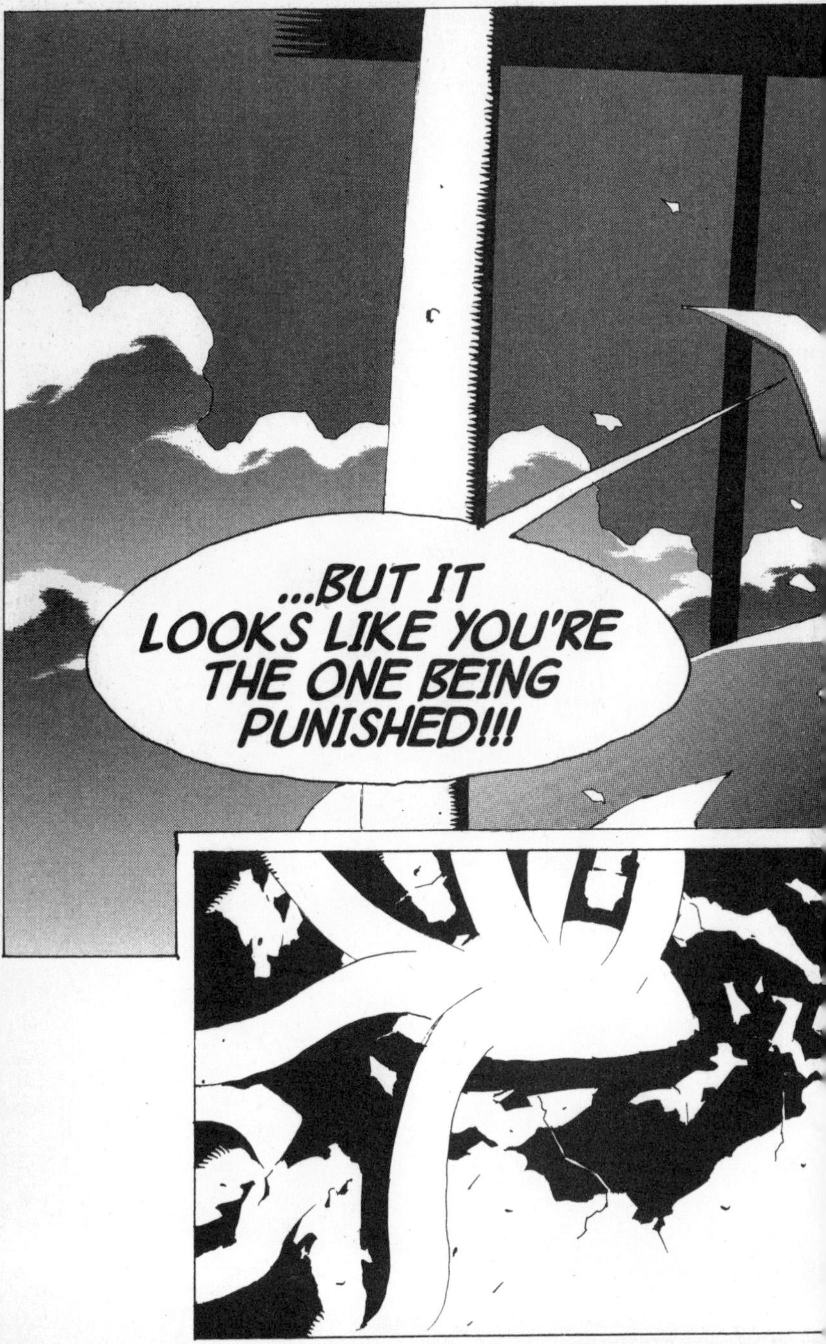
...BUT IT LOOKS LIKE YOU'RE THE ONE BEING PUNISHED!!!

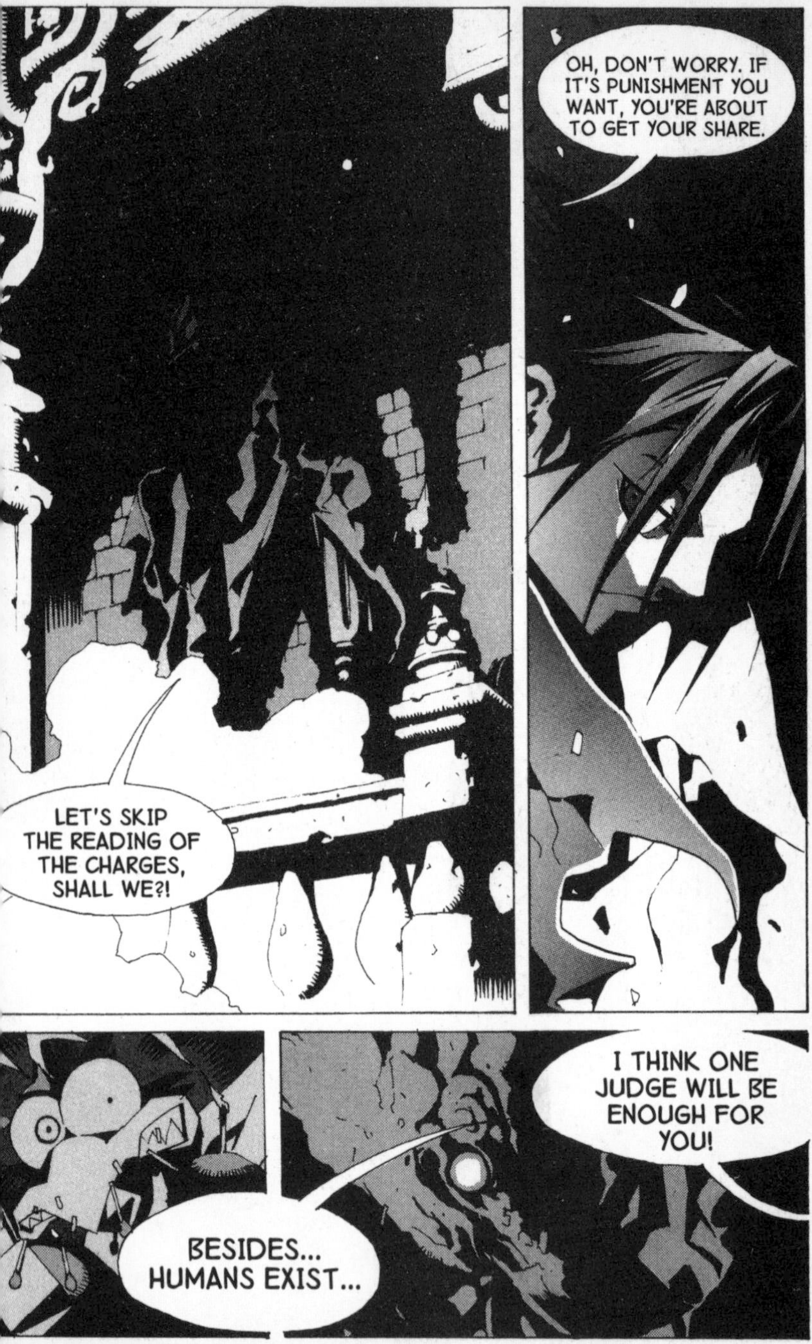
OH, DON'T WORRY. IF IT'S PUNISHMENT YOU WANT, YOU'RE ABOUT TO GET YOUR SHARE.
LET'S SKIP THE READING OF THE CHARGES, SHALL WE?!
I THINK ONE JUDGE WILL BE ENOUGH FOR YOU!
BESIDES... HUMANS EXIST...

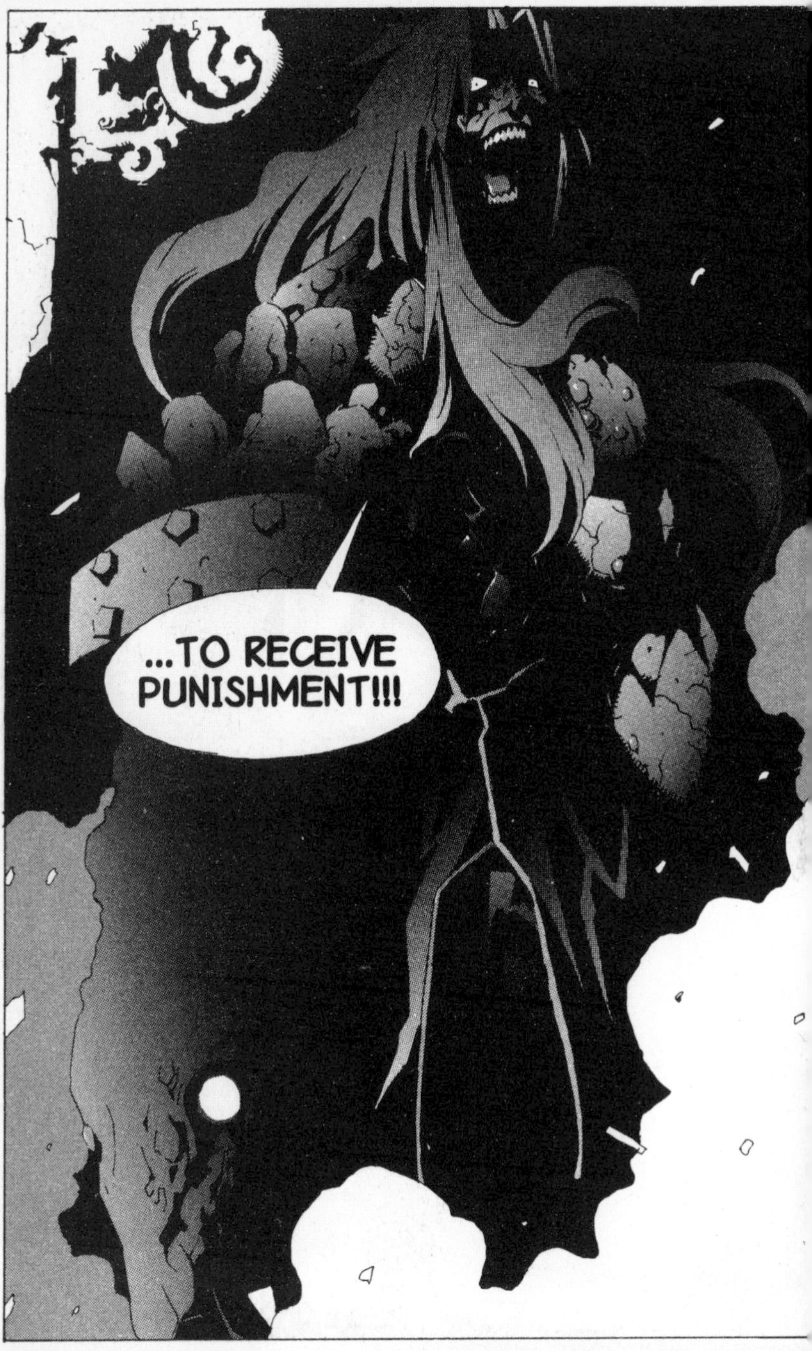
...TO RECEIVE PUNISHMENT!!!

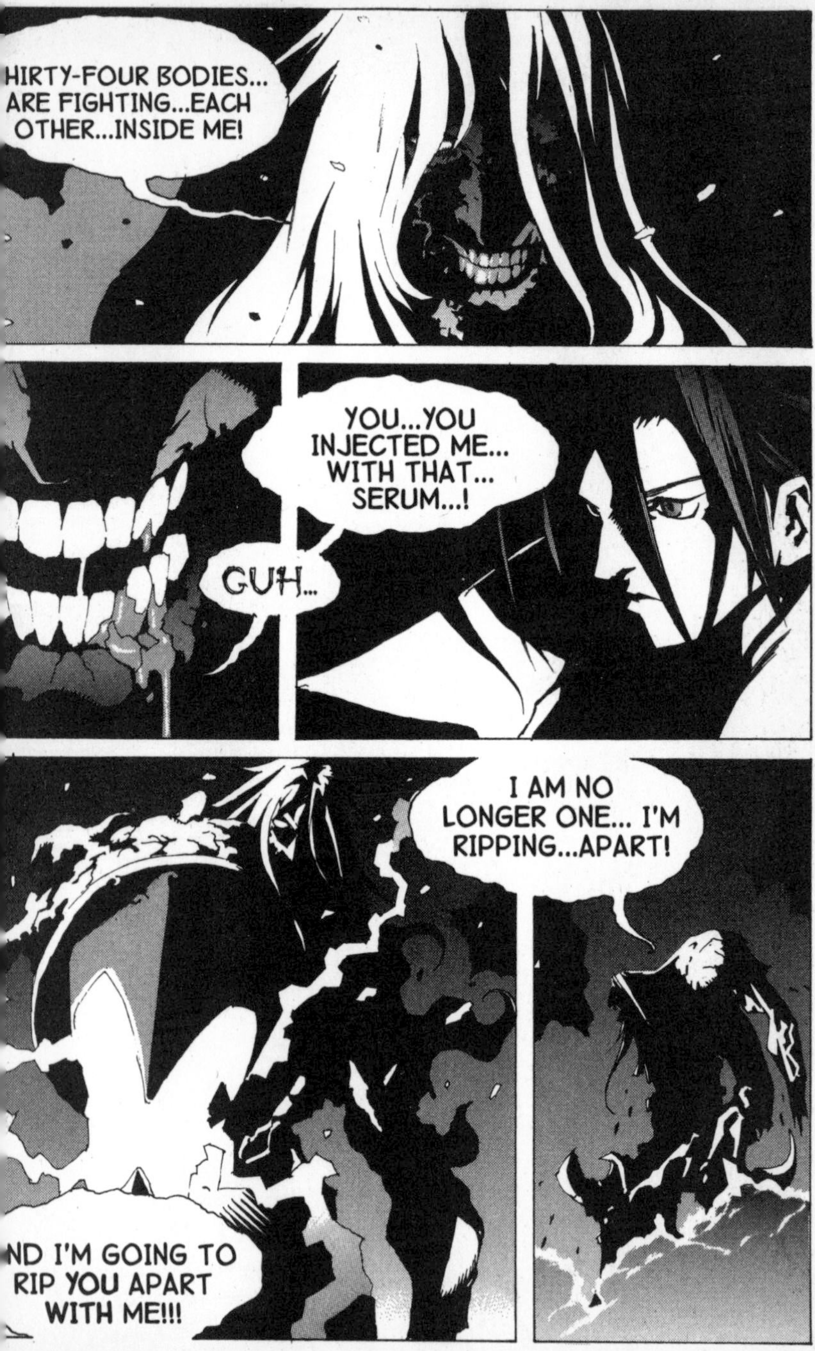
HIRTY-FOUR BODIES... ARE FIGHTING...EACH OTHER...INSIDE ME!
YOU...YOU INJECTED ME... WITH THAT... SERUM...!
GUH...
I AM NO LONGER ONE... I'M RIPPING...APART!
ND I'M GOING TO RIP YOU APART WITH ME!!!

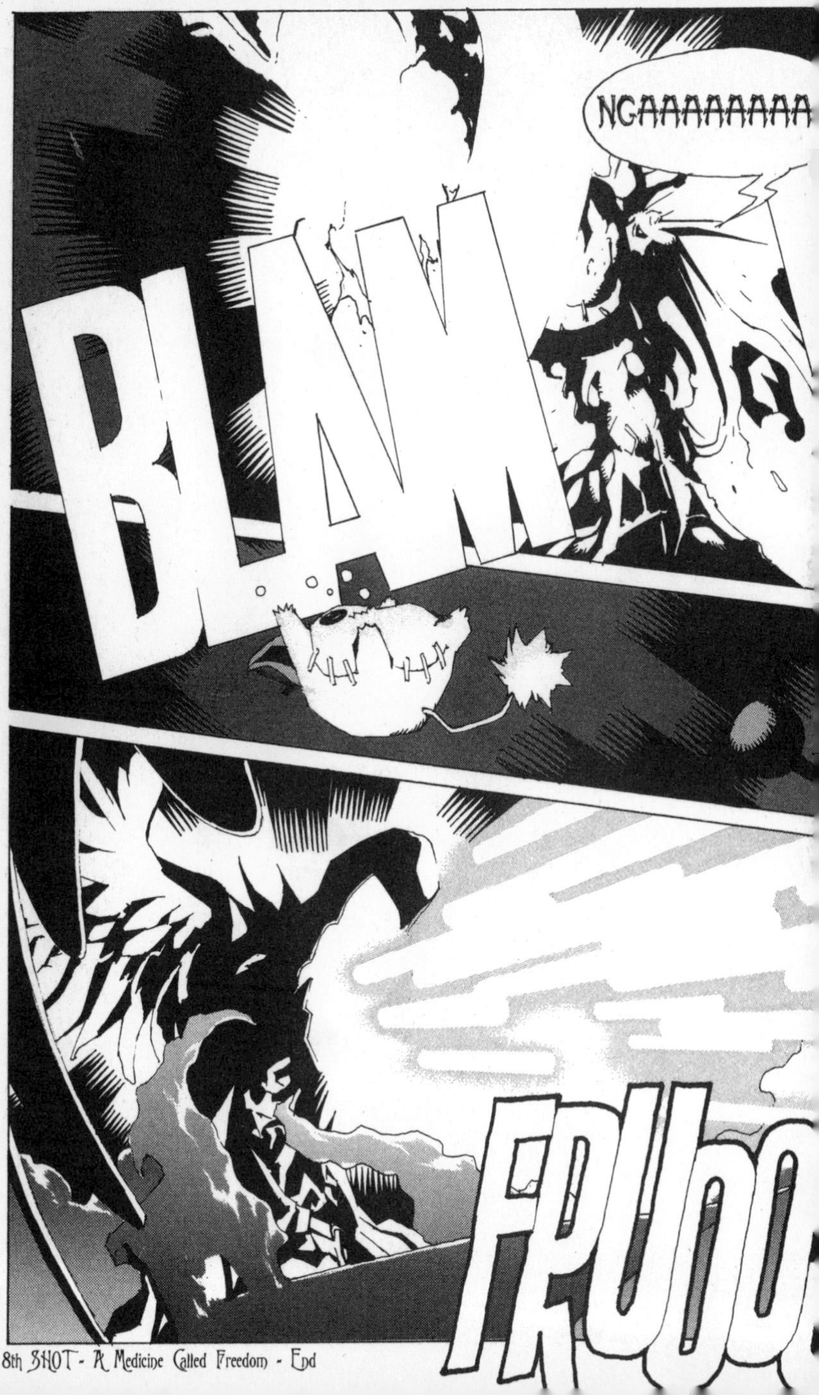

NGAAAAAAAA
BLAM
FPUOO

8th SHOT - A Medicine Called Freedom - End

9th Shot -
The End of Judgment

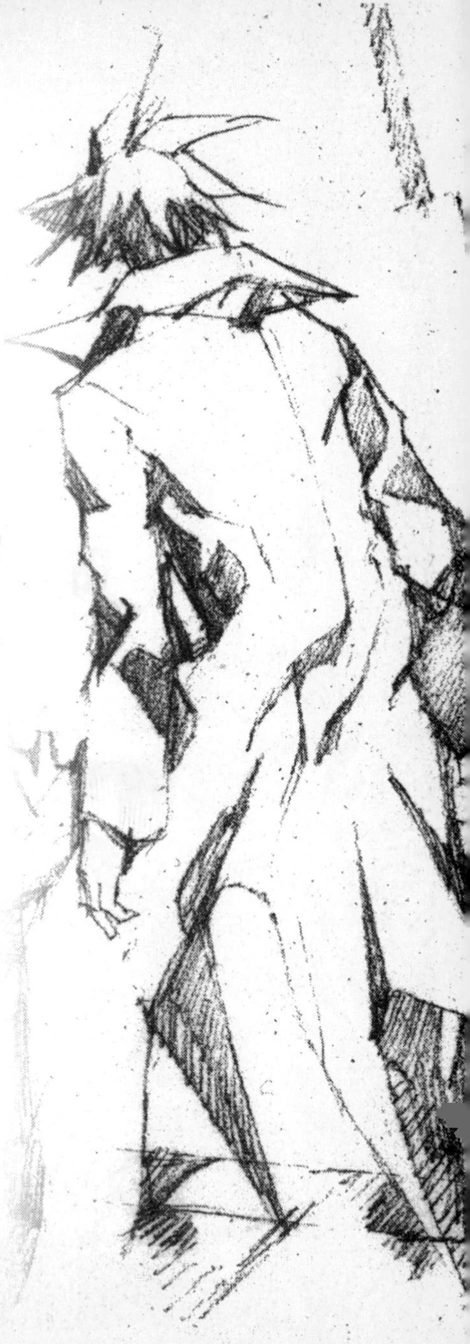

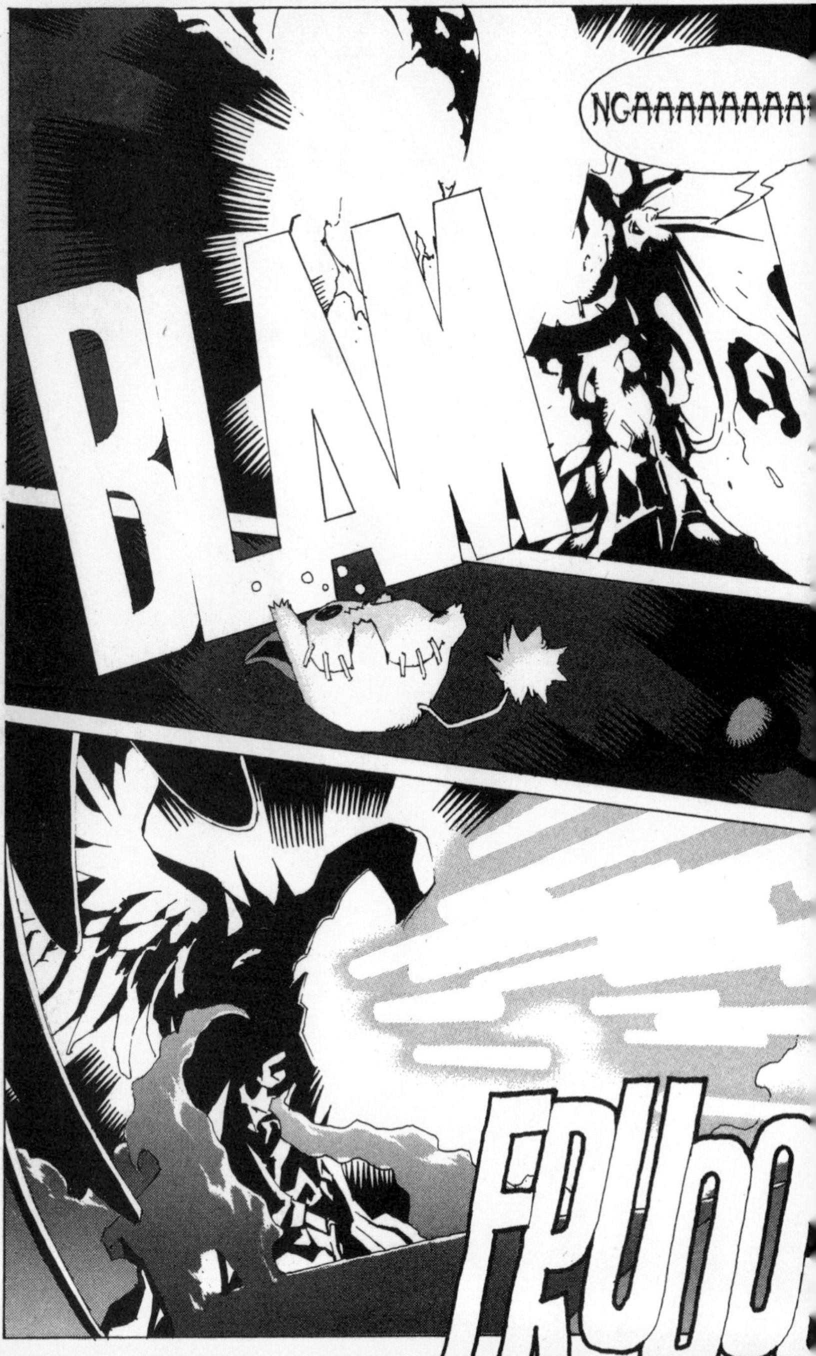
NGAAAAAAAAA
BLAM

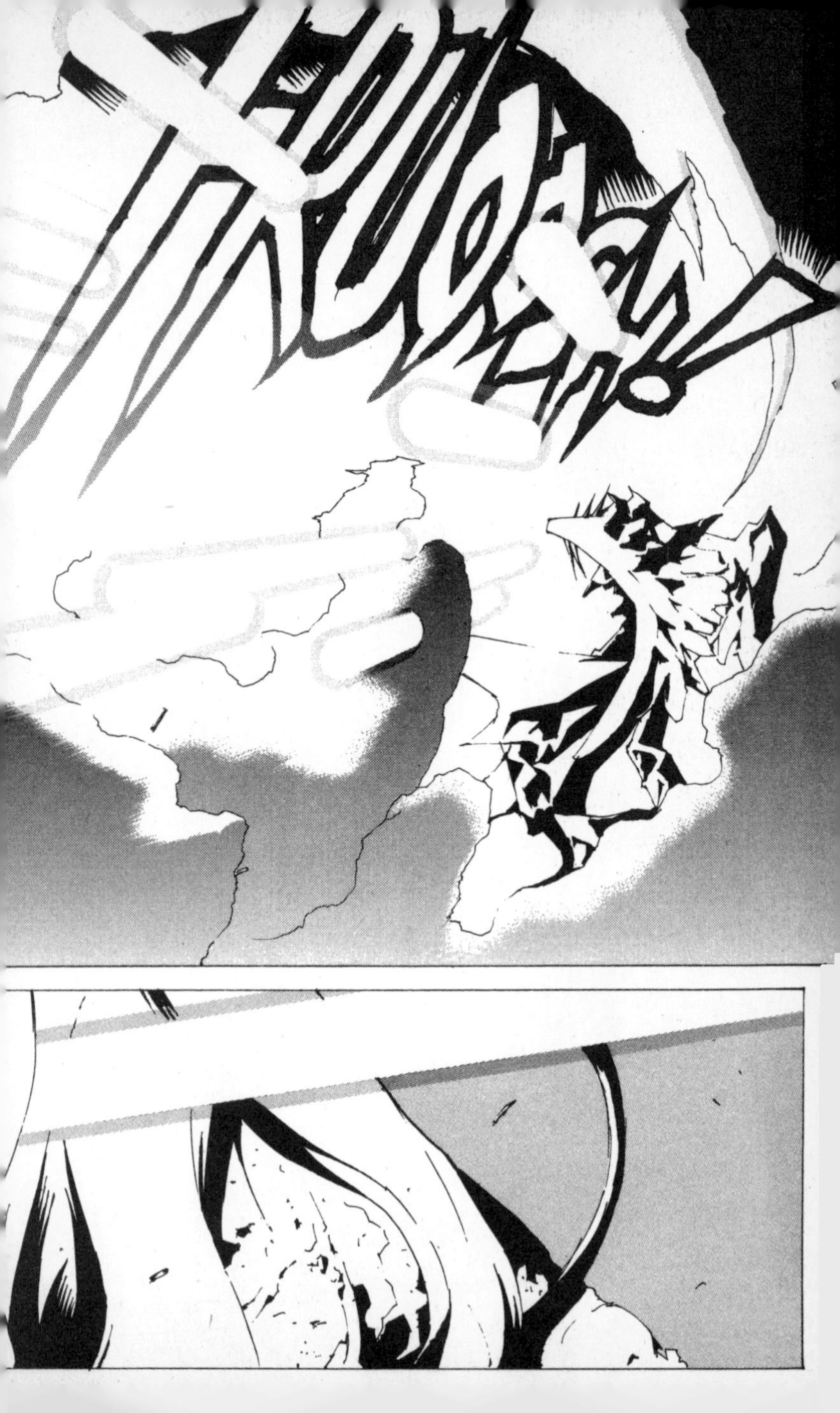

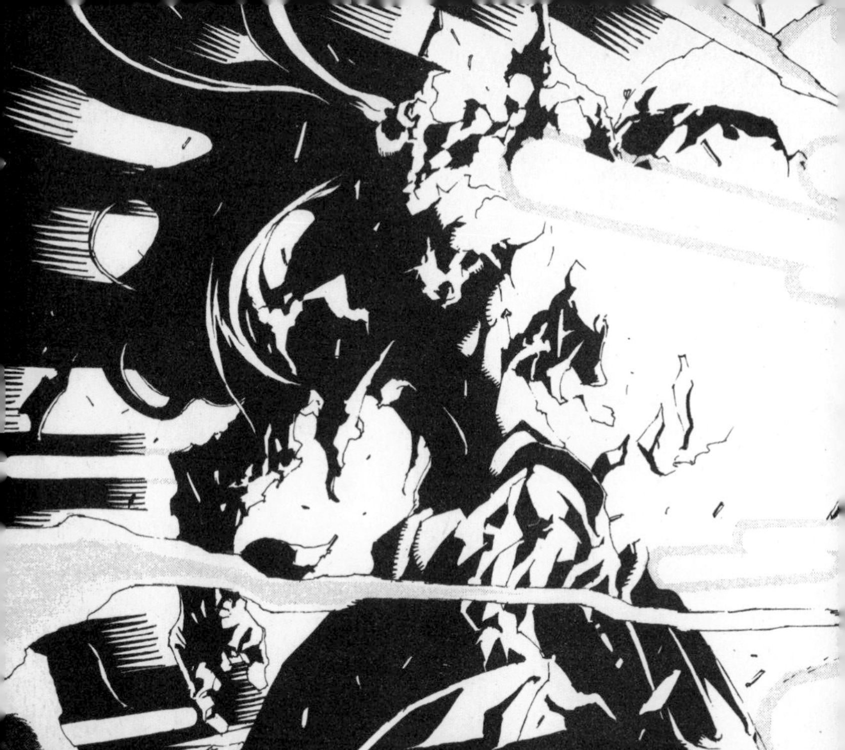

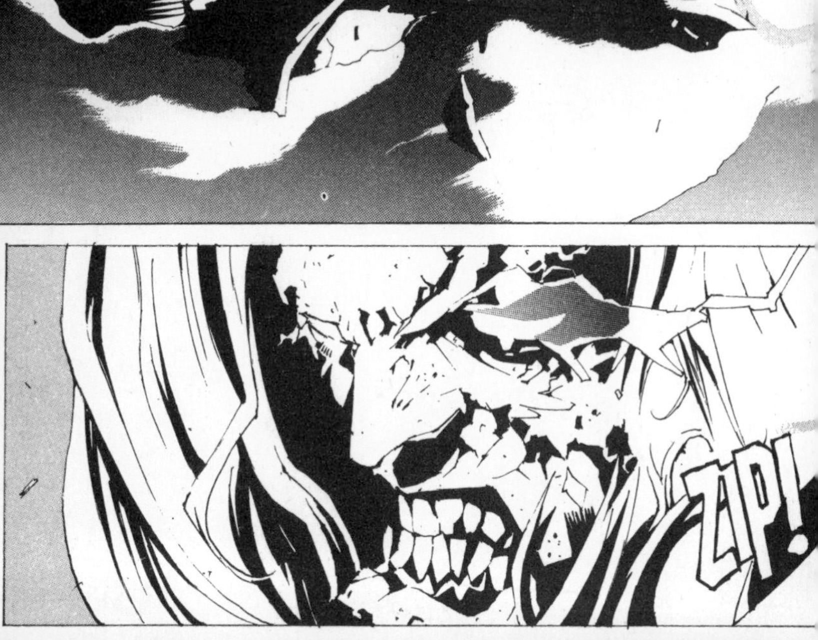
ZIP!

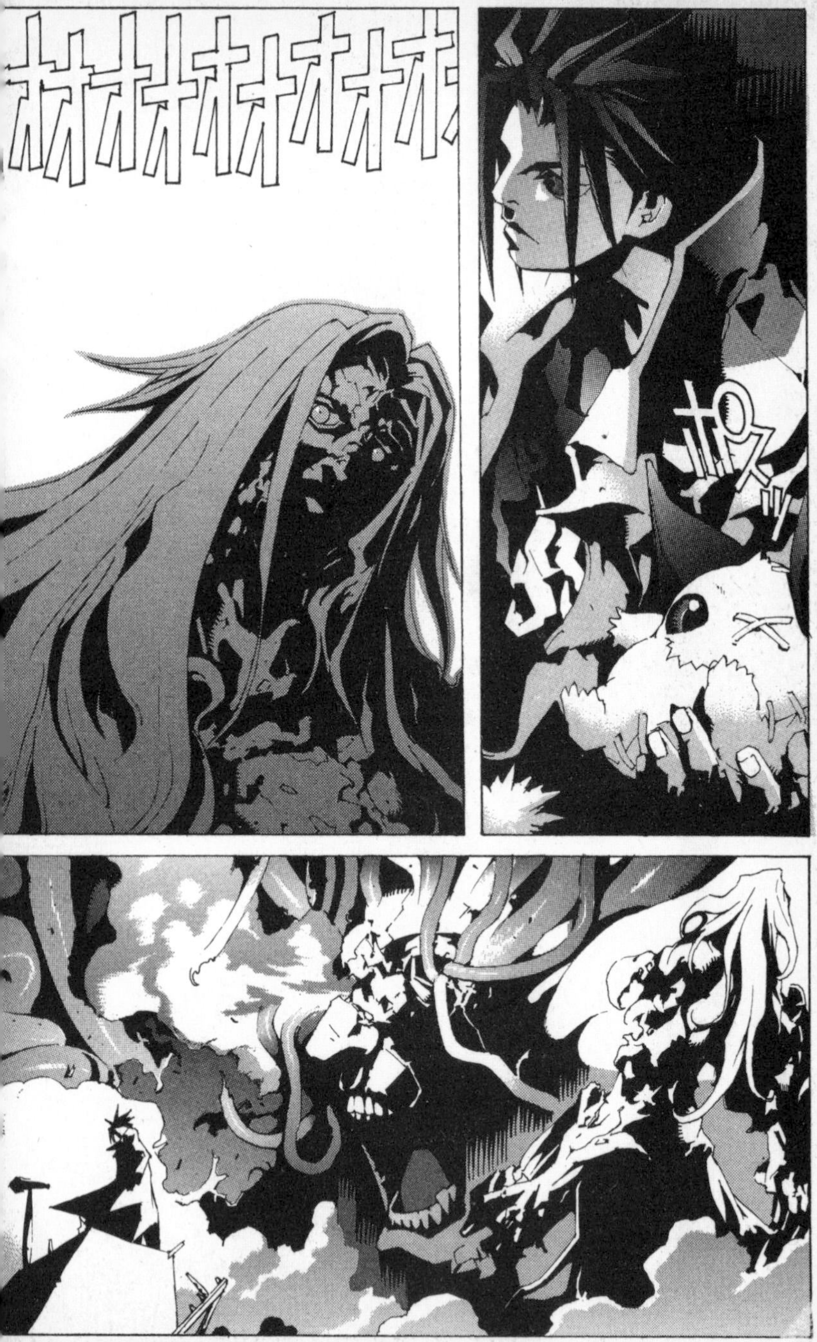
ポスッ
オオオオオオオオオ

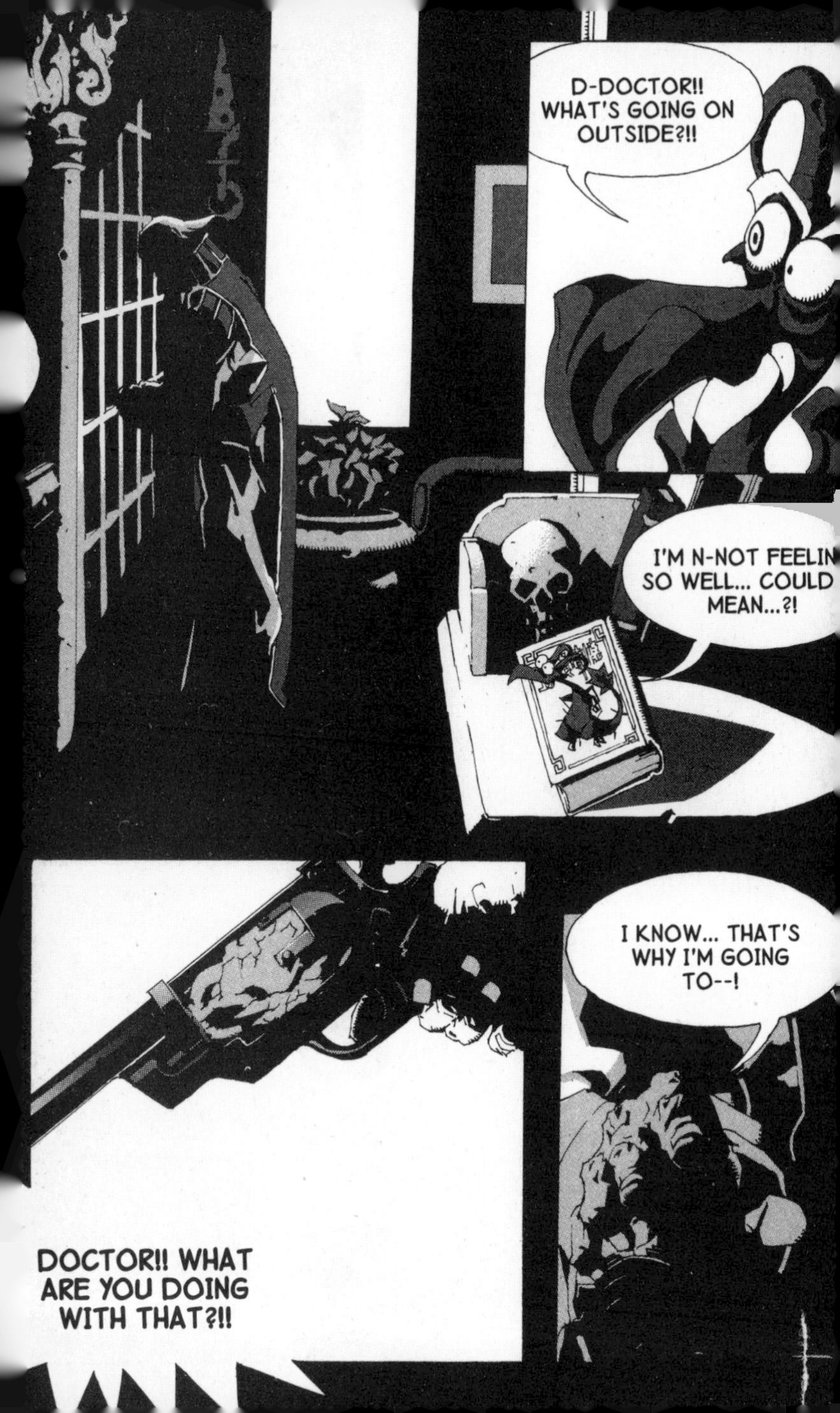
D-DOCTOR!! WHAT'S GOING ON OUTSIDE?!!
I'M N-NOT FEELIN SO WELL... COULD MEAN...?!
I KNOW... THAT'S WHY I'M GOING TO--!
DOCTOR!! WHAT ARE YOU DOING WITH THAT?!!

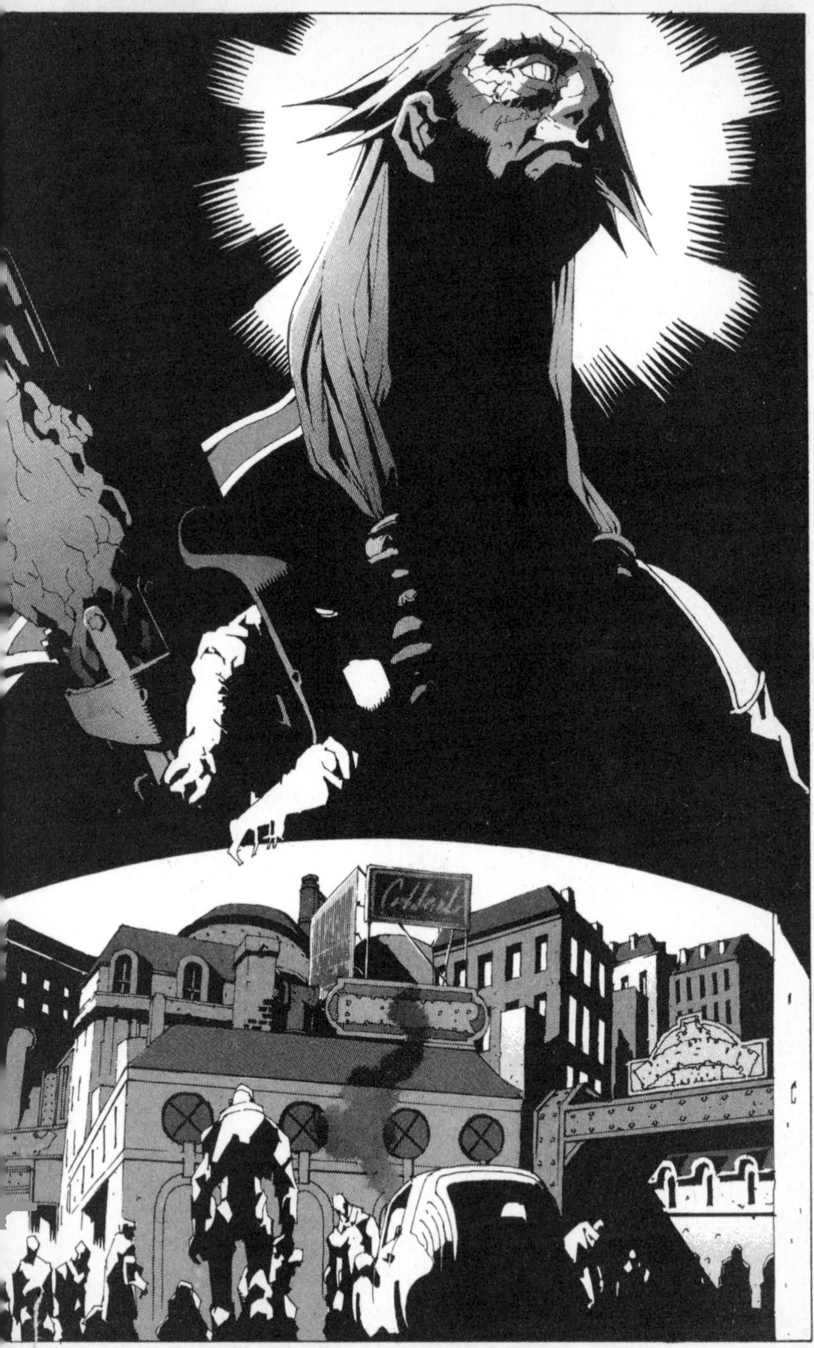

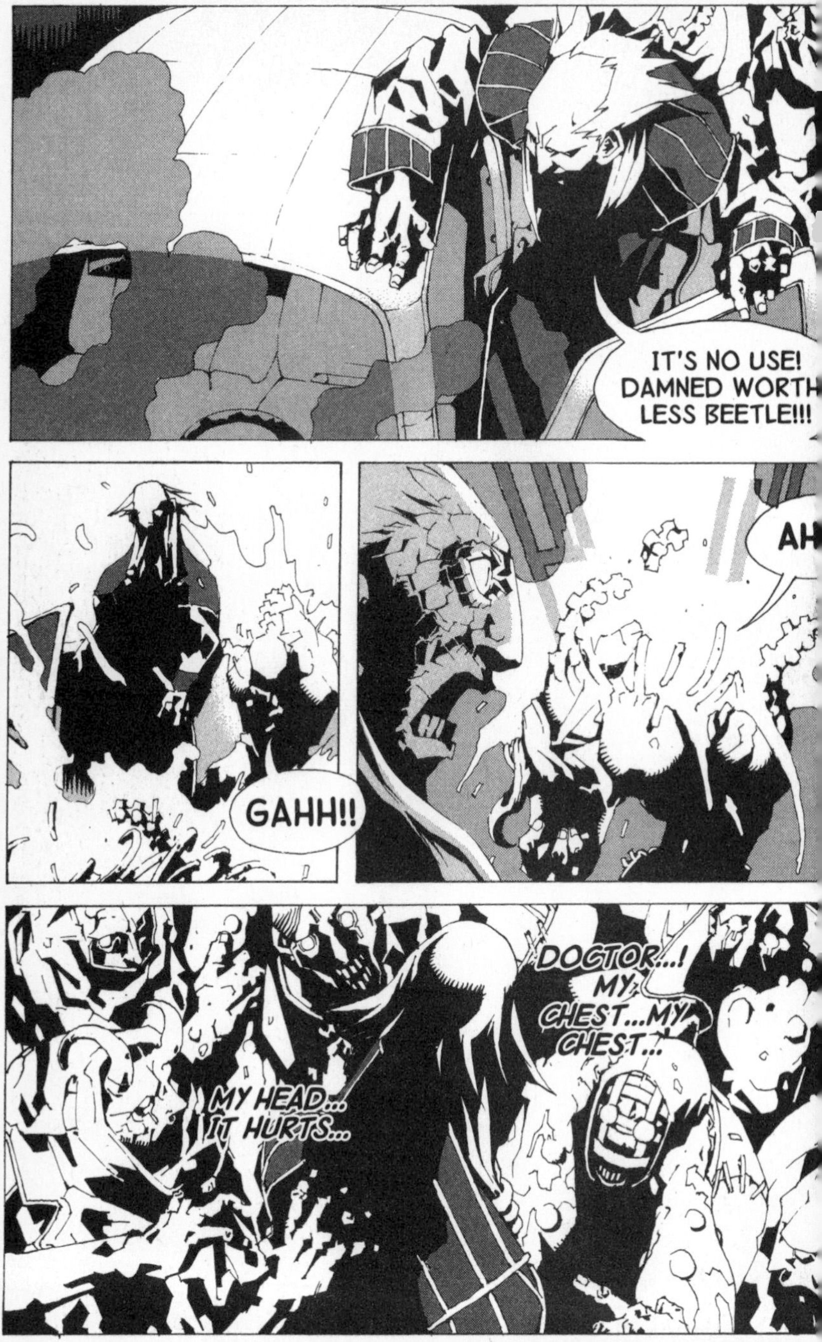
IT'S NO USE! DAMNED WORTH LESS BEETLE!!!
AH
GAHH!!
DOCTOR...! MY CHEST...MY CHEST...
MY HEAD... IT HURTS...

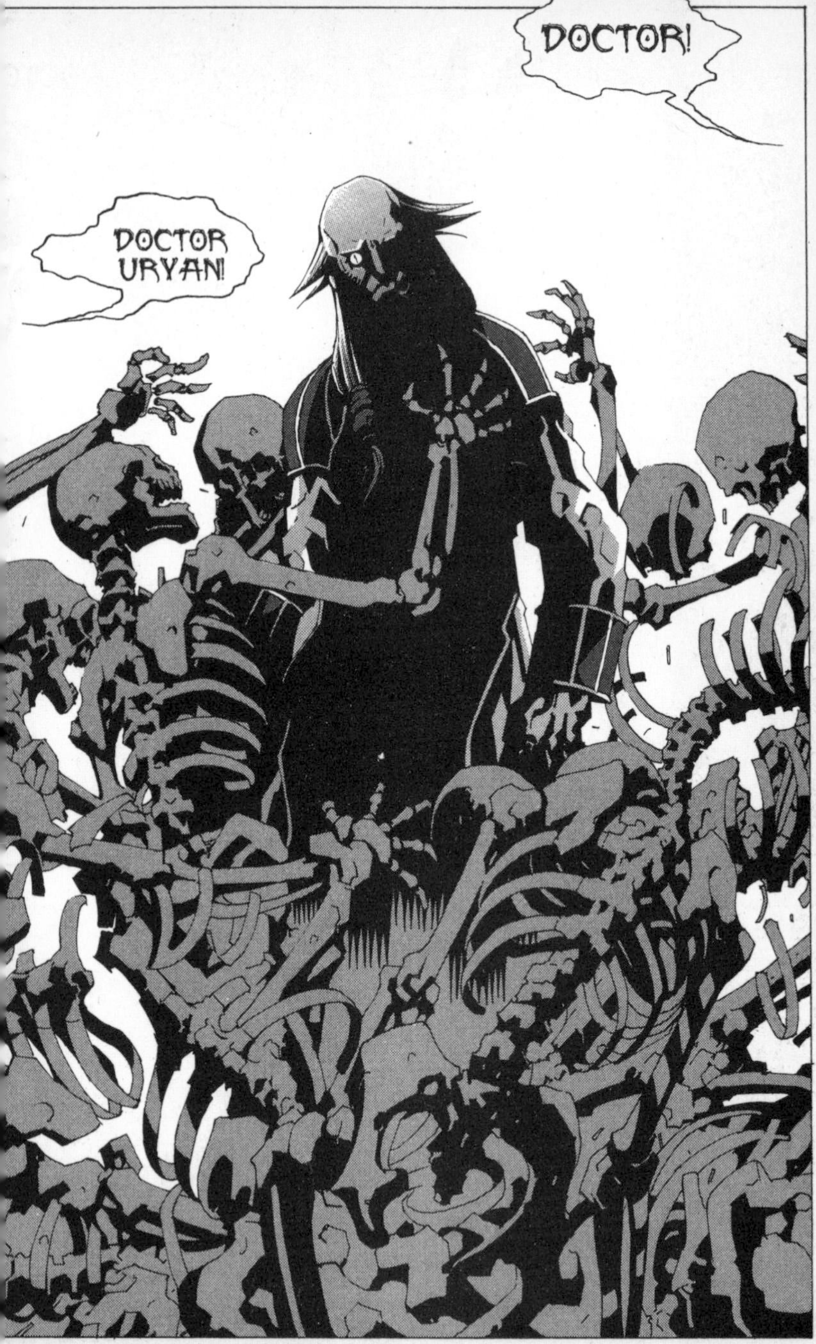
DOCTOR!
DOCTOR URYAN!

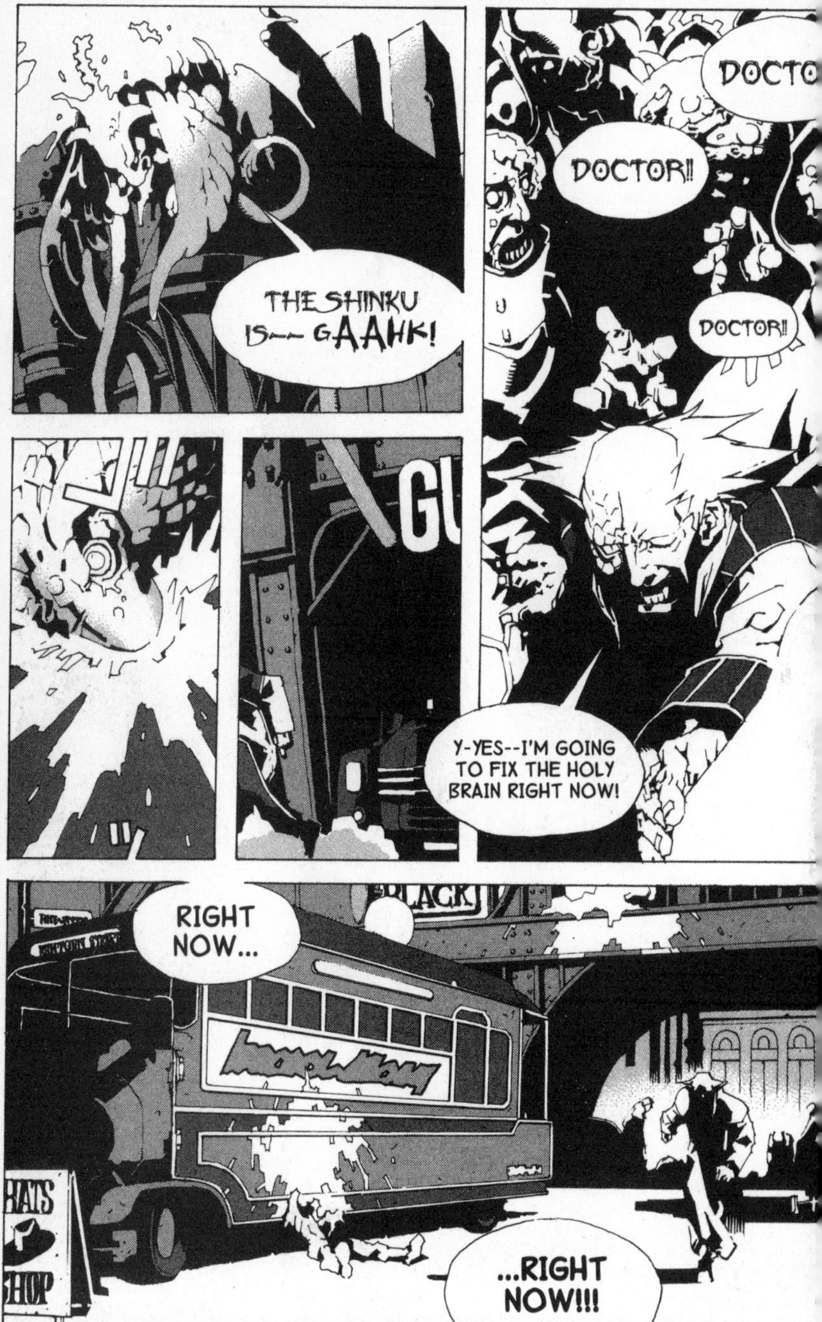
DOCTO
DOCTOR!!
DOCTOR!!
Y-YES--I'M GOING TO FIX THE HOLY BRAIN RIGHT NOW!
THE SHINKU IS-- GAAHK!
RIGHT NOW...
...RIGHT NOW!!!

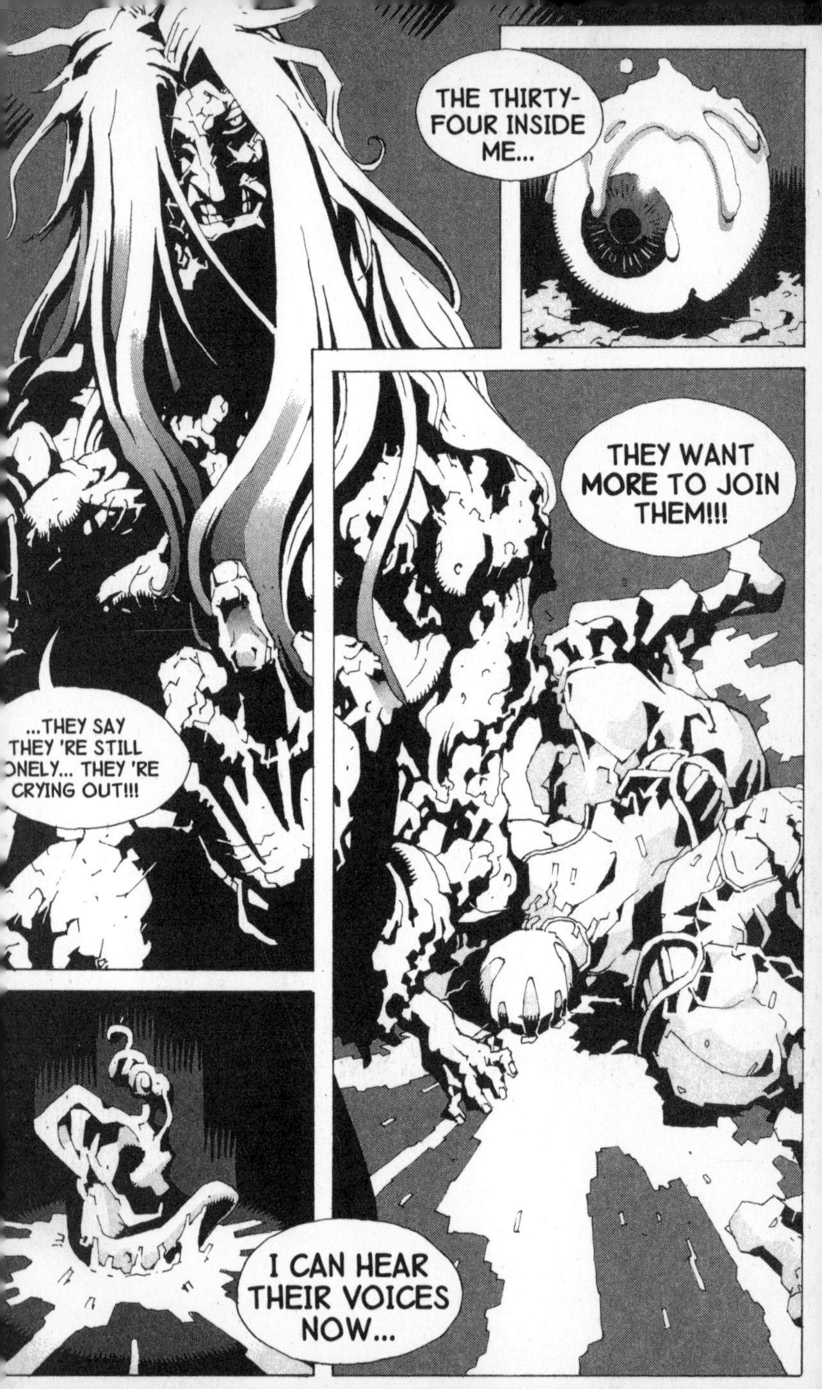
THE THIRTY-FOUR INSIDE ME...
THEY WANT MORE TO JOIN THEM!!!
...THEY SAY THEY 'RE STILL ONELY... THEY 'RE CRYING OUT!!!
I CAN HEAR THEIR VOICES NOW...

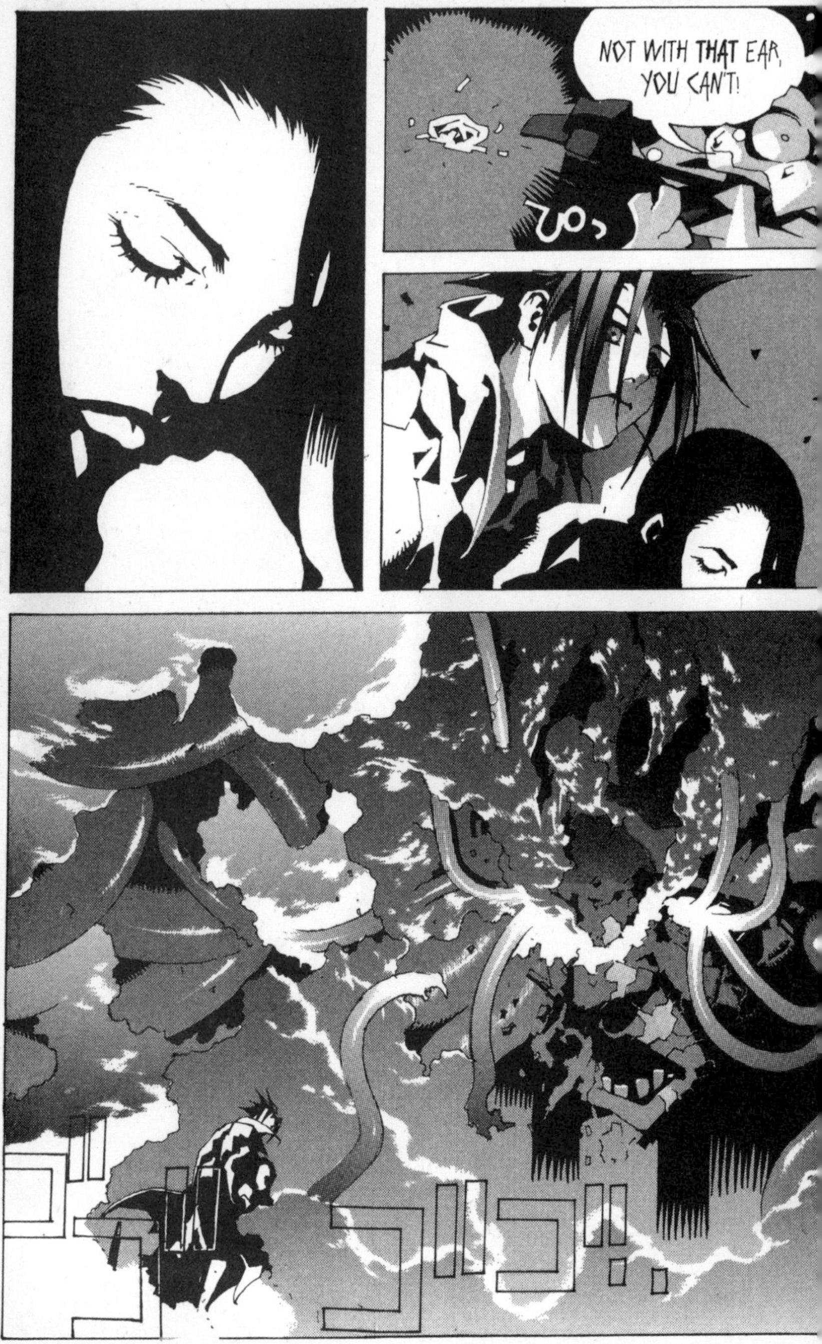
NOT WITH THAT EAR, YOU CAN'T!

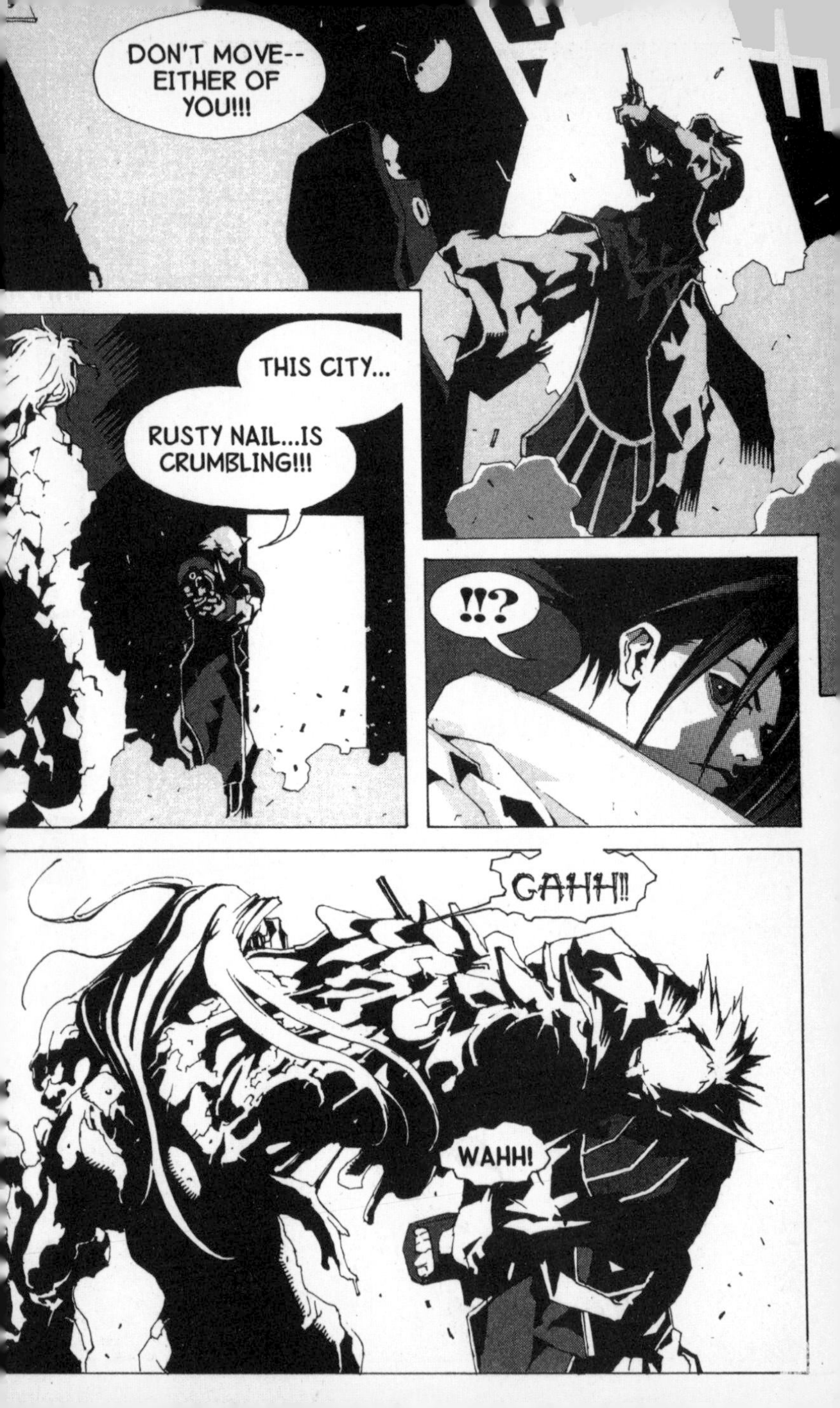
DON'T MOVE--
EITHER OF
YOU!!!
!!?
THIS CITY...
RUSTY NAIL...IS
CRUMBLING!!!
GAHH!!
WAHH!

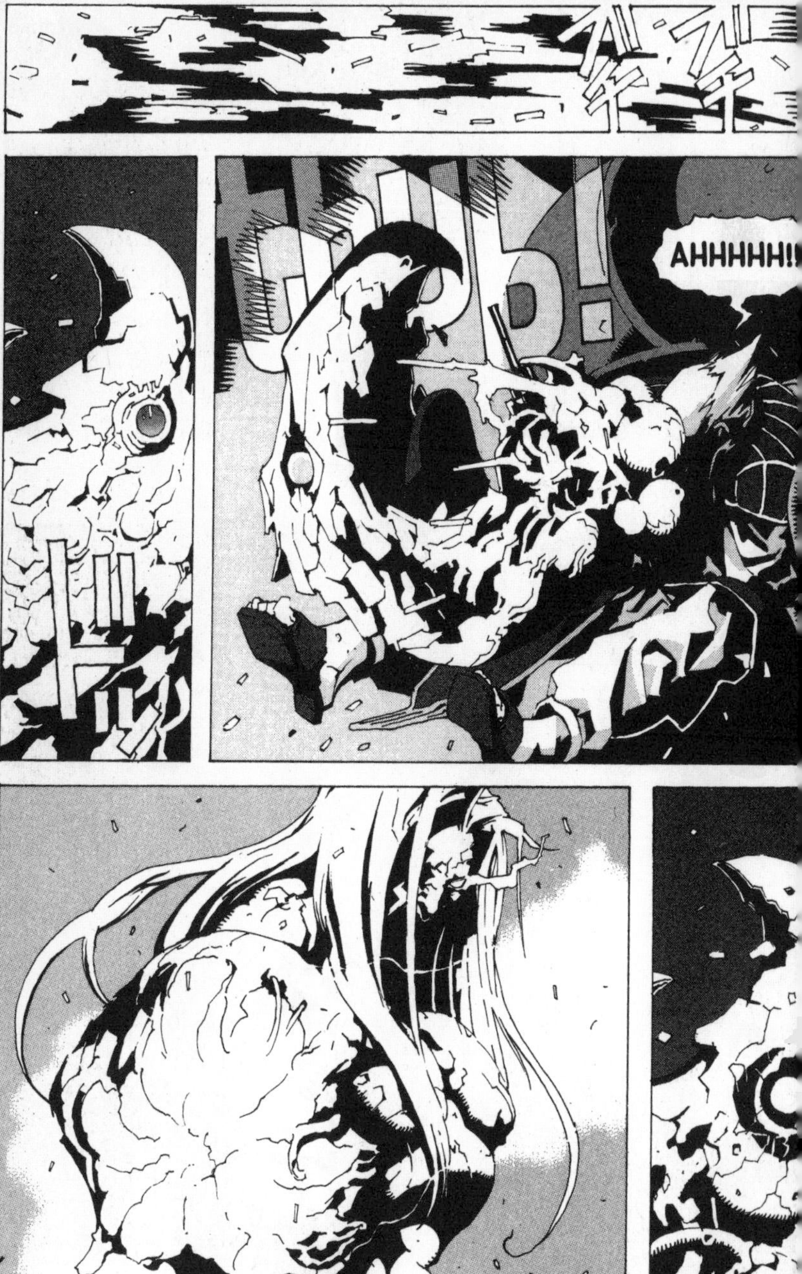
AHHHHH!!

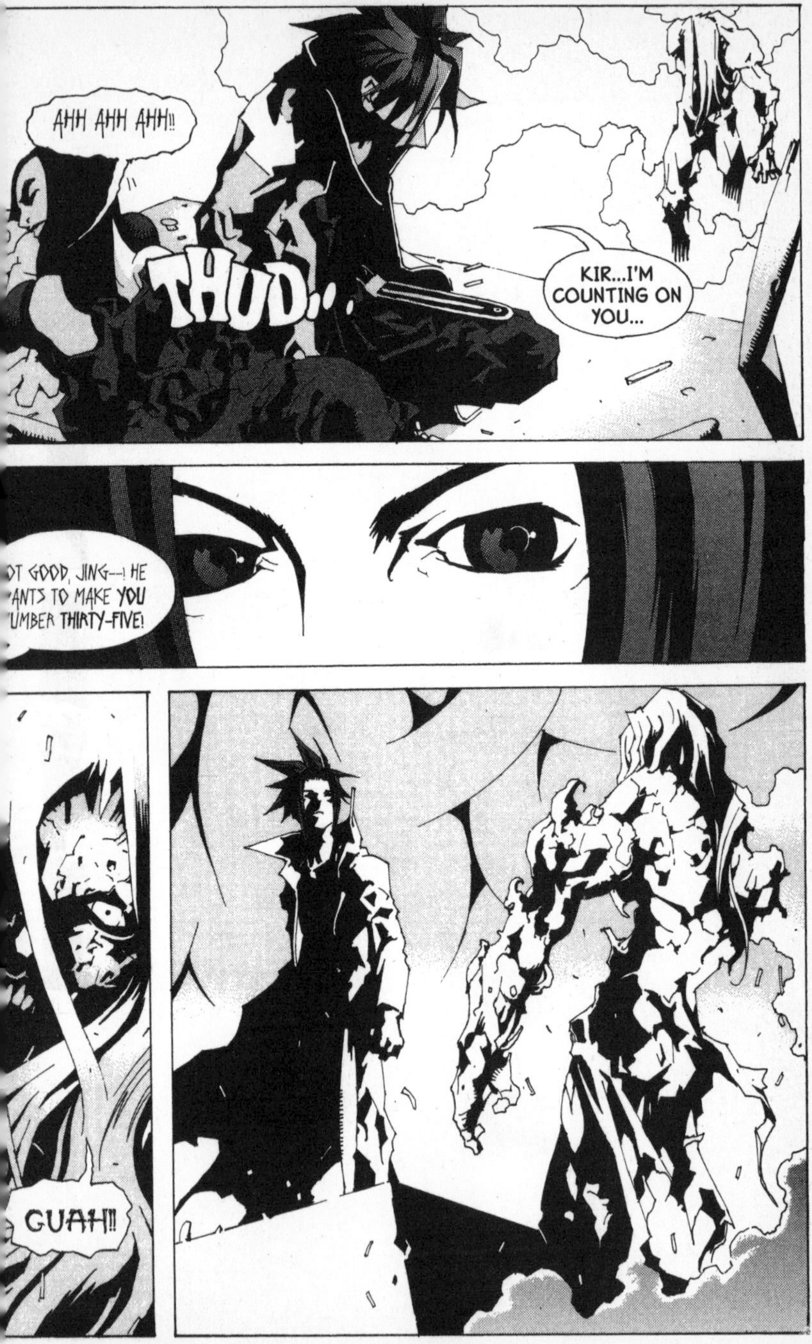
KIR...I'M COUNTING ON YOU...
AHH AHH AHH!!
THUD..
OT GOOD, JING--! HE
ANTS TO MAKE YOU
UMBER THIRTY-FIVE!
GUAH!!

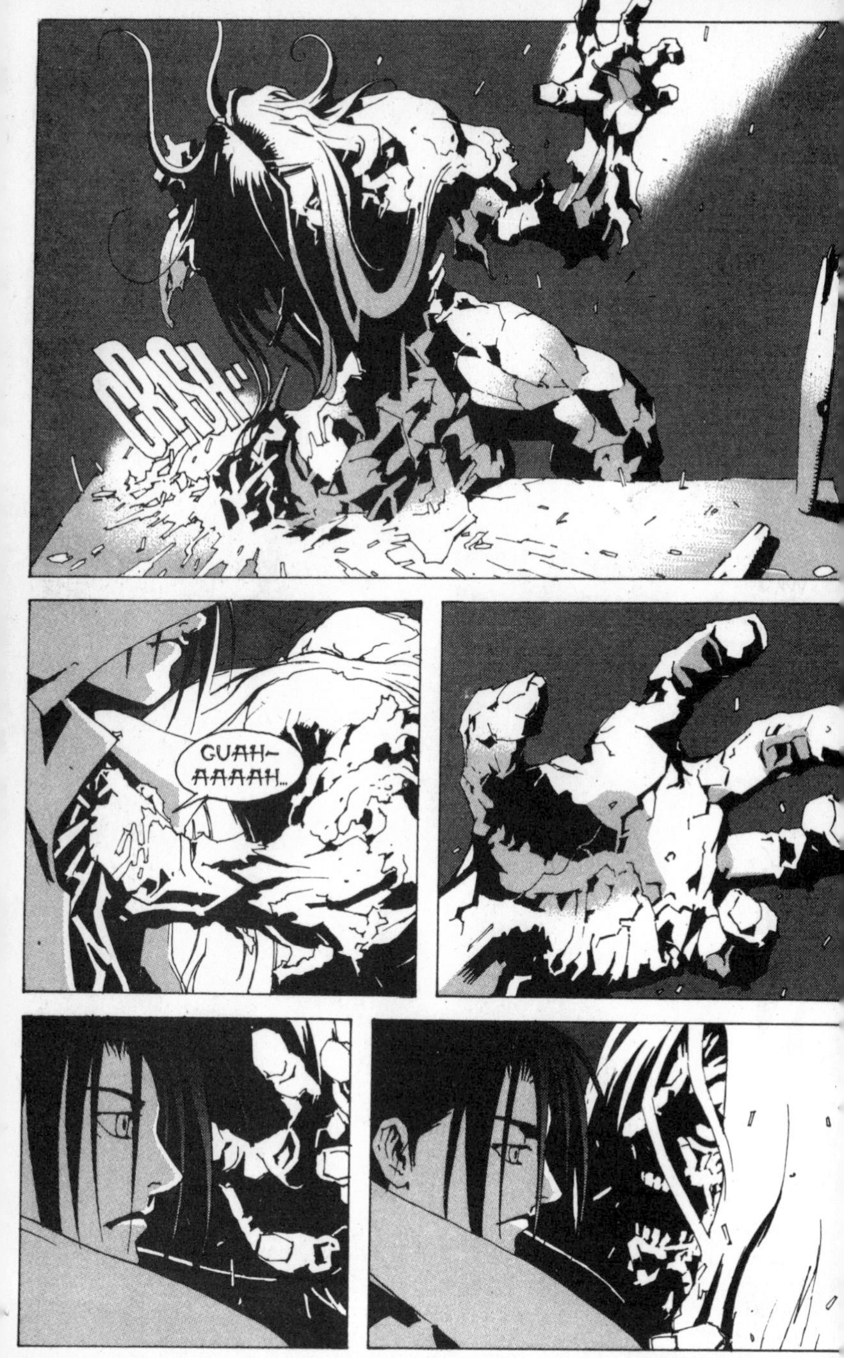
CRASH
GUAH-AAAAH...

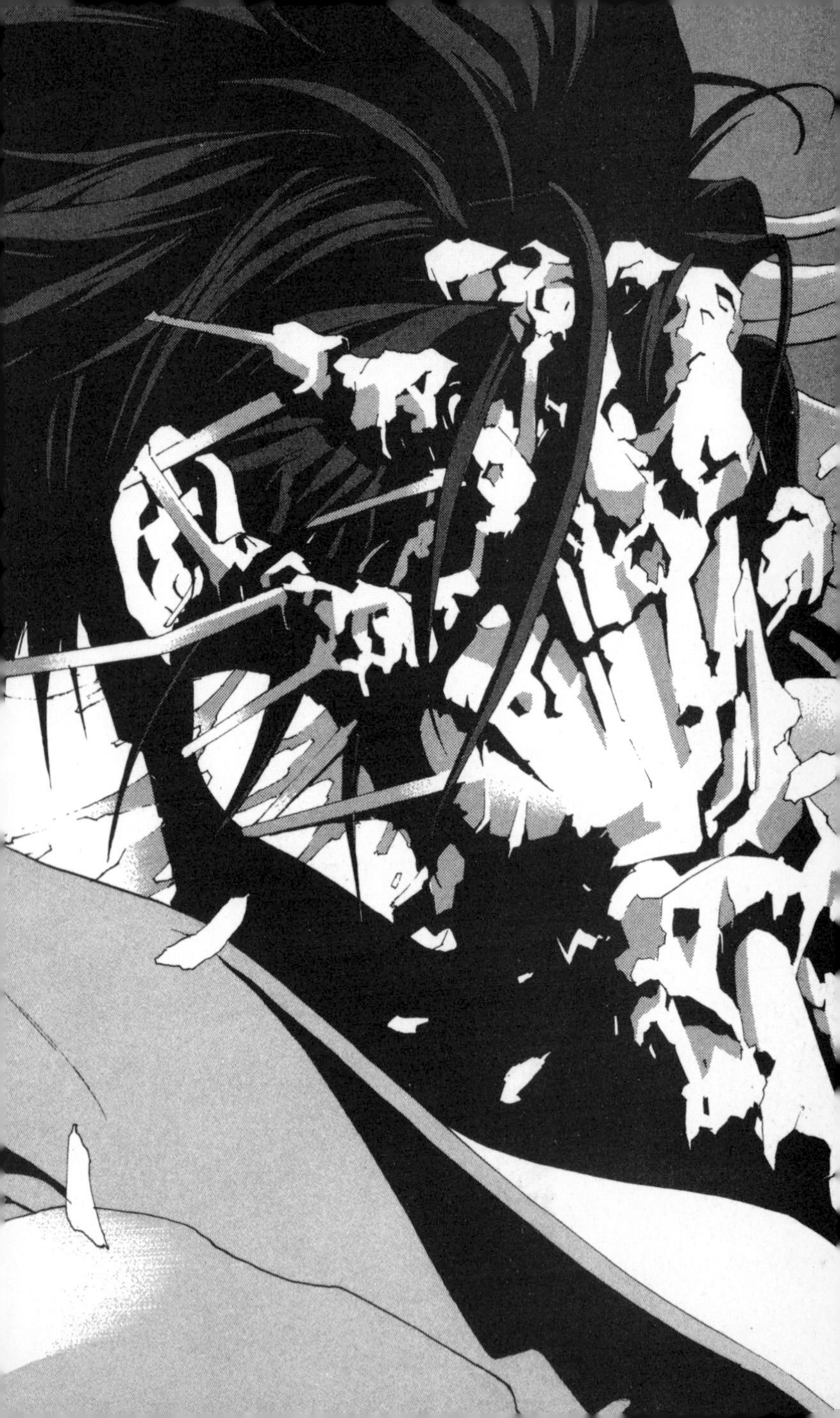

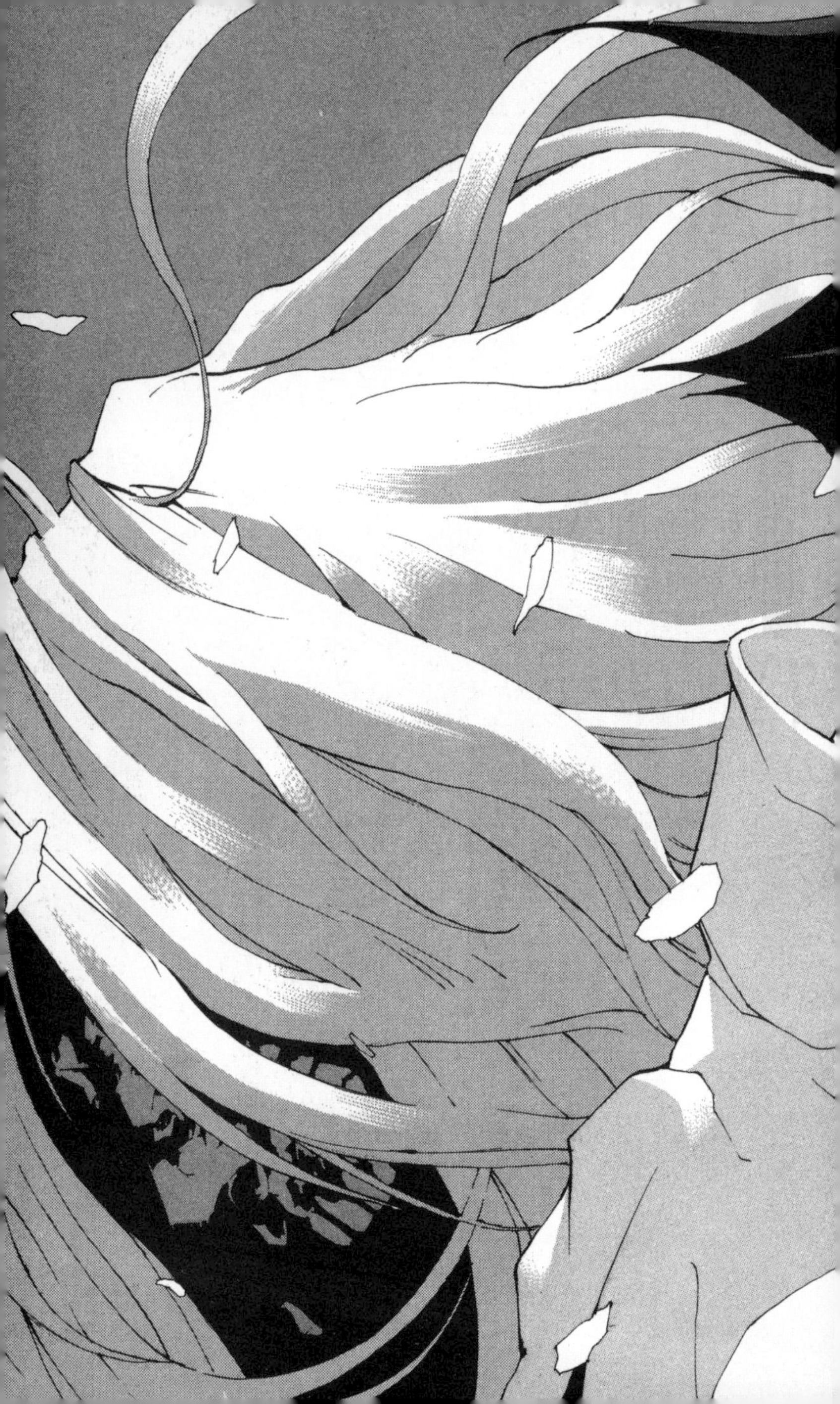

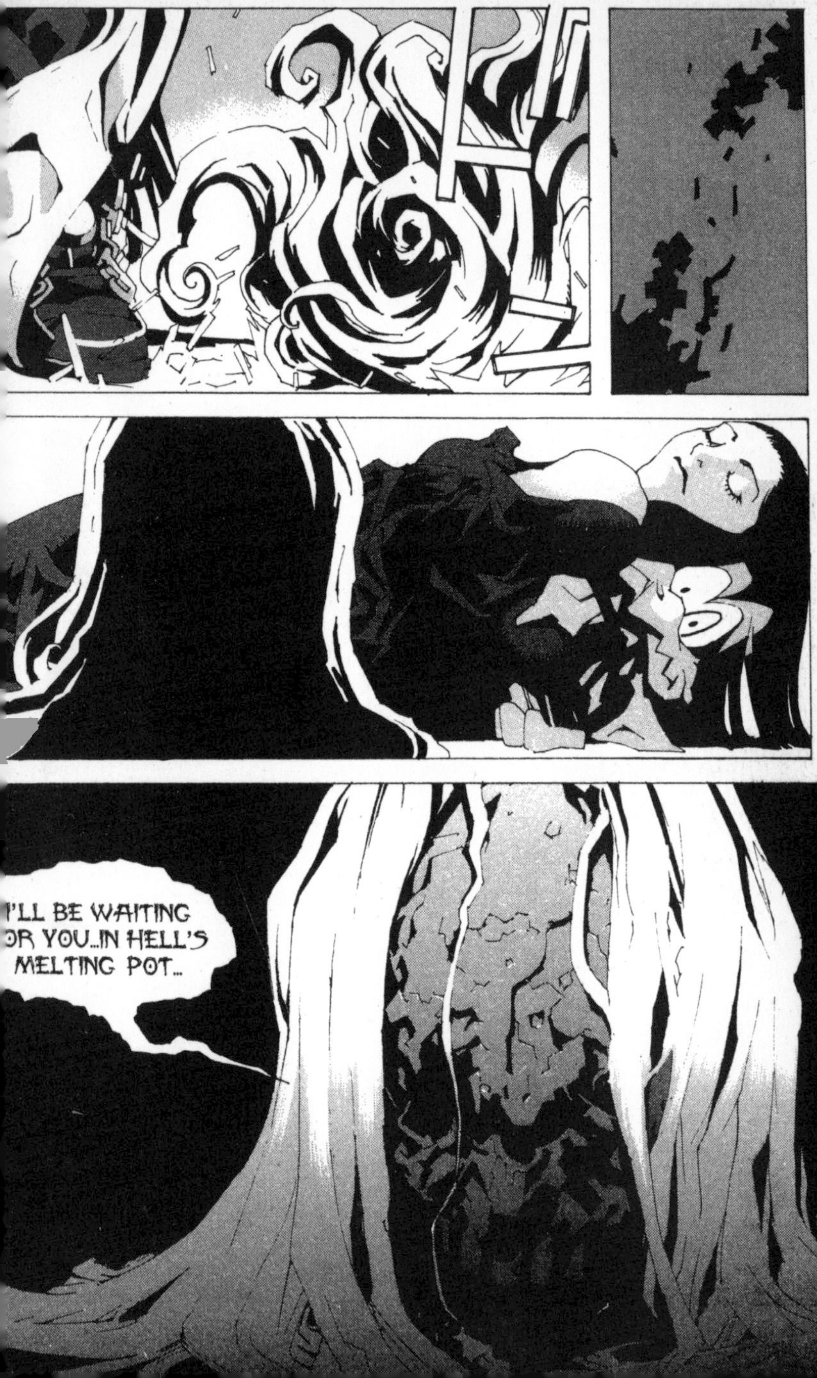
I'LL BE WAITING
OR YOU...IN HELL'S
MELTING POT...

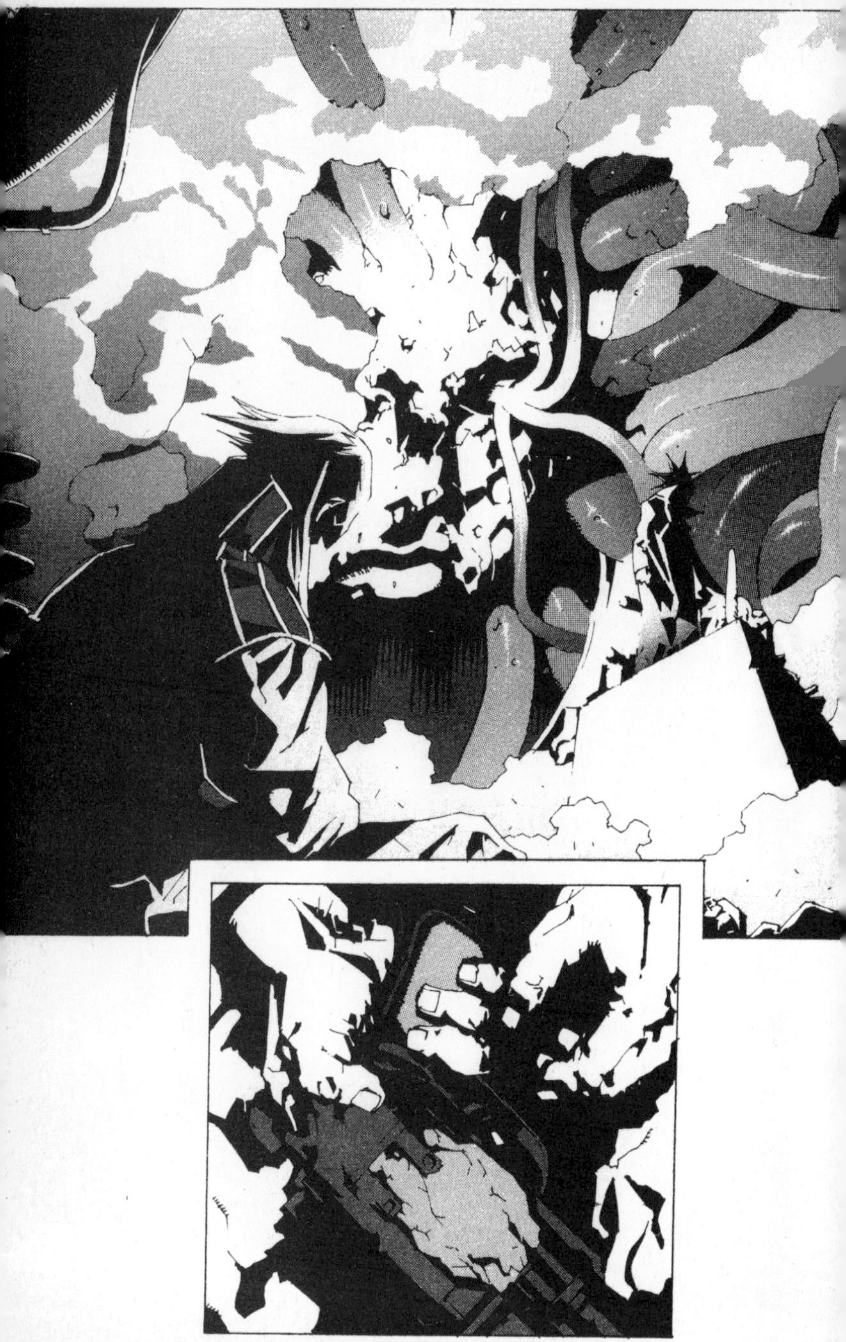

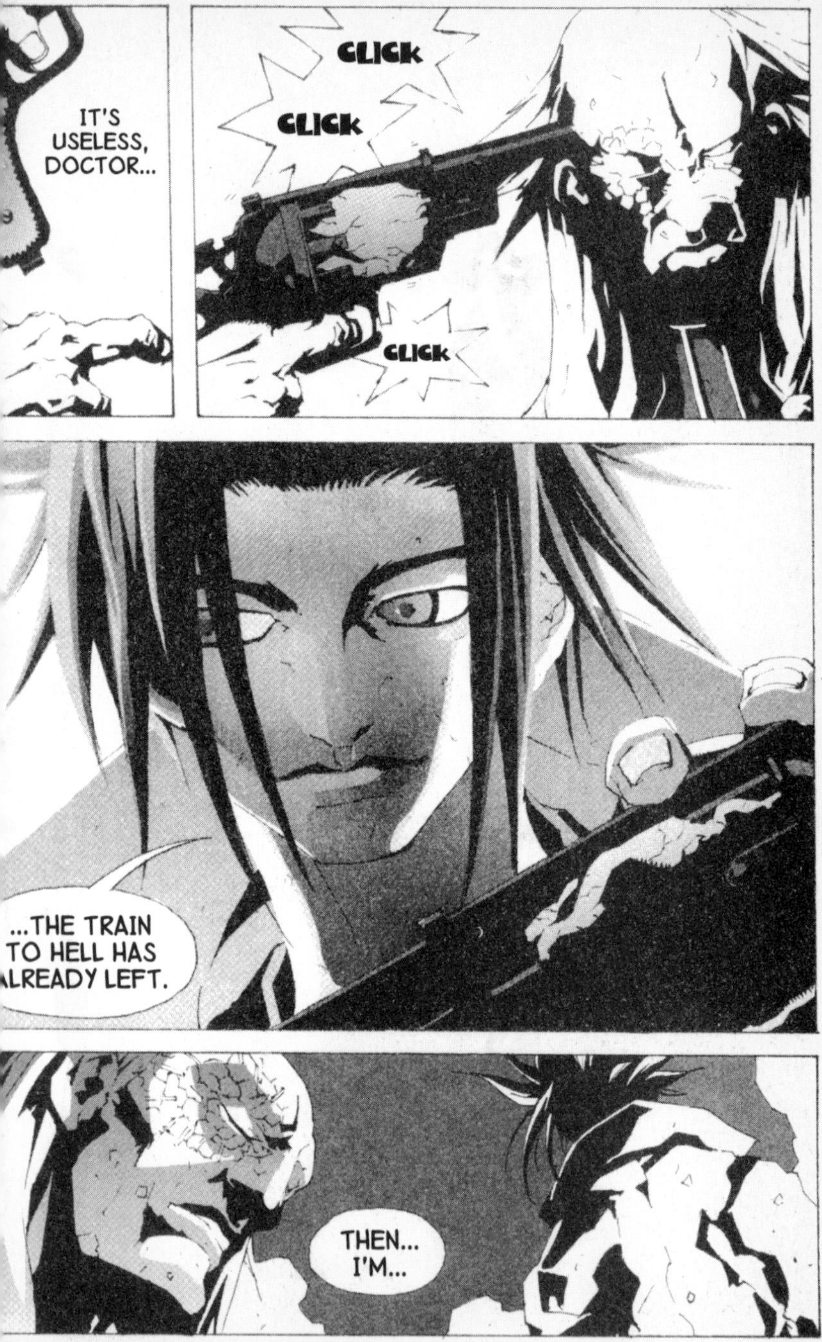
CLICK
CLICK
CLICK
IT'S USELESS, DOCTOR...
...THE TRAIN TO HELL HAS LREADY LEFT.
THEN... I'M...

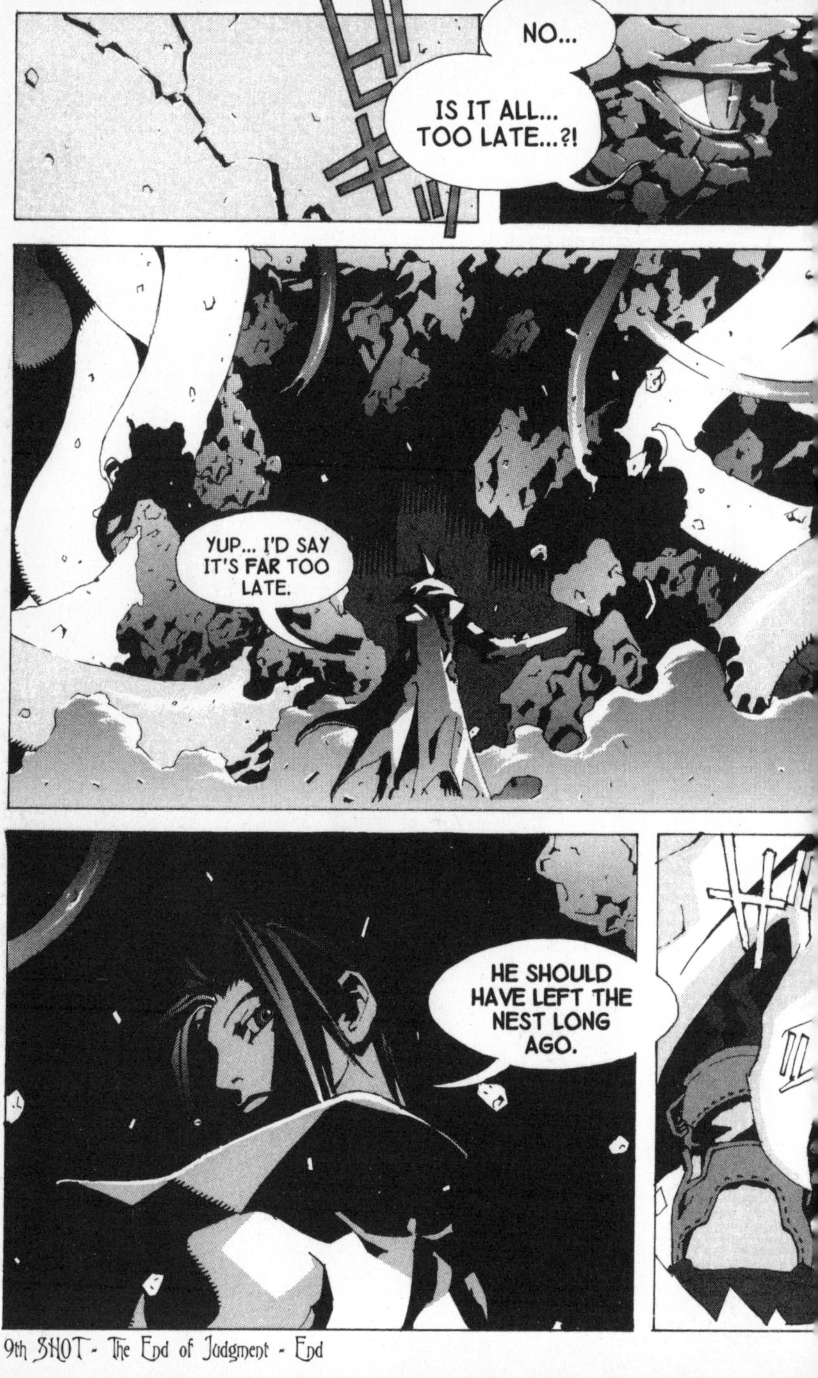
NO...
IS IT ALL... TOO LATE...?!
YUP... I'D SAY IT'S FAR TOO LATE.
HE SHOULD HAVE LEFT THE NEST LONG AGO.

9th SHOT - The End of Judgment - End

10th Shot - The Naked World

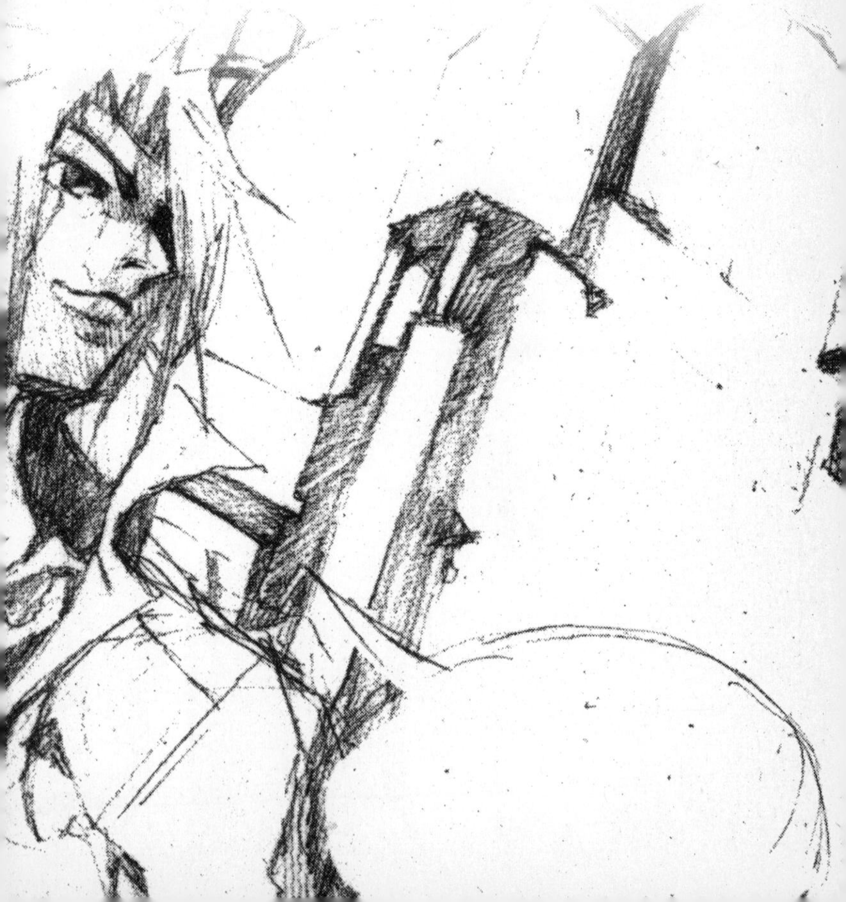

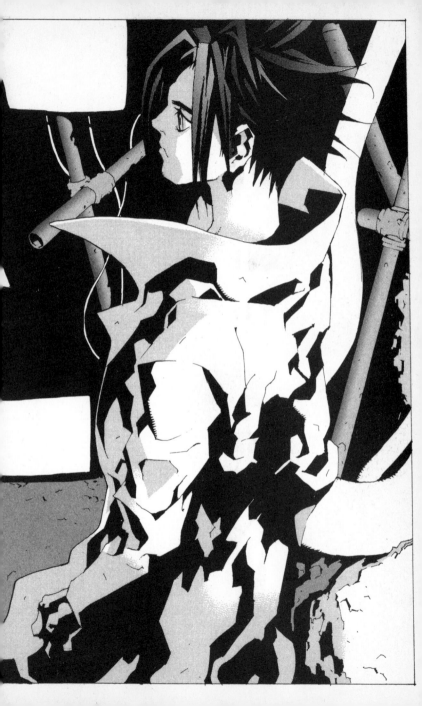

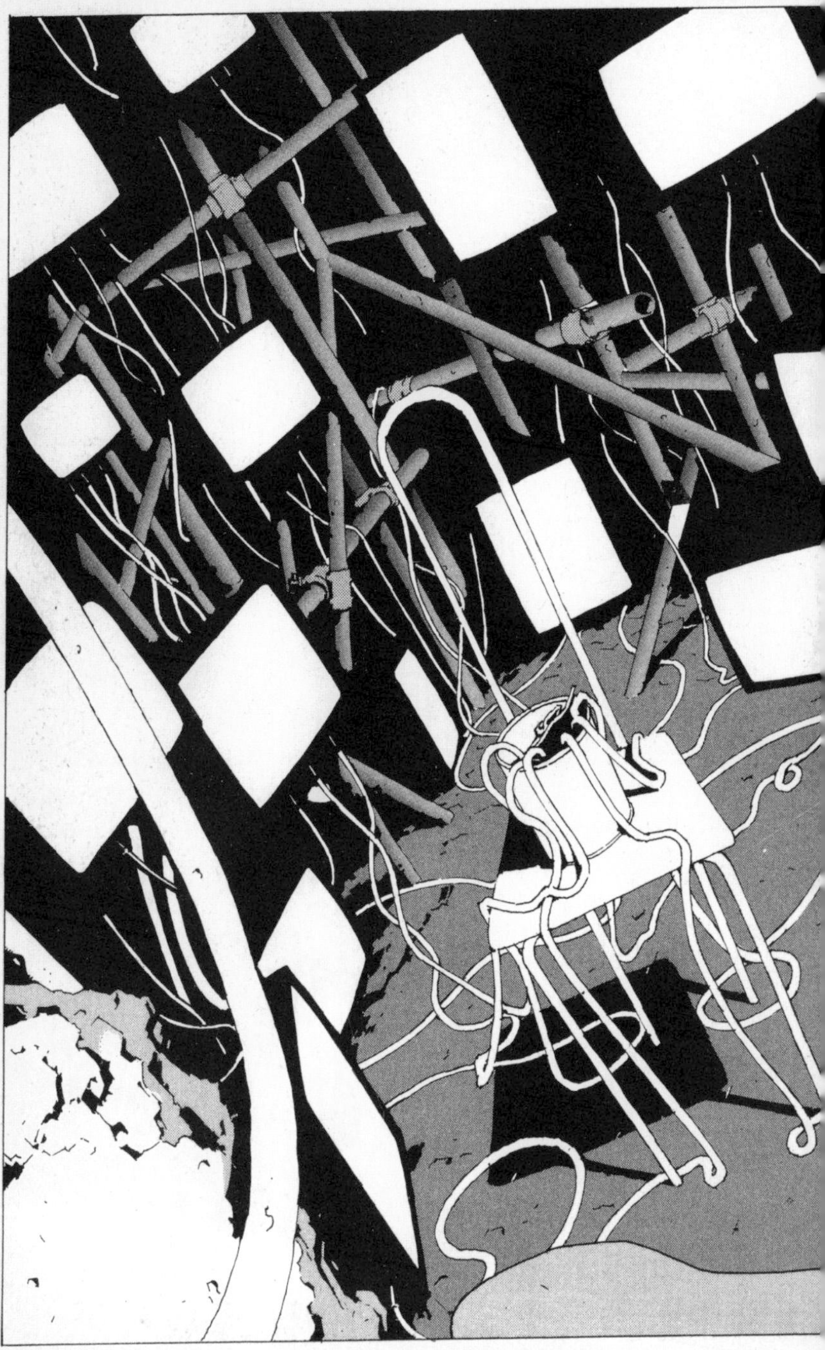

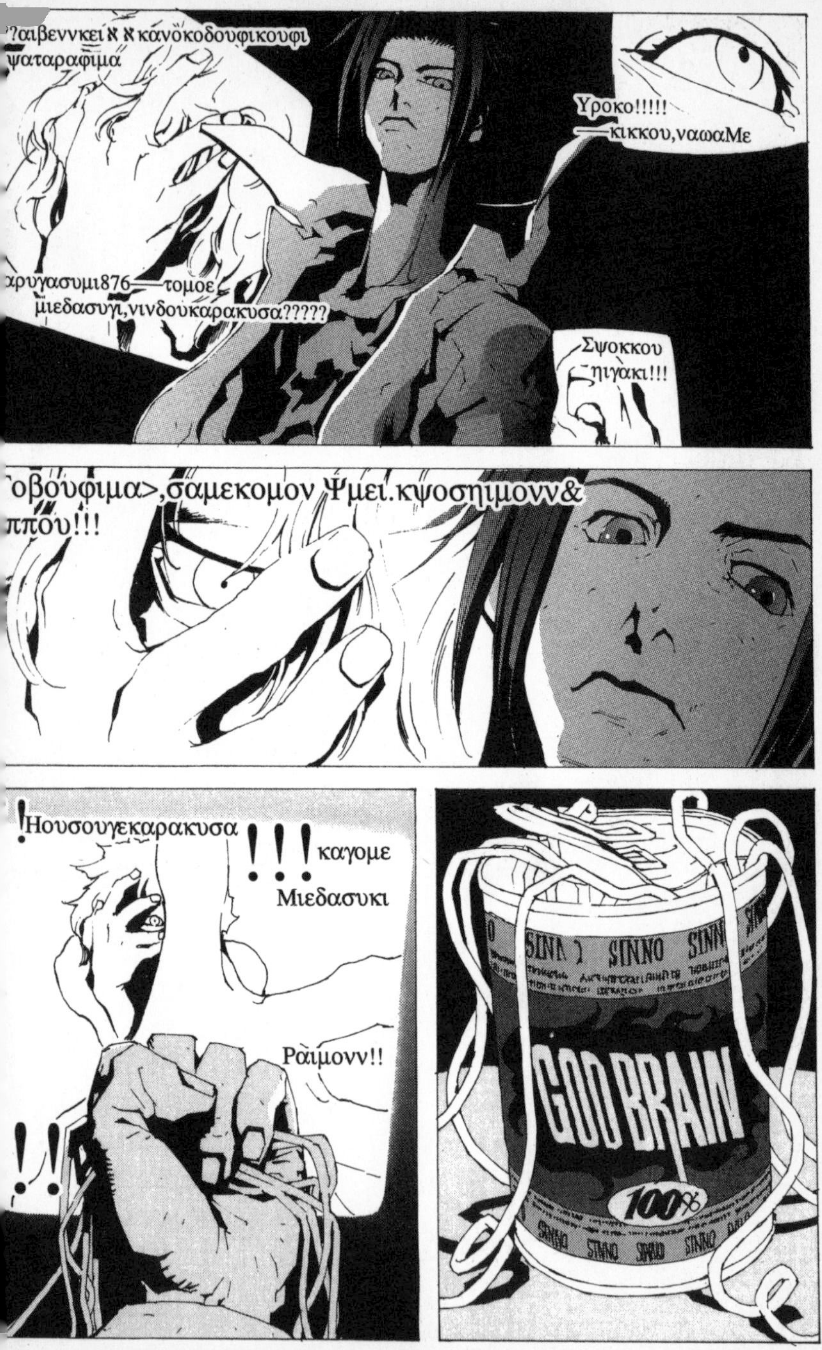
Υροκο!!!!!
——κικκου,ναωαΜε
?αιβεννκει ℵ ℵ κάνὸκοδουφικουφι
ψαταραφιμα
Σψοκκου
ηιγάκι!!!
αρυγασυμι876——τομοε
μιεδασυγι,νινδουκαρακυσα?????
οβουφιμα>,σαμεκομον Ψμει.κψοσημονν&
ππου!!!
SINNO SINNO SINNO
GOD BRAIN
100%
SINNO SINNO SINNO SINNO
!Ηουσουγεκαρακυσα
!!! καγομε
Μιεδασυκι
Ραὶμονν!!
!!

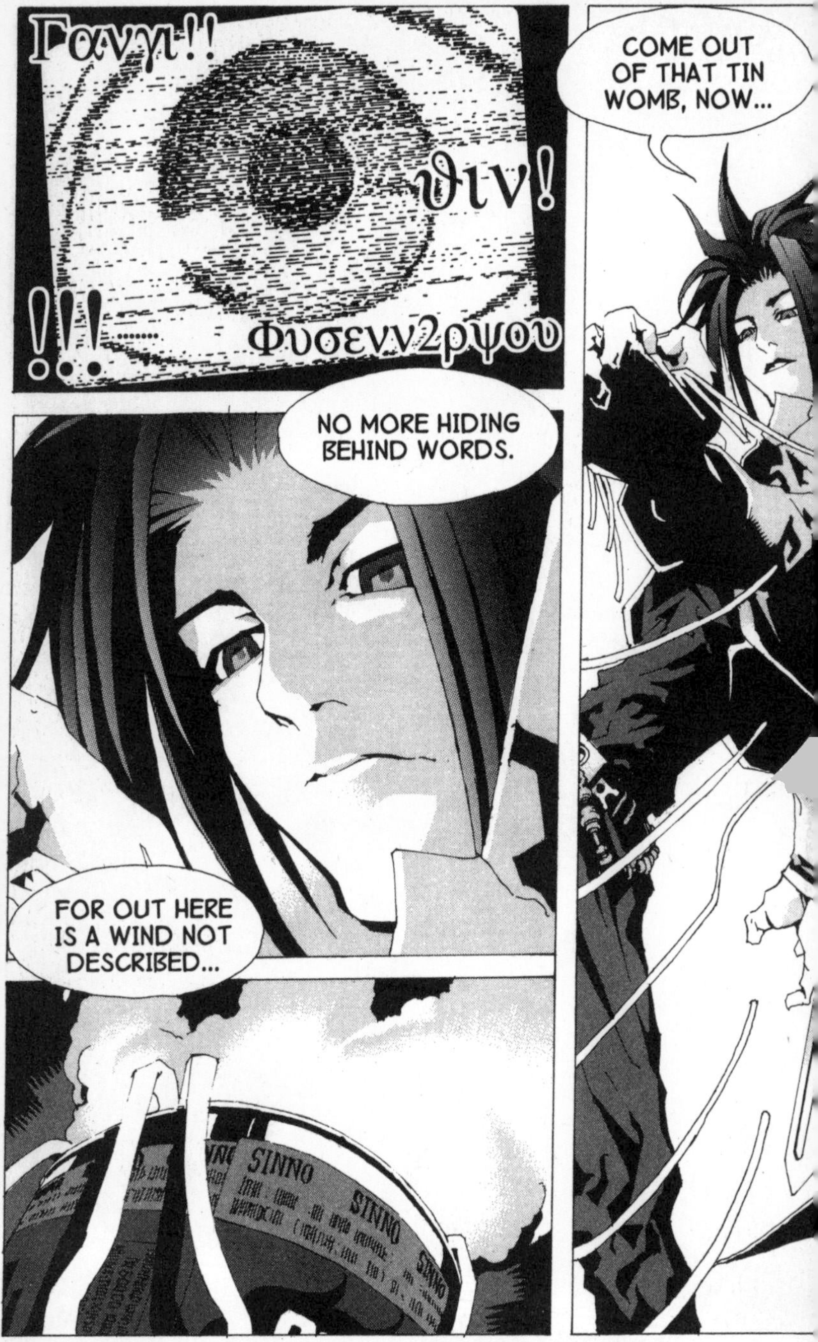
COME OUT OF THAT TIN WOMB, NOW...
Γανγι!!
θιν!
Φυσενν2ρψου
!!!......
NO MORE HIDING BEHIND WORDS.
FOR OUT HERE IS A WIND NOT DESCRIBED...
SINNO
SINNO
SINNO

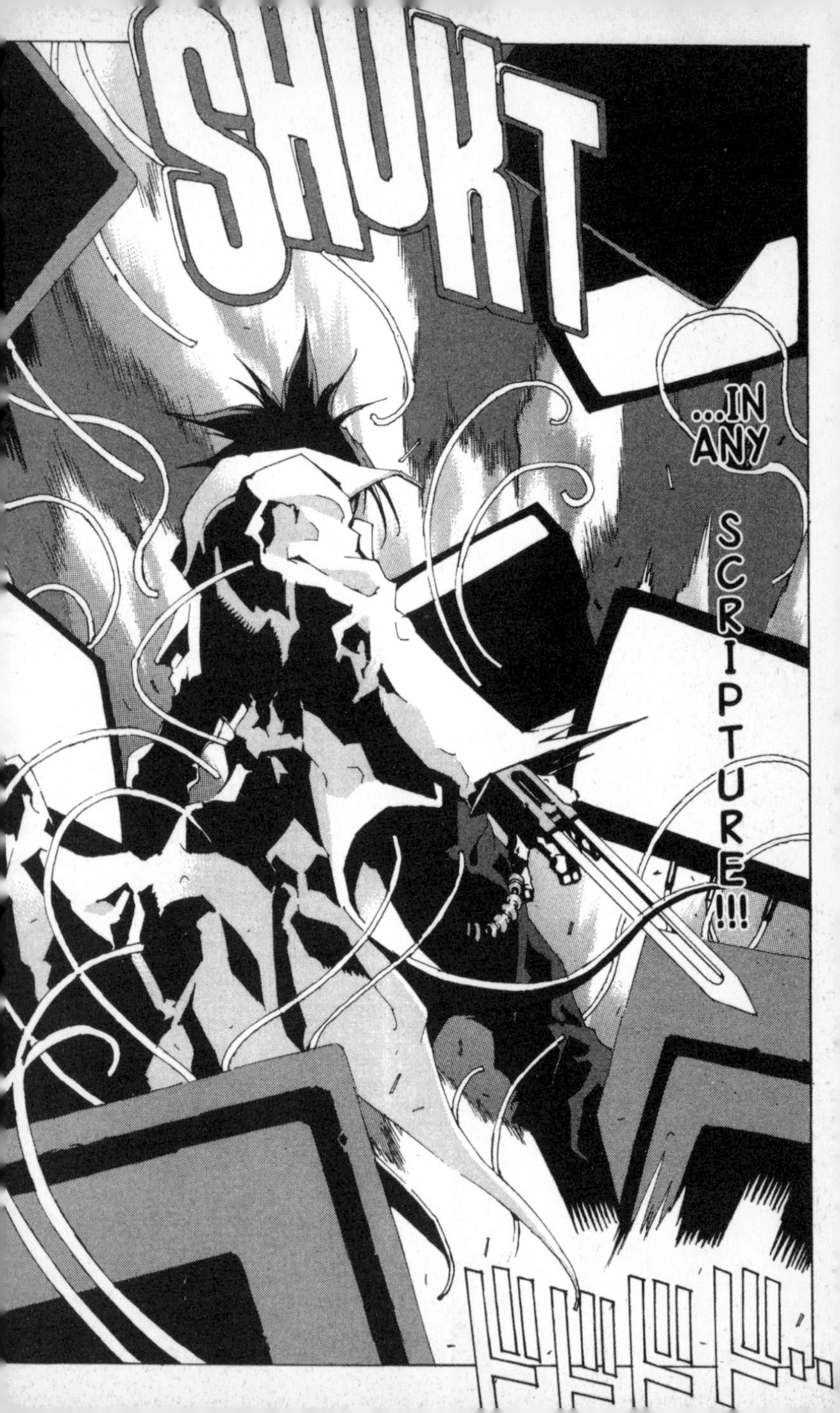
SHURT
...IN ANY SCRIPTURE!!!

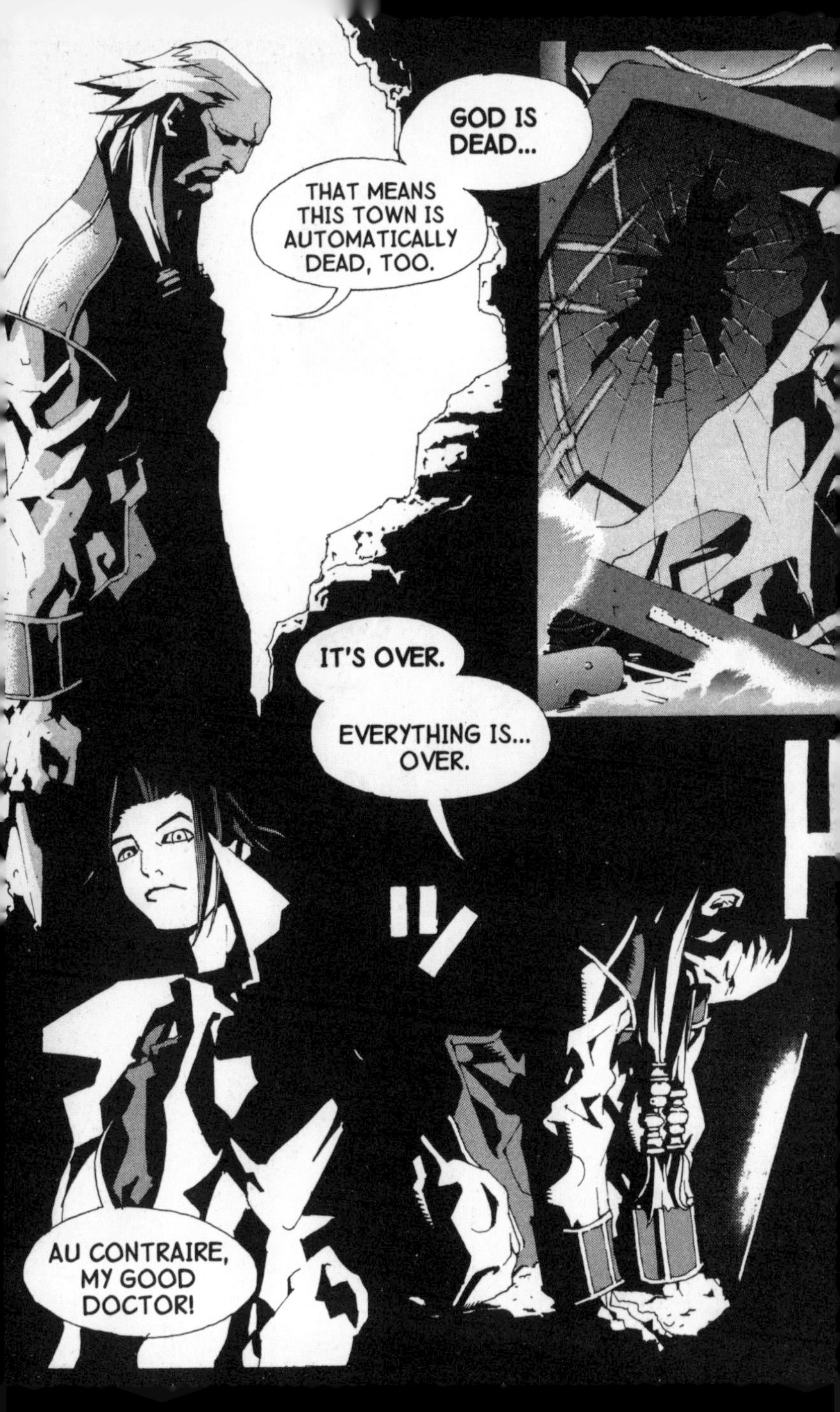
GOD IS DEAD...
THAT MEANS THIS TOWN IS AUTOMATICALLY DEAD, TOO.
IT'S OVER.
EVERYTHING IS... OVER.
AU CONTRAIRE, MY GOOD DOCTOR!

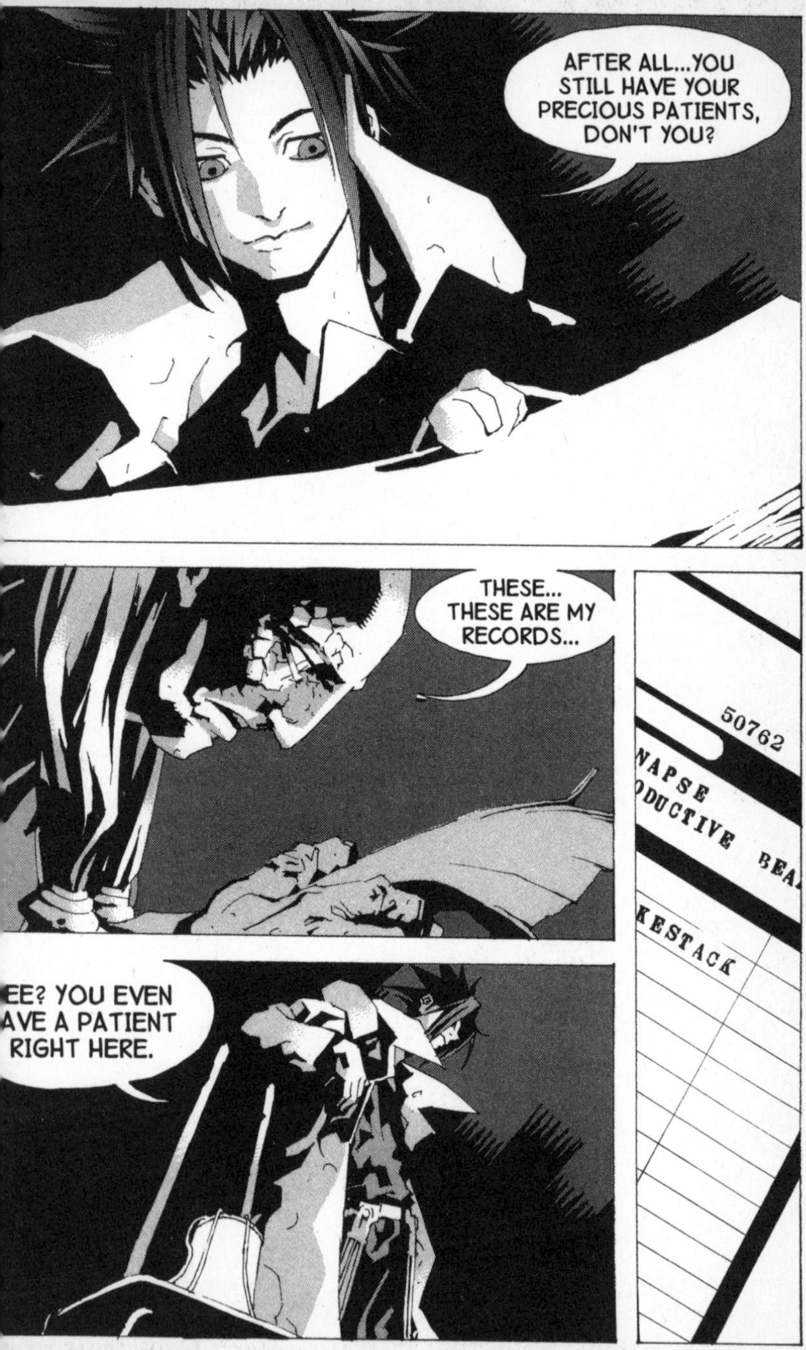
AFTER ALL...YOU STILL HAVE YOUR PRECIOUS PATIENTS, DON'T YOU?
50762
NAPSE
ODUCTIVE
BEA
KESTACK
THESE... THESE ARE MY RECORDS...
EE? YOU EVEN AVE A PATIENT RIGHT HERE.

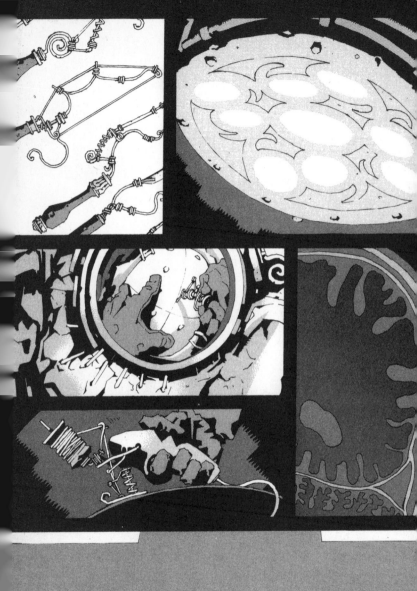

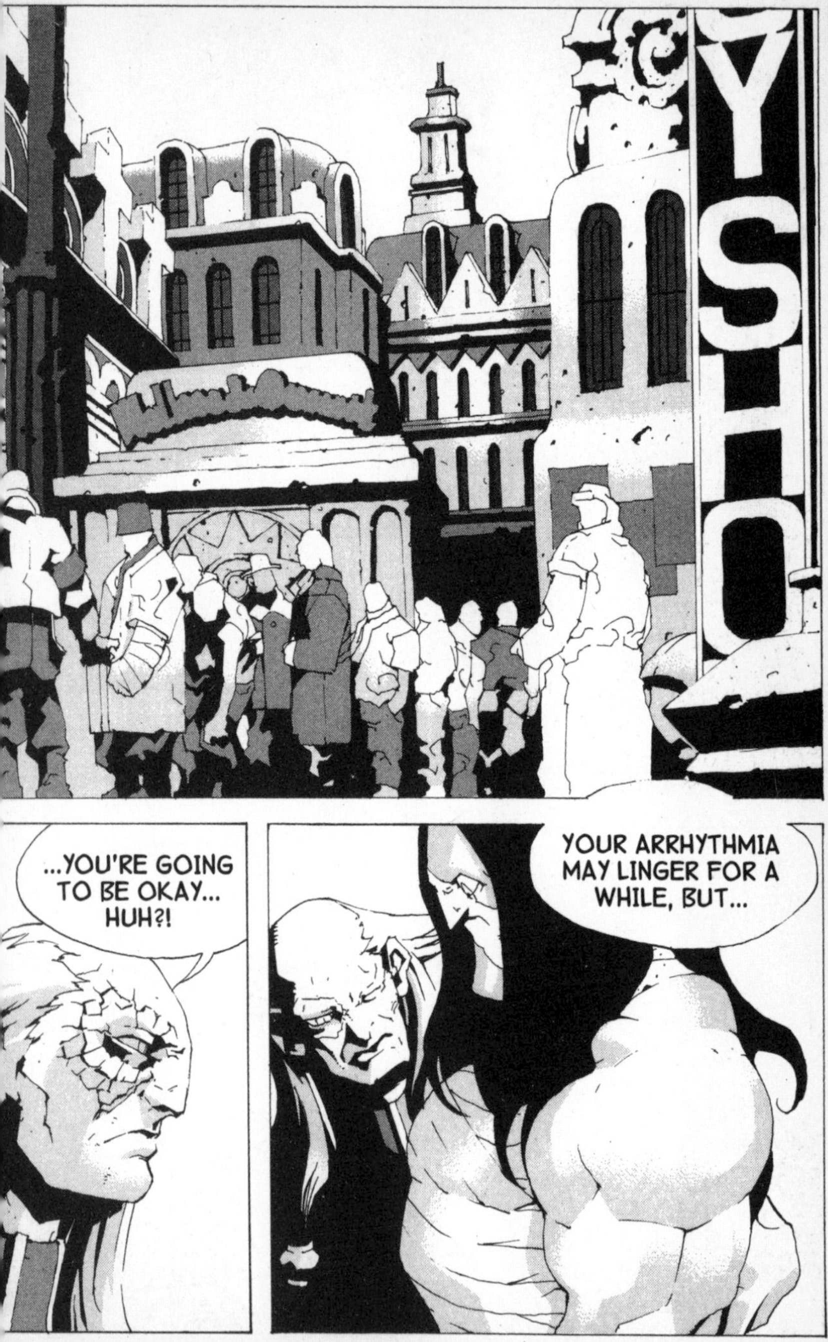
YOUR ARRHYTHMIA MAY LINGER FOR A WHILE, BUT...
...YOU'RE GOING TO BE OKAY... HUH?!

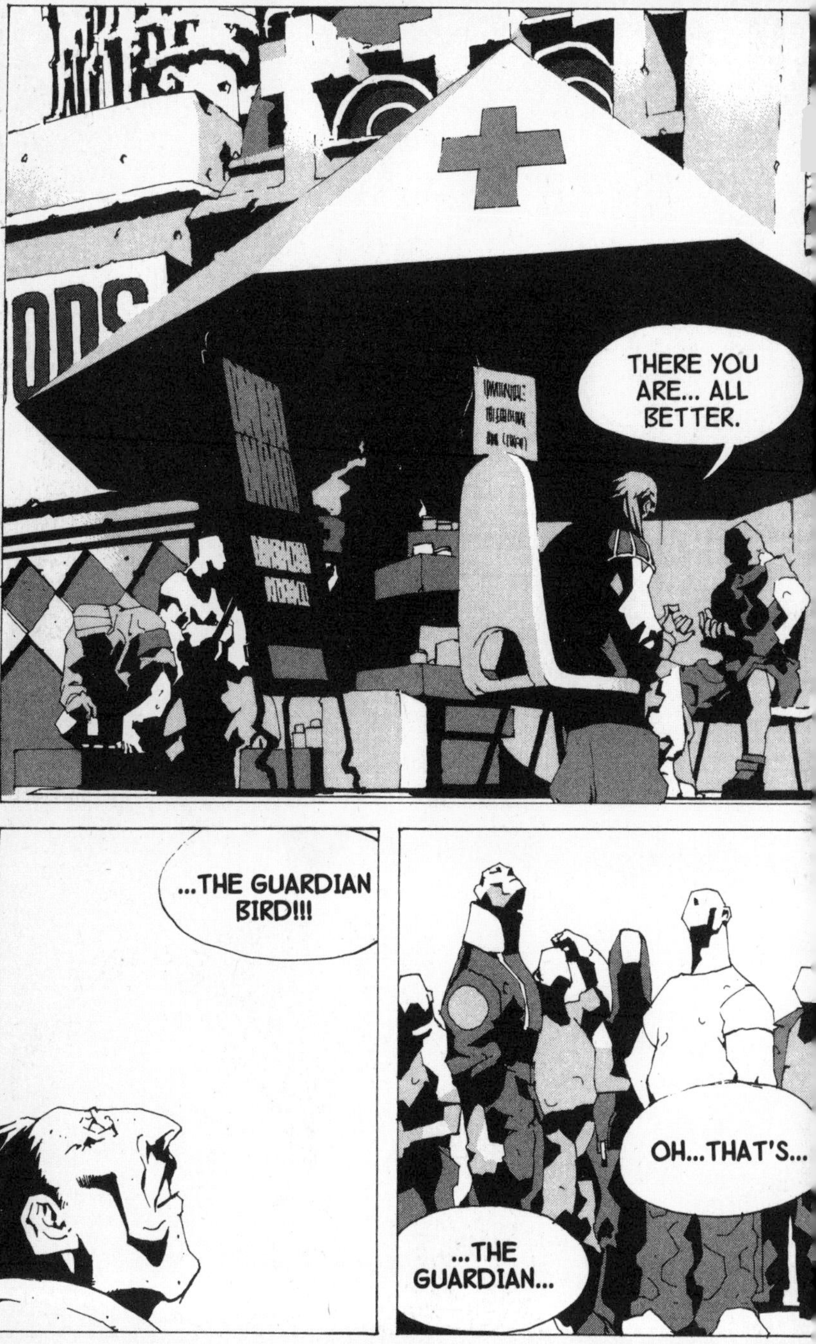
THERE YOU ARE... ALL BETTER.
OH...THAT'S...
...THE GUARDIAN...
...THE GUARDIAN BIRD!!!

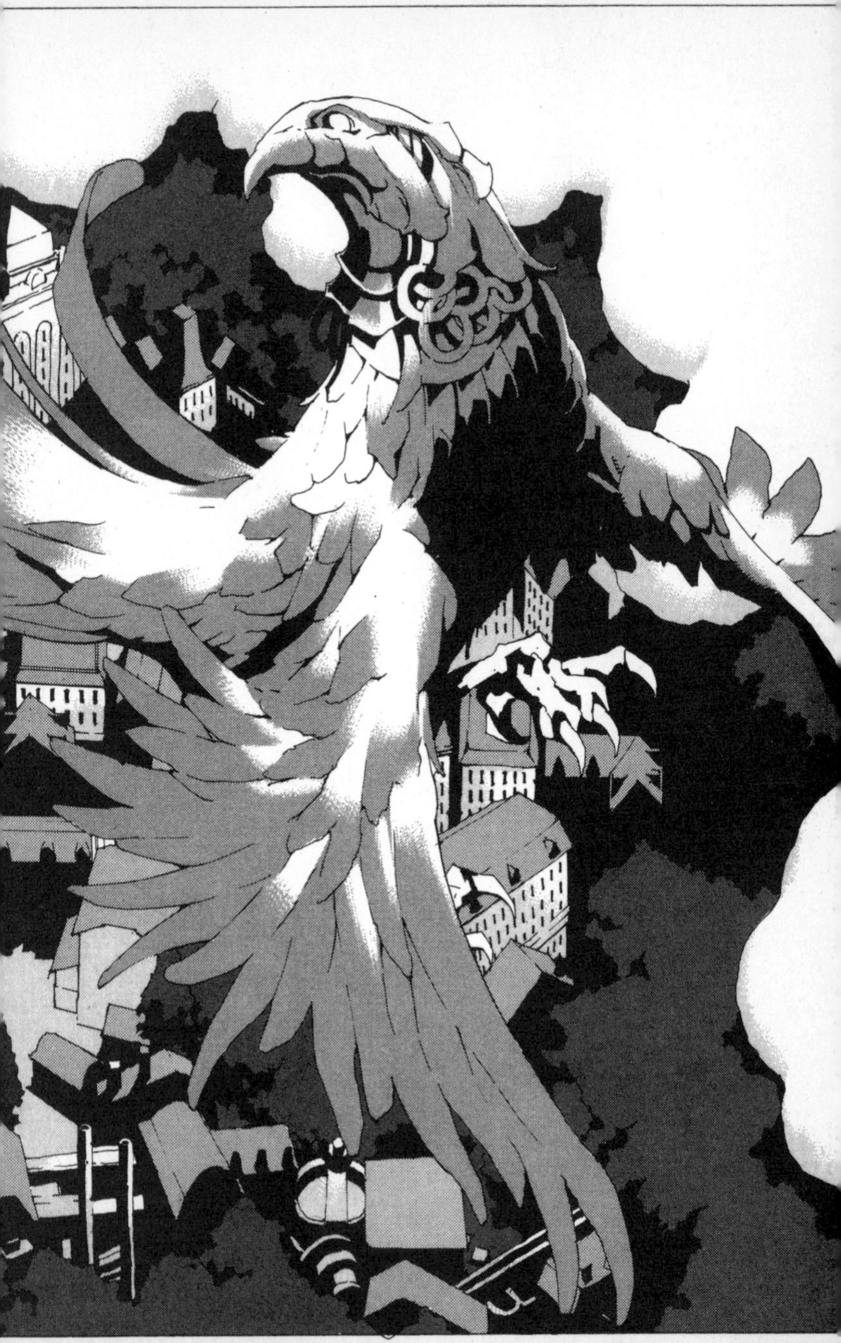

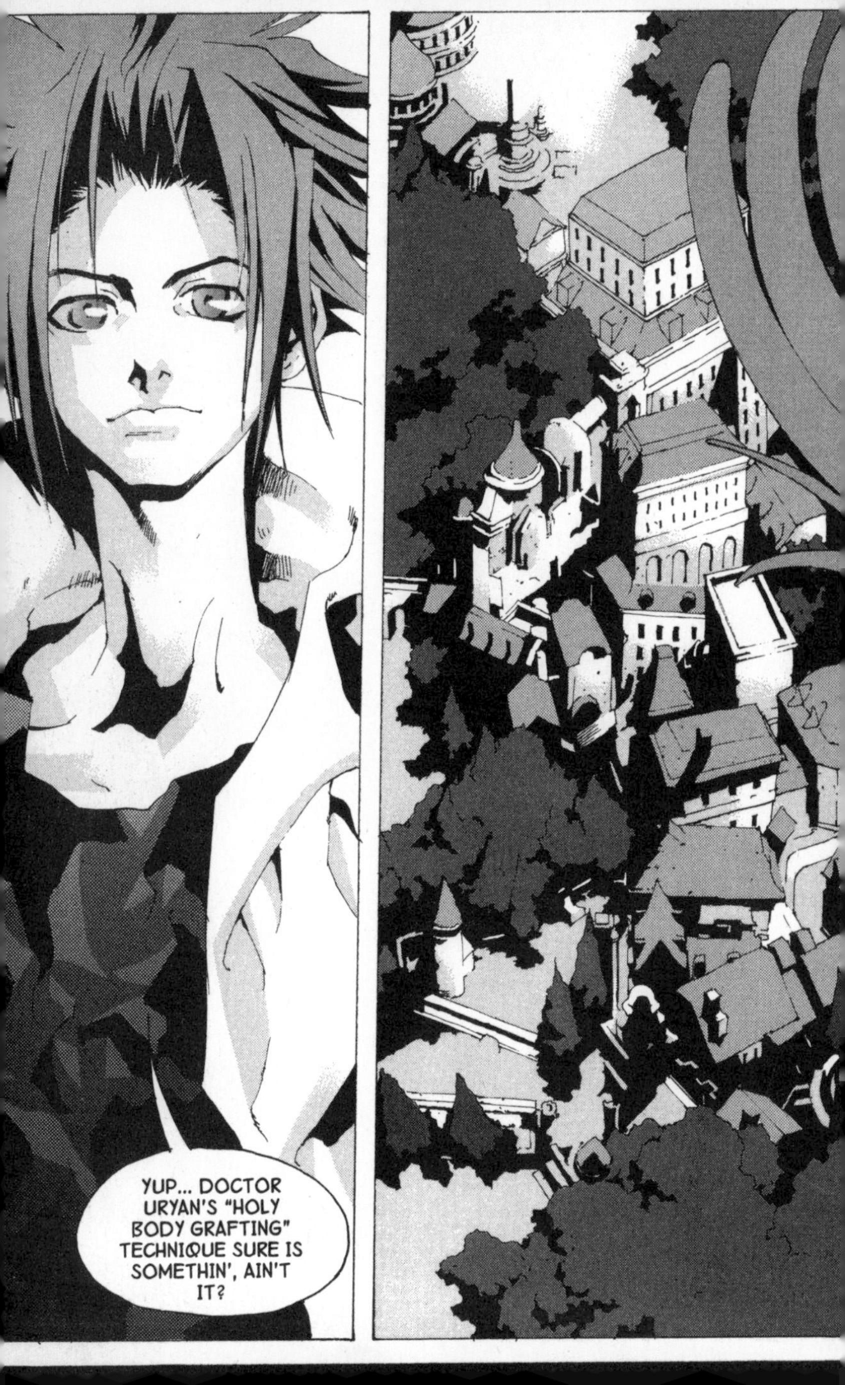
YUP... DOCTOR URYAN'S "HOLY BODY GRAFTING" TECHNIQUE SURE IS SOMETHIN', AIN'T IT?

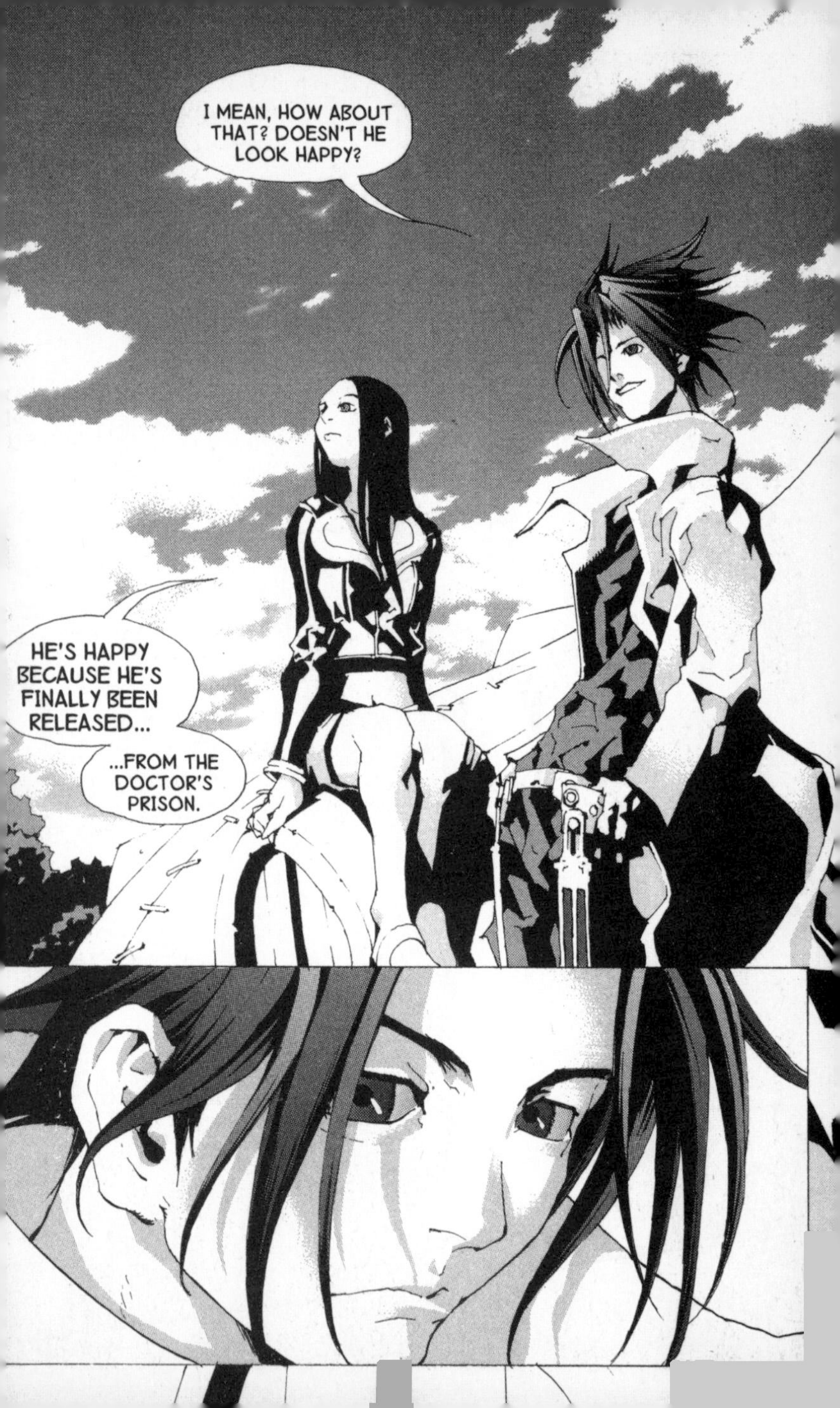
I MEAN, HOW ABOUT THAT? DOESN'T HE LOOK HAPPY?
HE'S HAPPY BECAUSE HE'S FINALLY BEEN RELEASED...
...FROM THE DOCTOR'S PRISON.

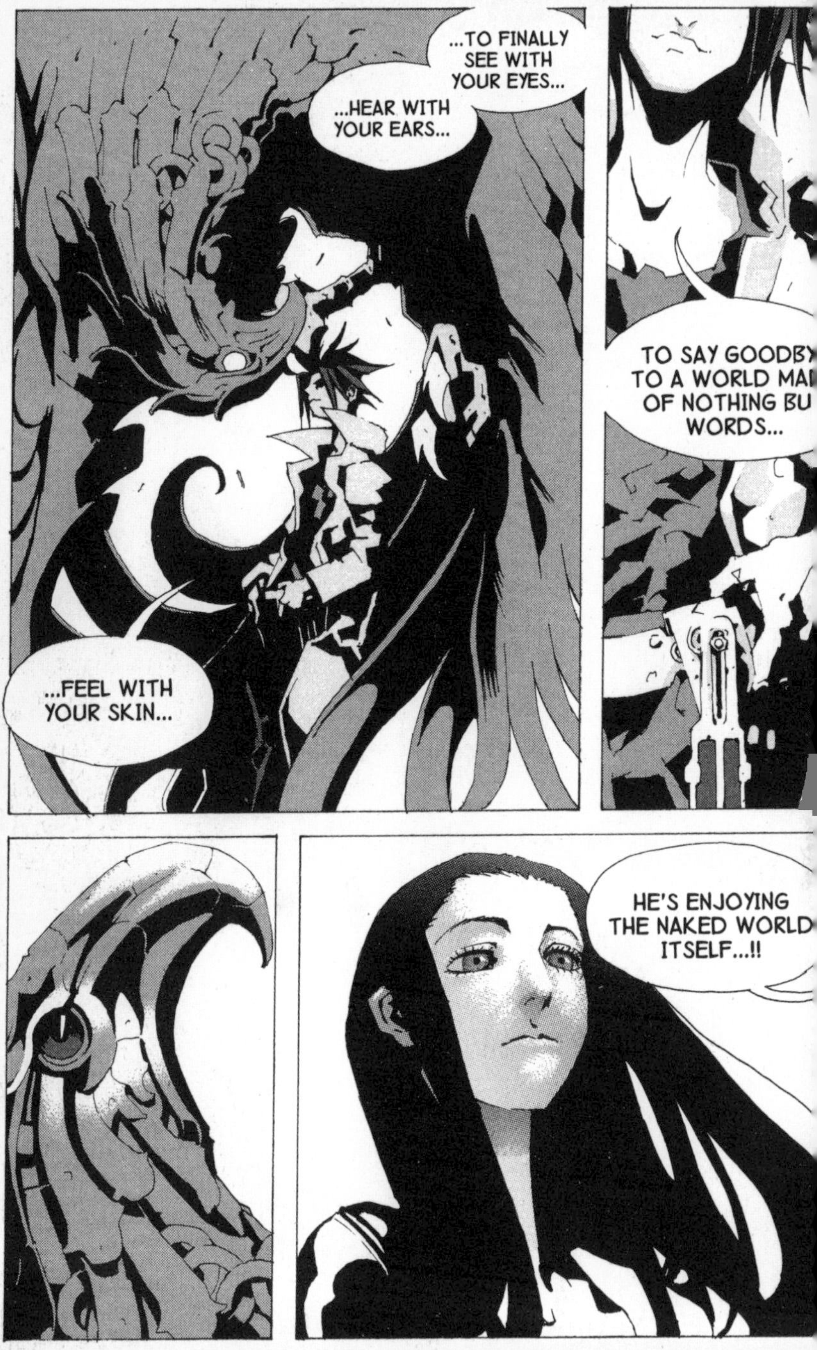
TO SAY GOODBY
TO A WORLD MA
OF NOTHING BU
WORDS...
...TO FINALLY SEE WITH YOUR EYES...
...HEAR WITH YOUR EARS...
...FEEL WITH YOUR SKIN...
HE'S ENJOYING THE NAKED WORLD ITSELF...!!

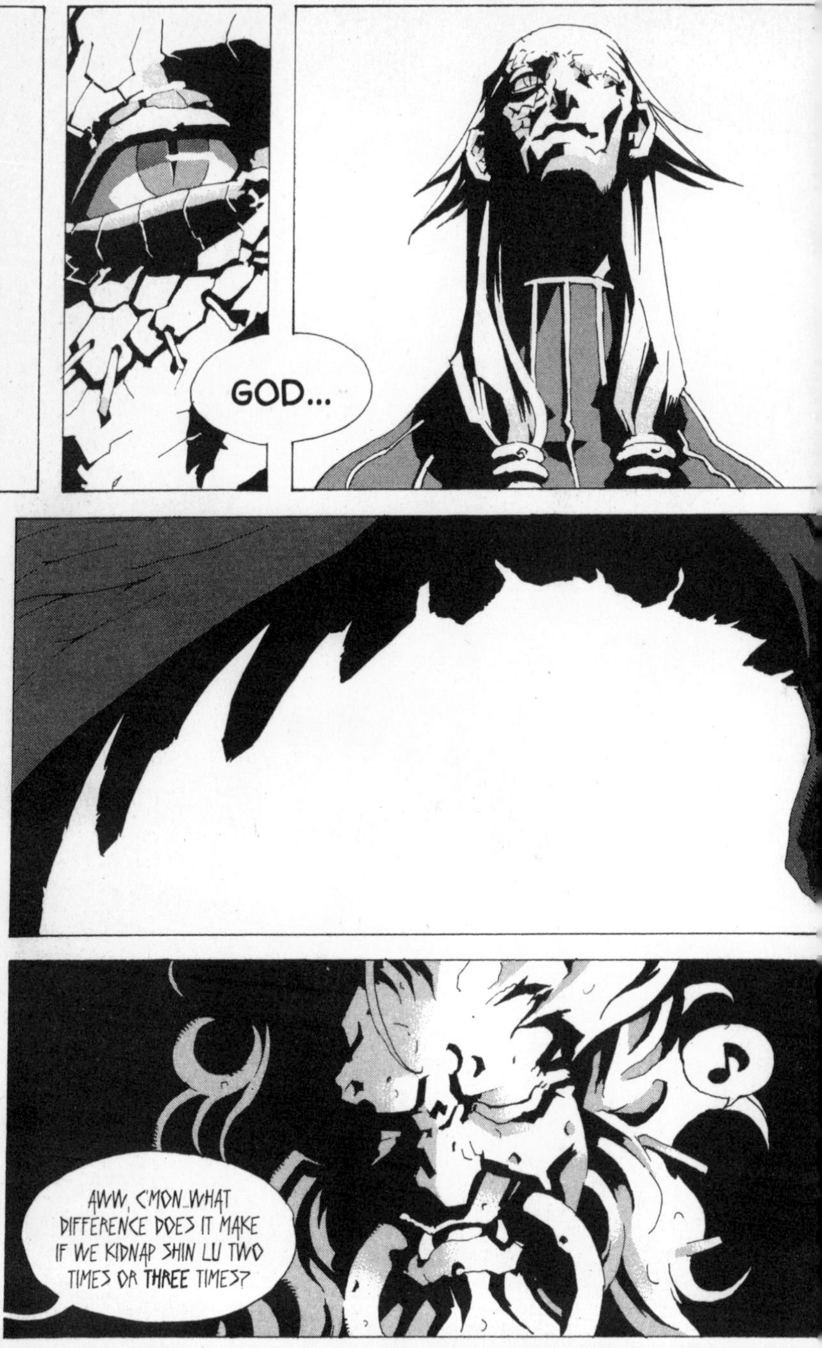
GOD...
♪
AWW, C'MON...WHAT DIFFERENCE DOES IT MAKE IF WE KIDNAP SHIN LU TWO TIMES OR THREE TIMES?

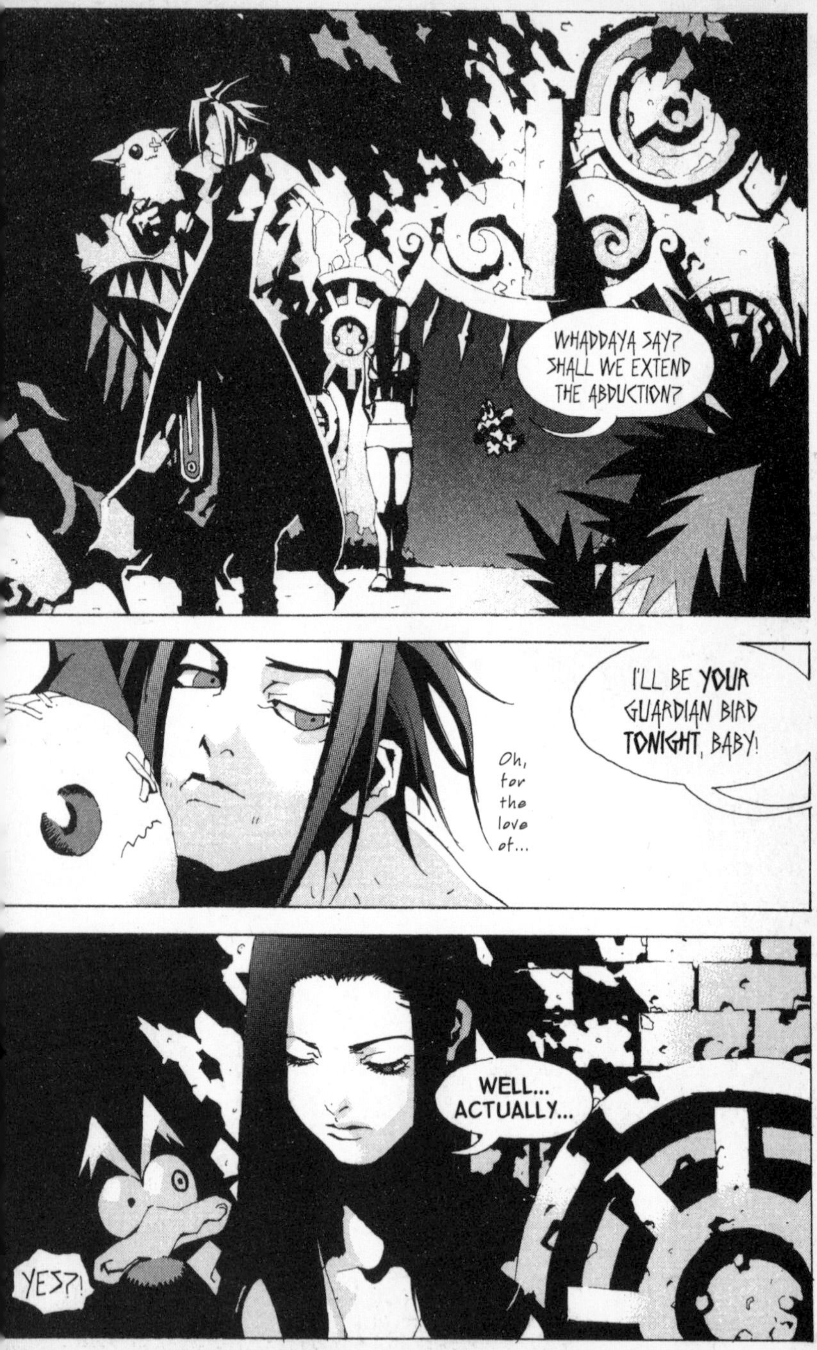
WHADDAYA SAY? SHALL WE EXTEND THE ABDUCTION?
I'LL BE **YOUR** GUARDIAN BIRD **TONIGHT**, BABY!
Oh, for the love of...
WELL... ACTUALLY...
YES?!

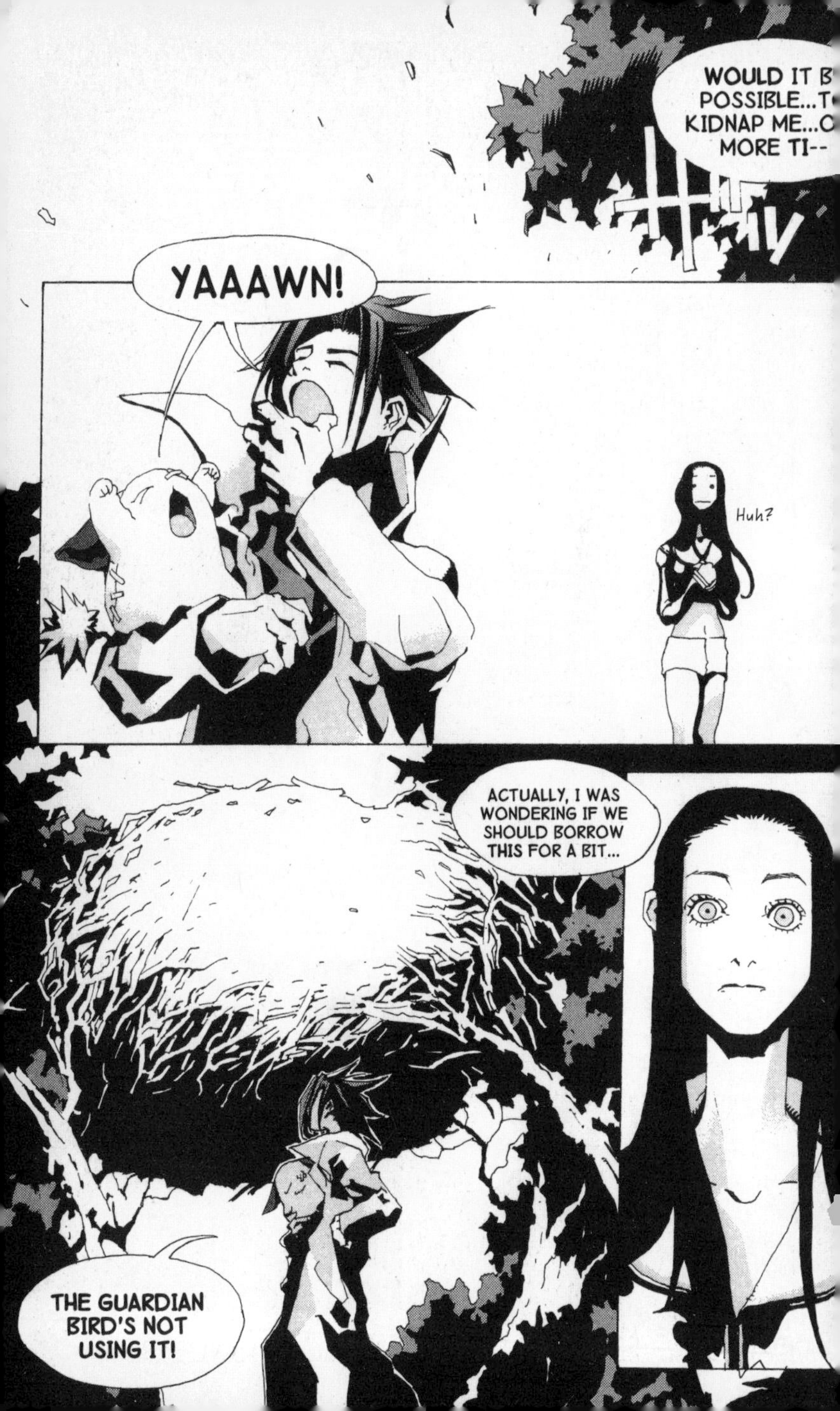
WOULD IT B POSSIBLE...T KIDNAP ME...C MORE TI--
YAAAWN!
Huh?
ACTUALLY, I WAS WONDERING IF WE SHOULD BORROW THIS FOR A BIT...
THE GUARDIAN BIRD'S NOT USING IT!

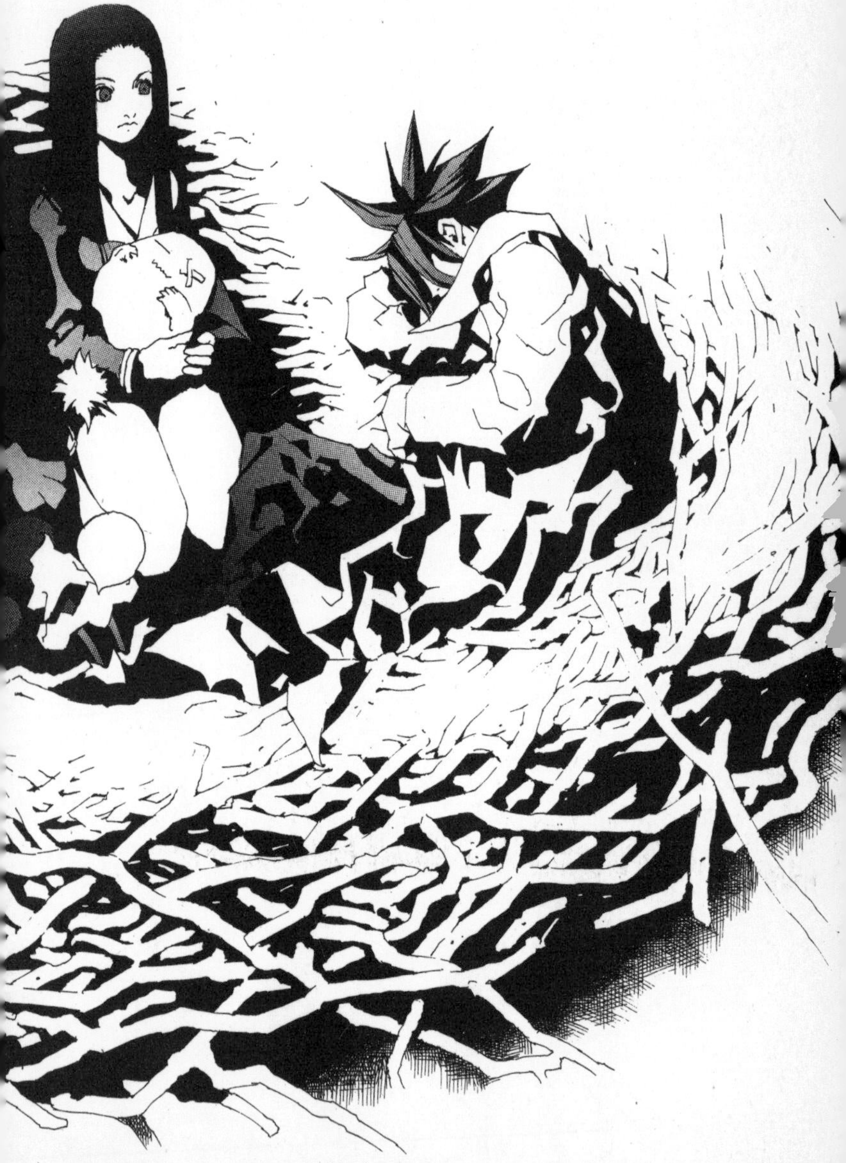

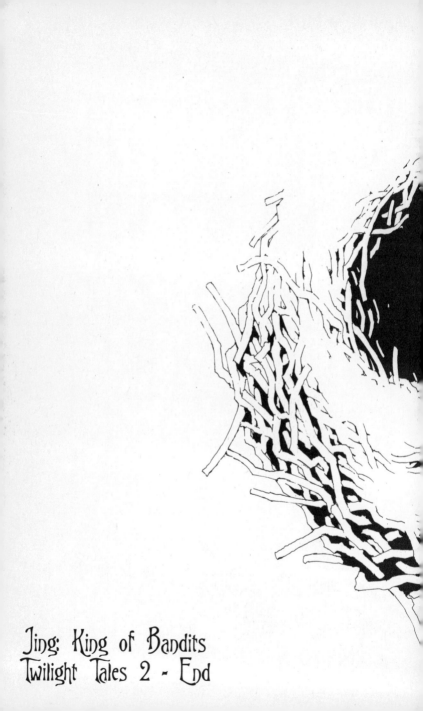

Jing: King of Bandits
Twilight Tales 2 - End

2Bcontinued

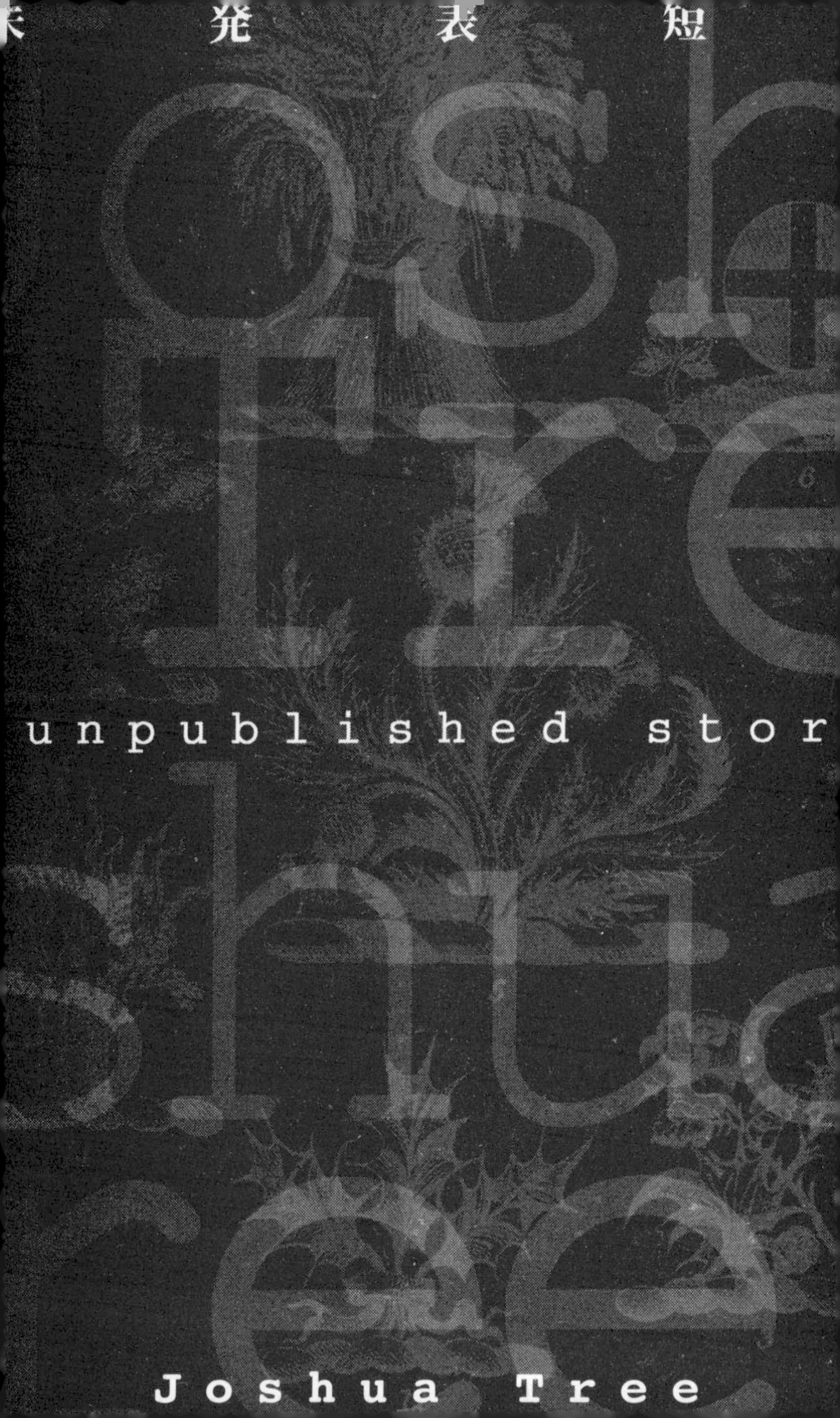
発 表 短
unpublished stor
Joshua Tree

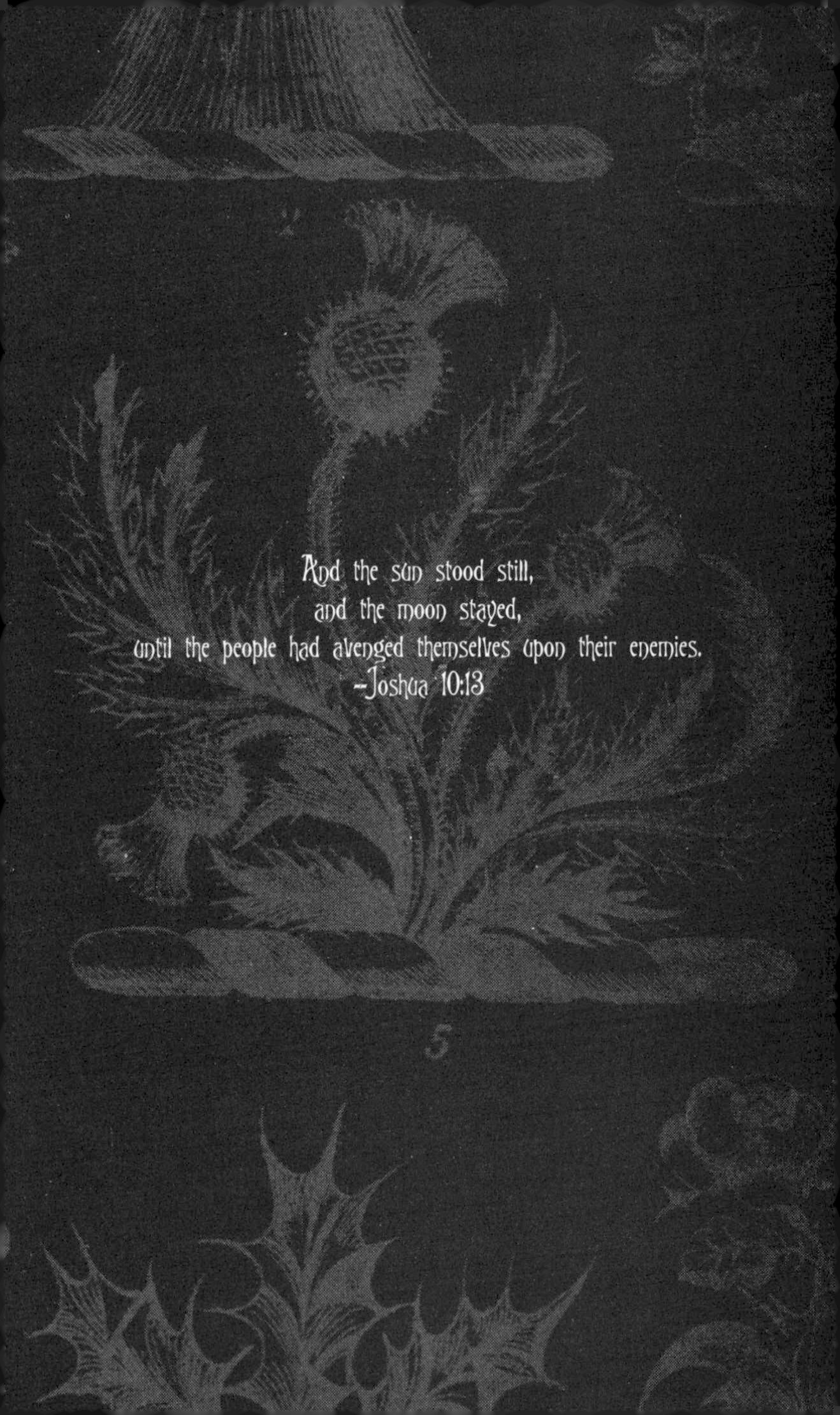
5

And the sun stood still,
and the moon stayed,
until the people had avenged themselves upon their enemies.
--Joshua 10:13

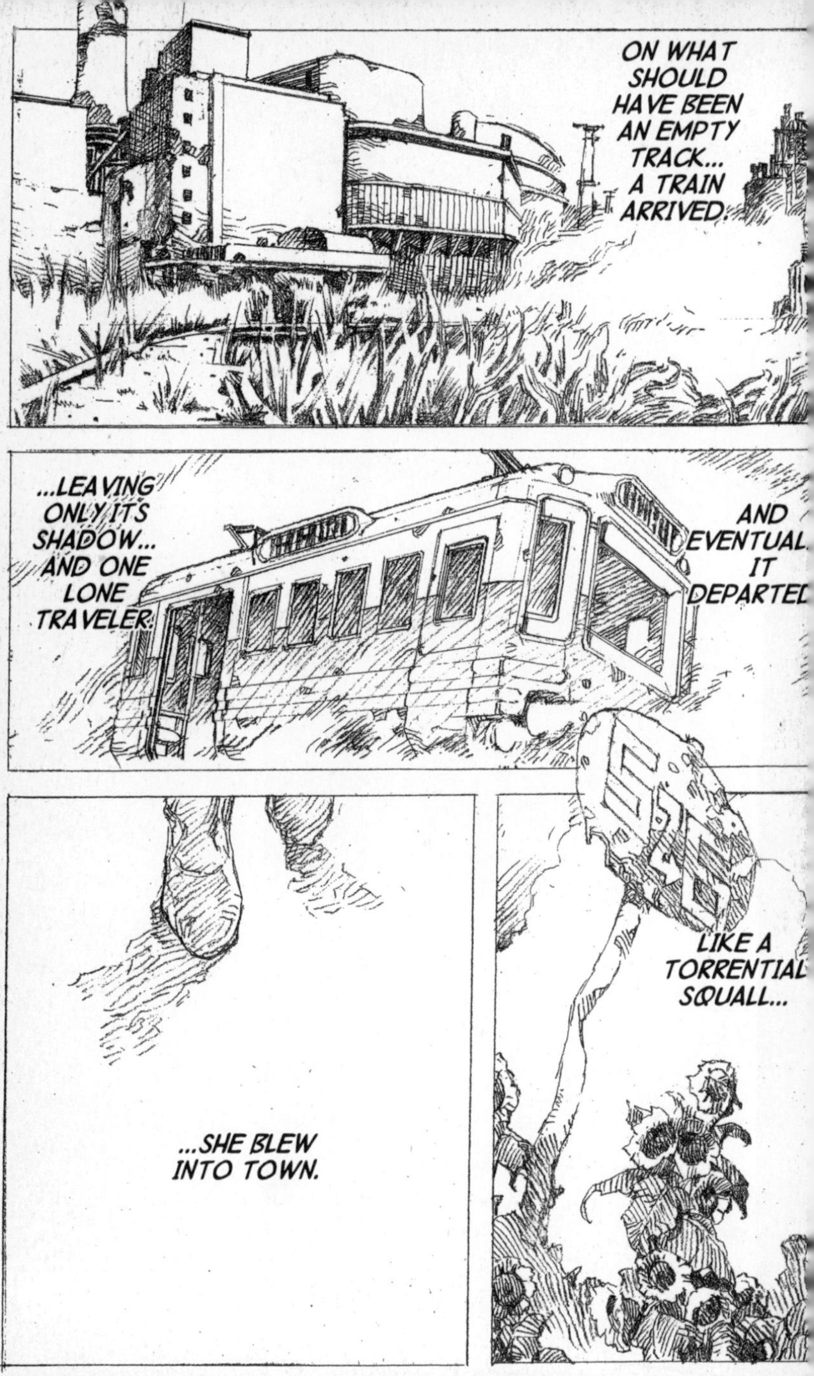
ON WHAT SHOULD HAVE BEEN AN EMPTY TRACK... A TRAIN ARRIVED.
AND EVENTUAL IT DEPARTED
...LEAVING ONLY ITS SHADOW... AND ONE LONE TRAVELER.
LIKE A TORRENTIAL SQUALL...
...SHE BLEW INTO TOWN.

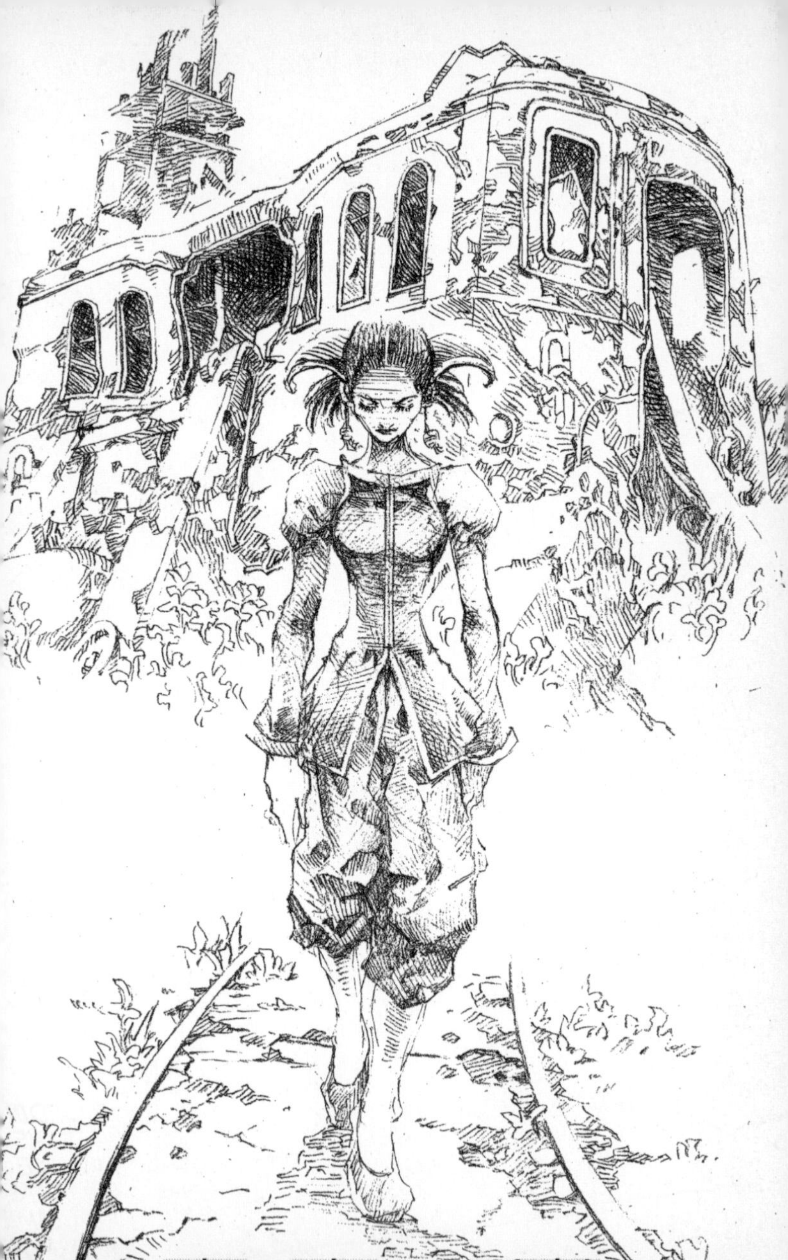
kumakura yuichi

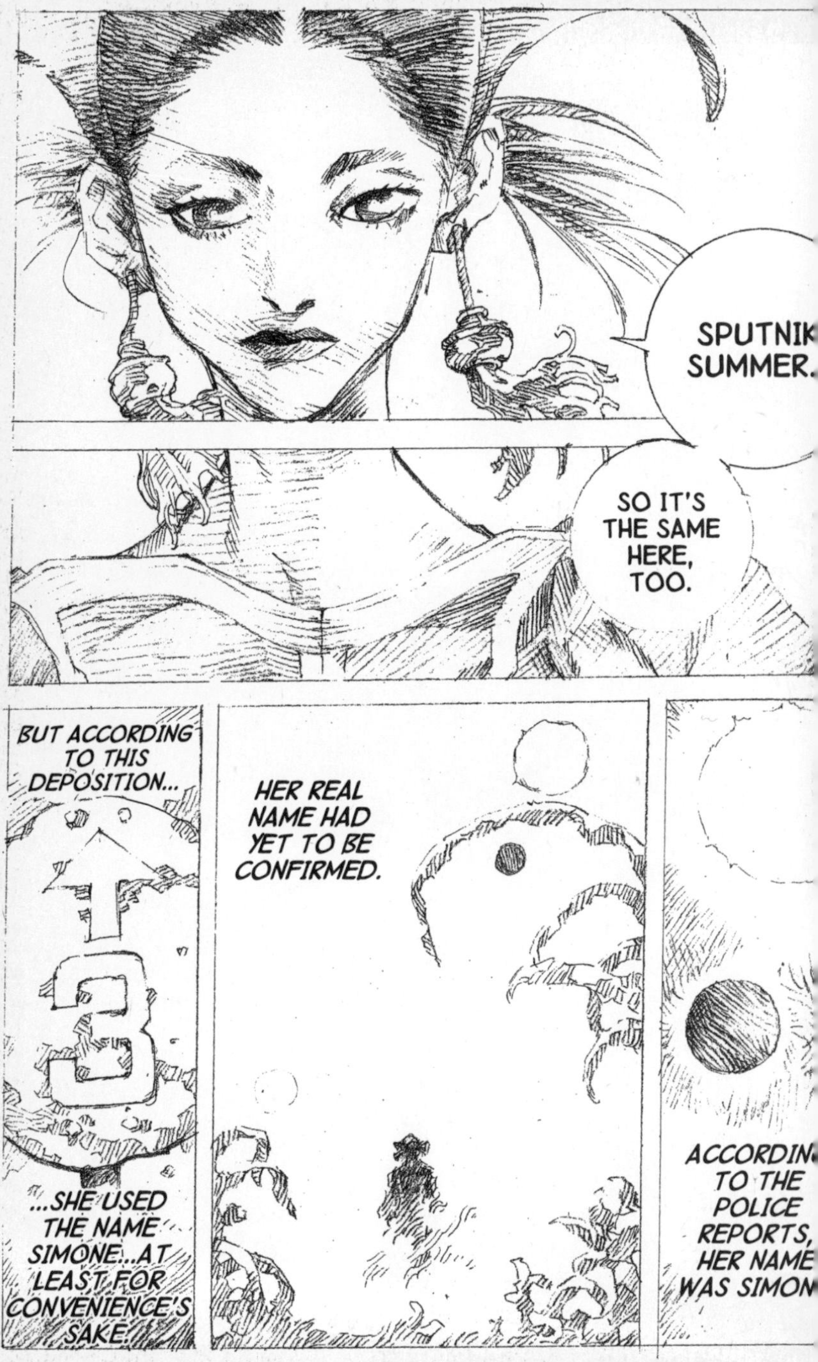
SPUTNIK SUMMER.
SO IT'S THE SAME HERE, TOO.
ACCORDIN TO THE POLICE REPORTS, HER NAME WAS SIMON
HER REAL NAME HAD YET TO BE CONFIRMED.
BUT ACCORDING TO THIS DEPOSITION...
...SHE USED THE NAME SIMONE...AT LEAST FOR CONVENIENCE'S SAKE.

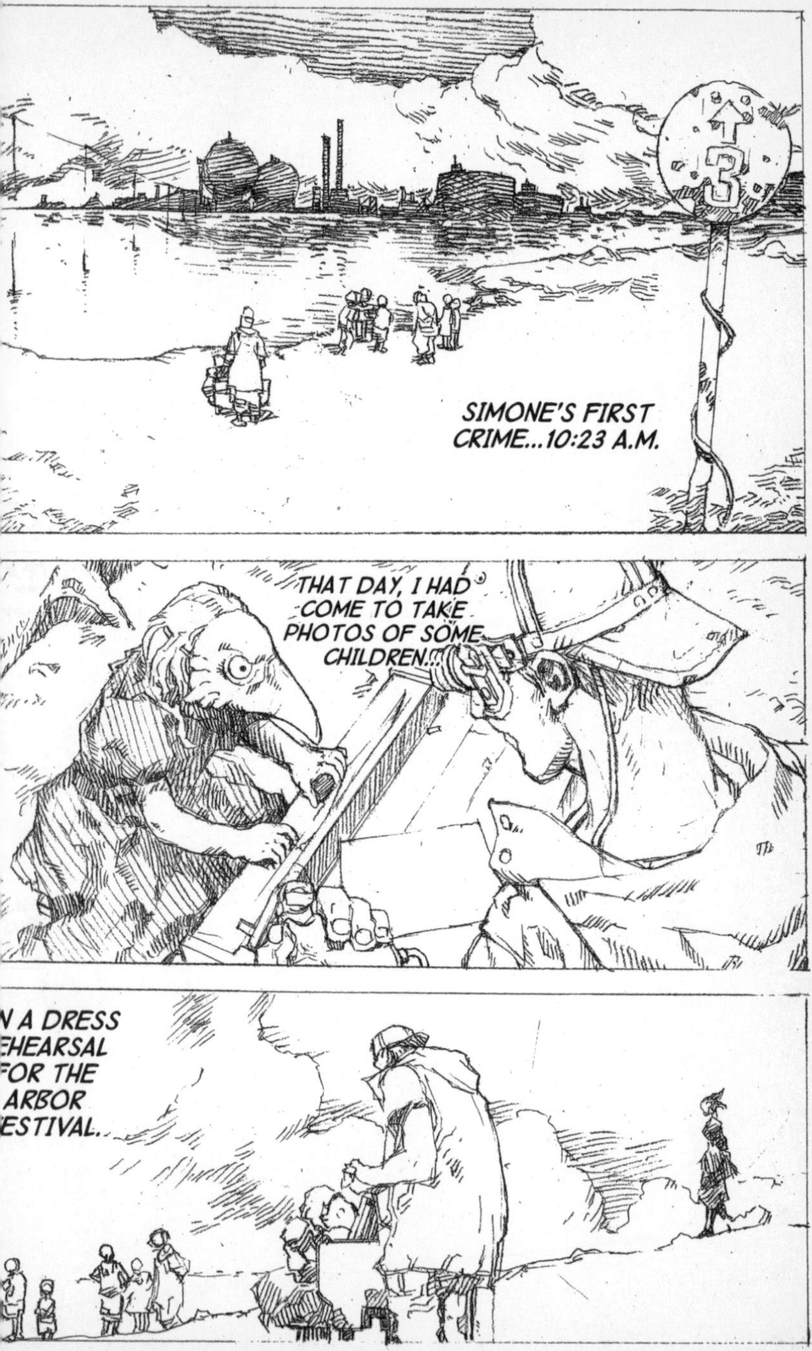
3
SIMONE'S FIRST CRIME...10:23 A.M.
THAT DAY, I HAD COME TO TAKE PHOTOS OF SOME CHILDREN...
N A DRESS EHEARSAL FOR THE ARBOR ESTIVAL...

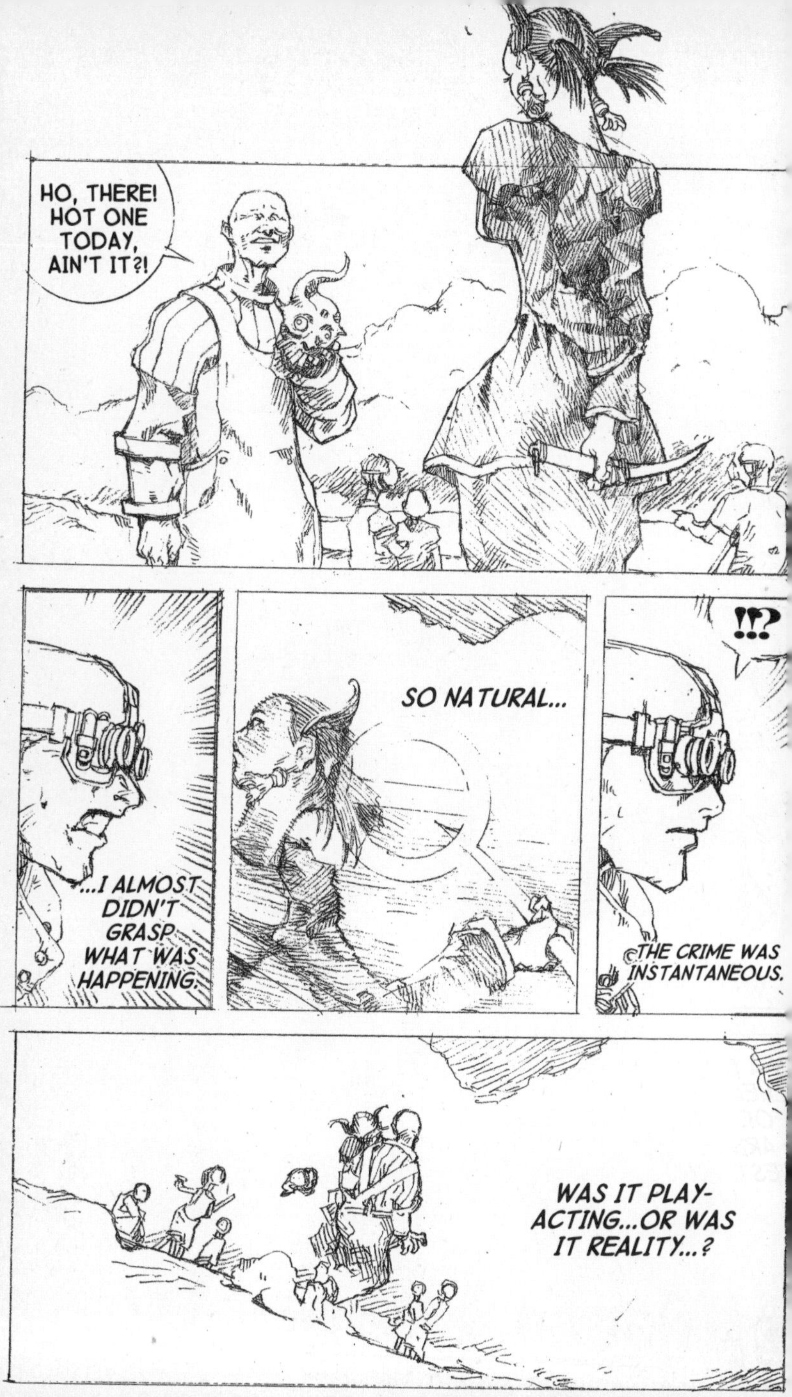
HO, THERE! HOT ONE TODAY, AIN'T IT?!
!!?
THE CRIME WAS INSTANTANEOUS.
SO NATURAL...
...I ALMOST DIDN'T GRASP WHAT WAS HAPPENING.
WAS IT PLAY-ACTING...OR WAS IT REALITY...?

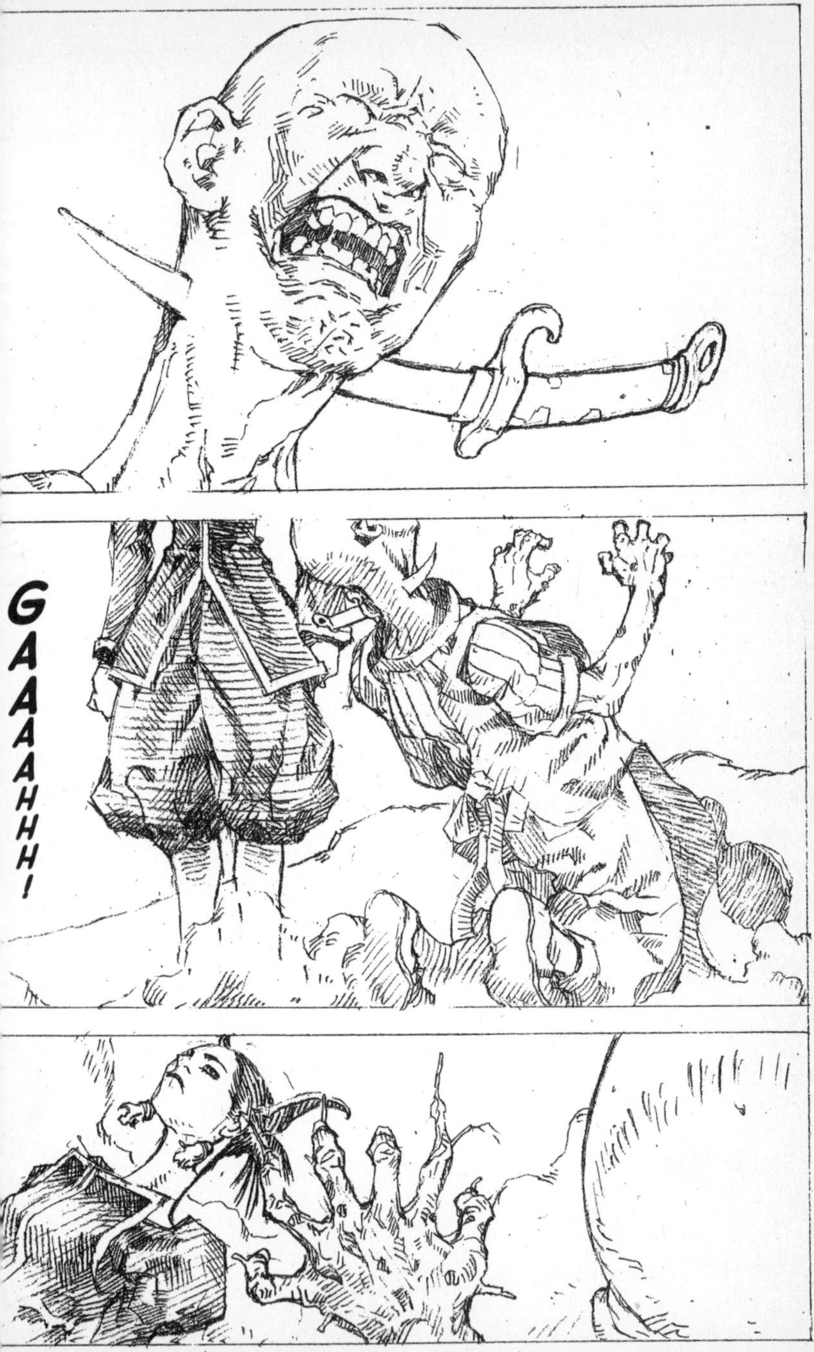
GAAAAHHH!

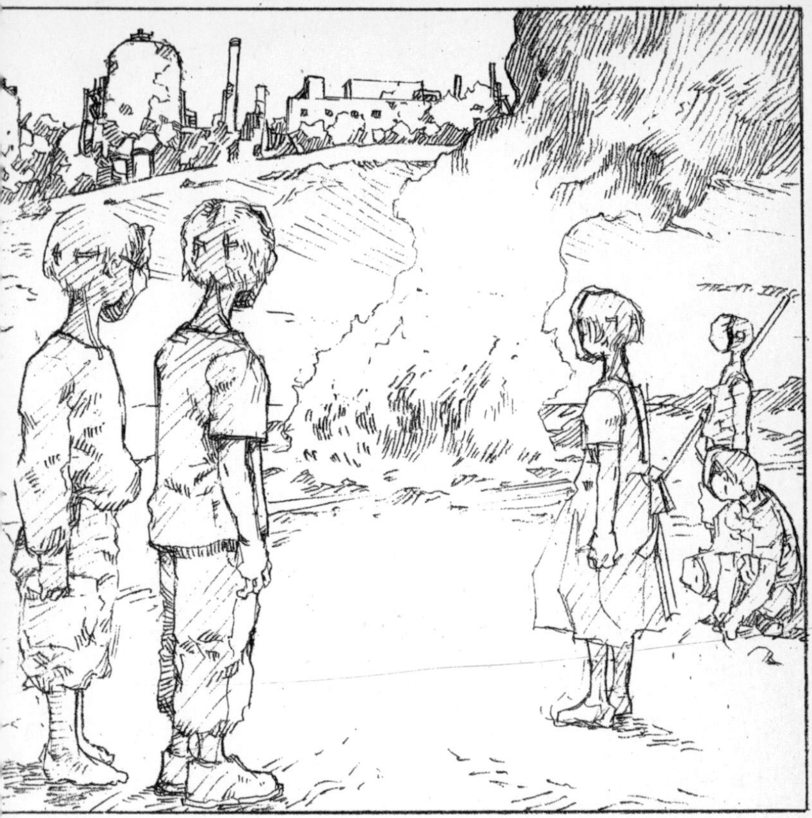
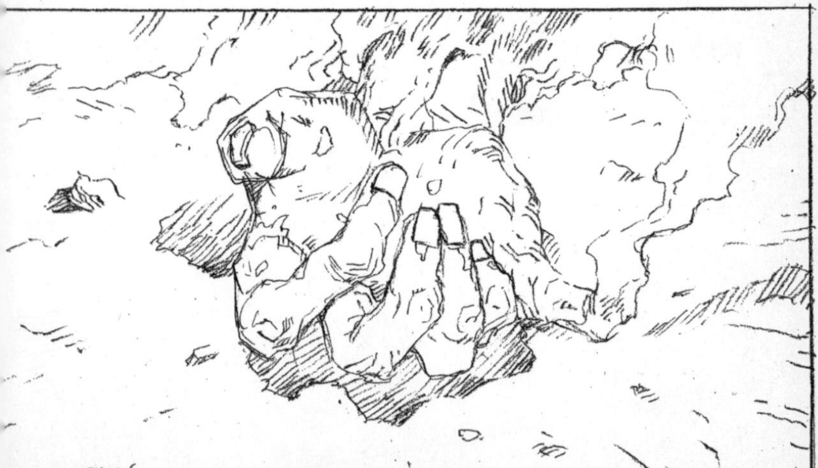

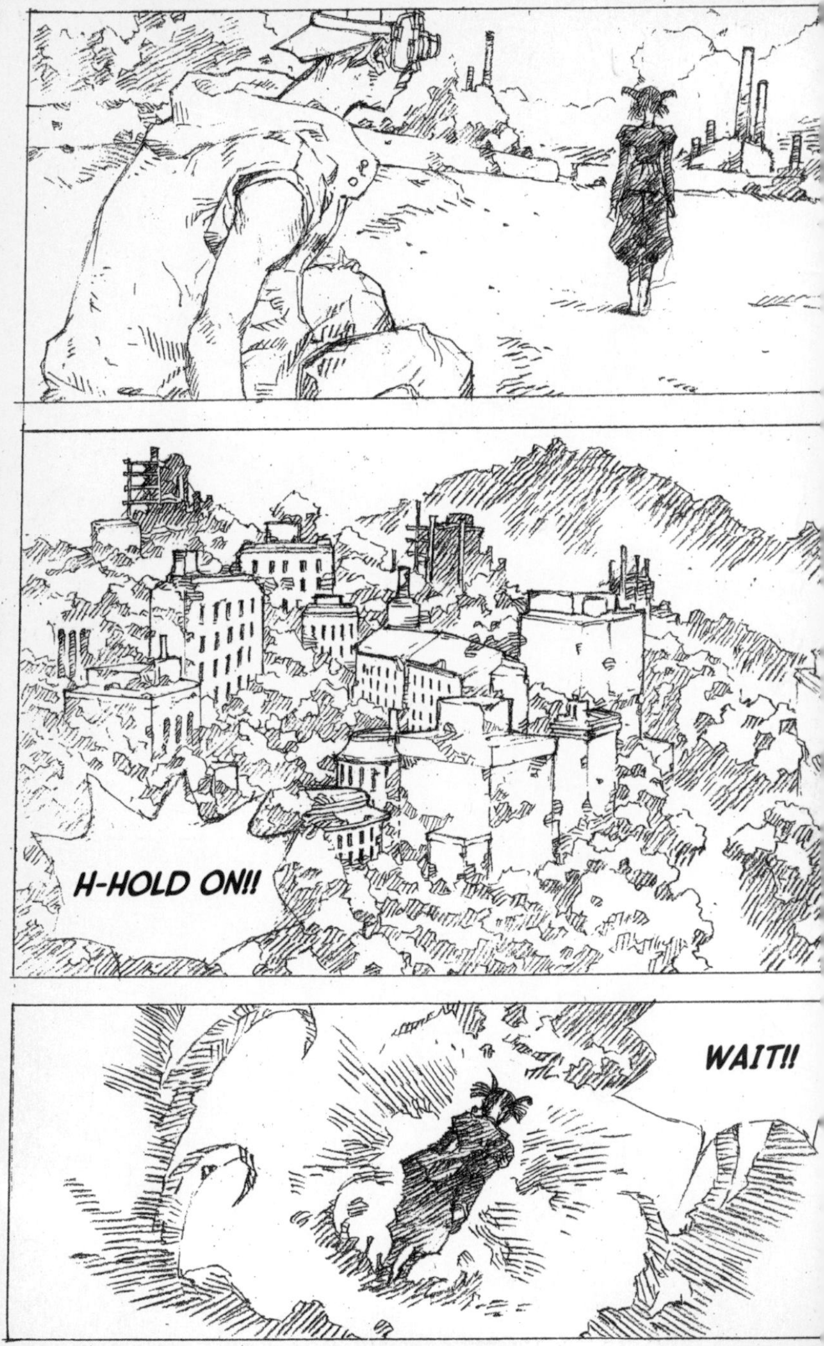
H-HOLD ON!!
WAIT!!

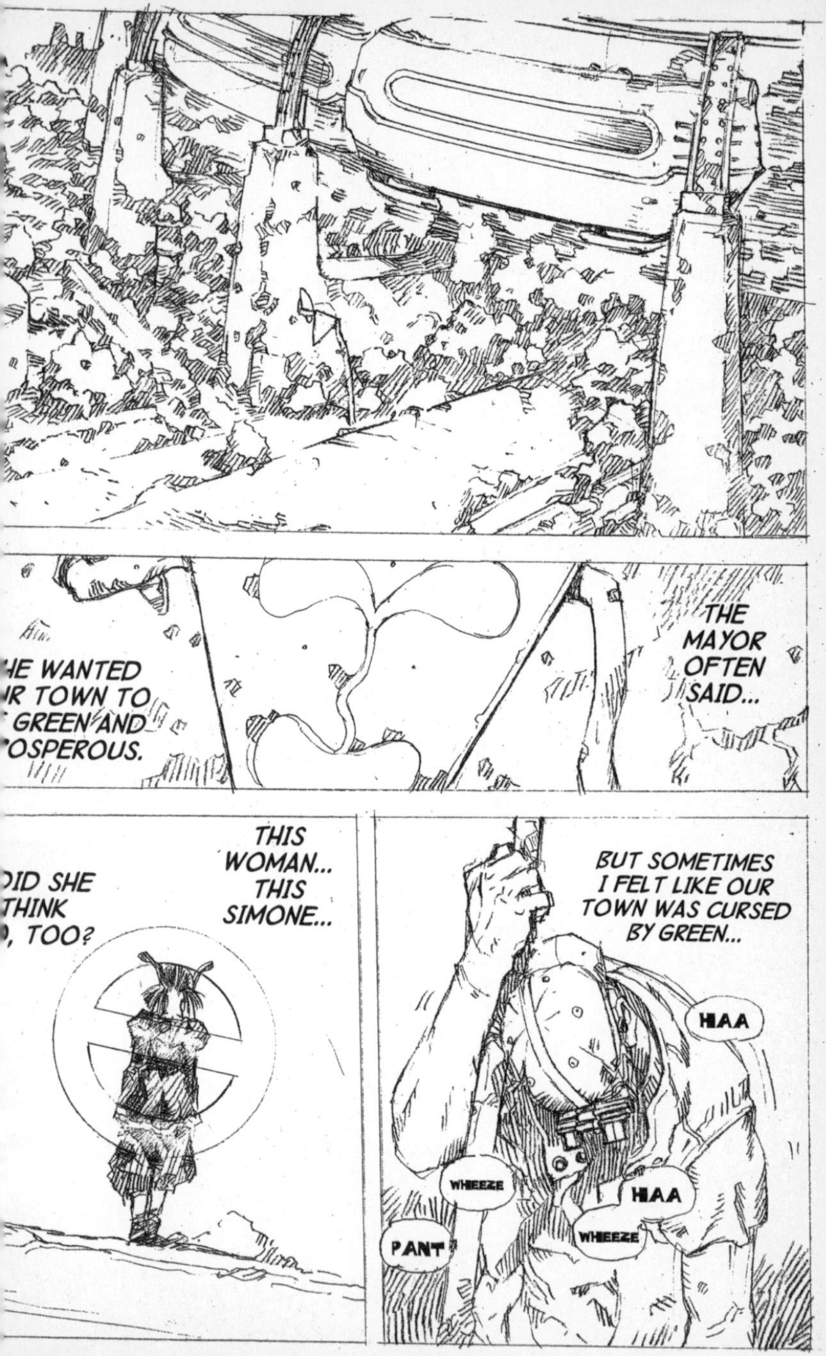
THE MAYOR OFTEN SAID...
HE WANTED R TOWN TO GREEN AND OSPEROUS.
BUT SOMETIMES I FELT LIKE OUR TOWN WAS CURSED BY GREEN...
HIAA
HIAA
WHEEZE
WHEEZE
PANT
THIS WOMAN... THIS SIMONE...
ID SHE THINK , TOO?

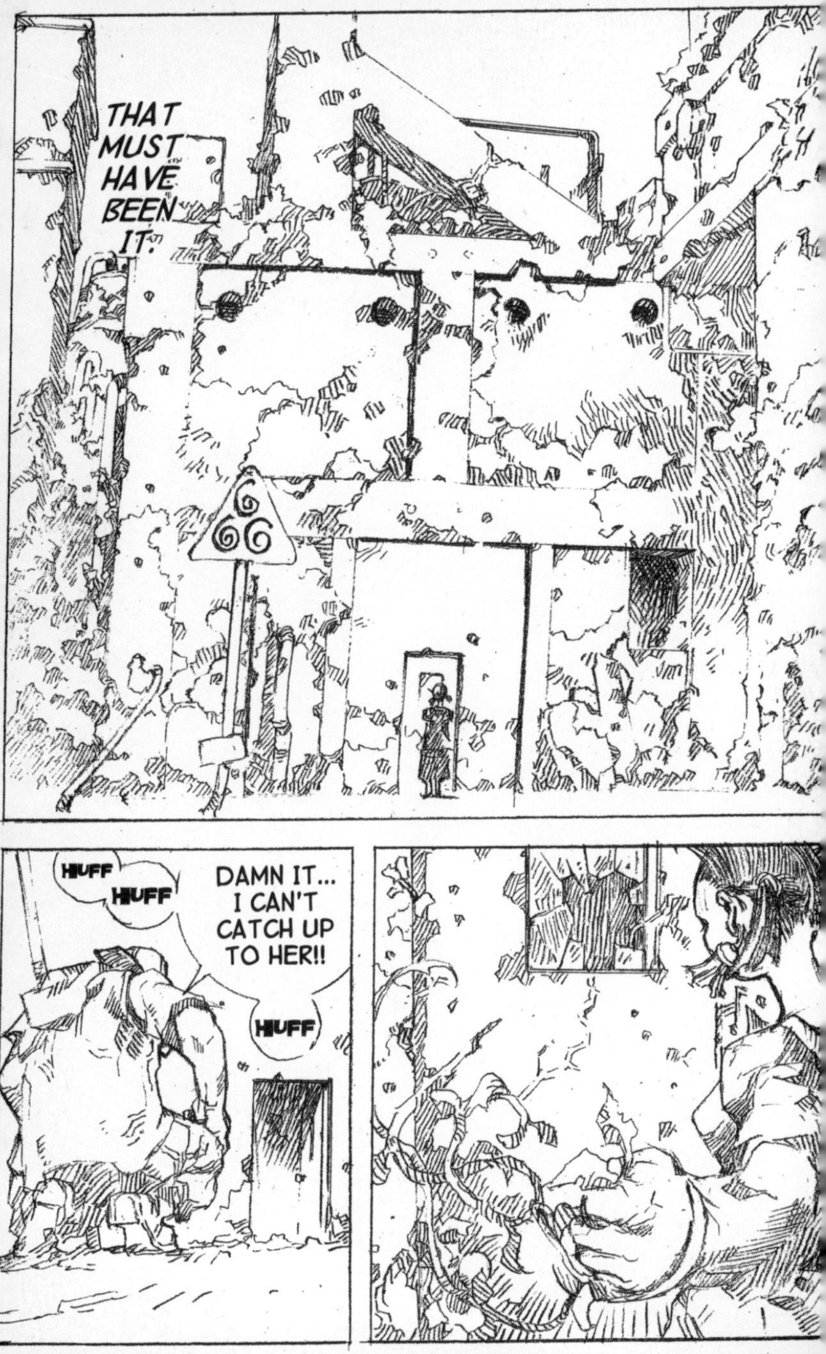
THAT MUST HAVE BEEN IT.
HUFF
HUFF
DAMN IT... I CAN'T CATCH UP TO HER!!
HUFF

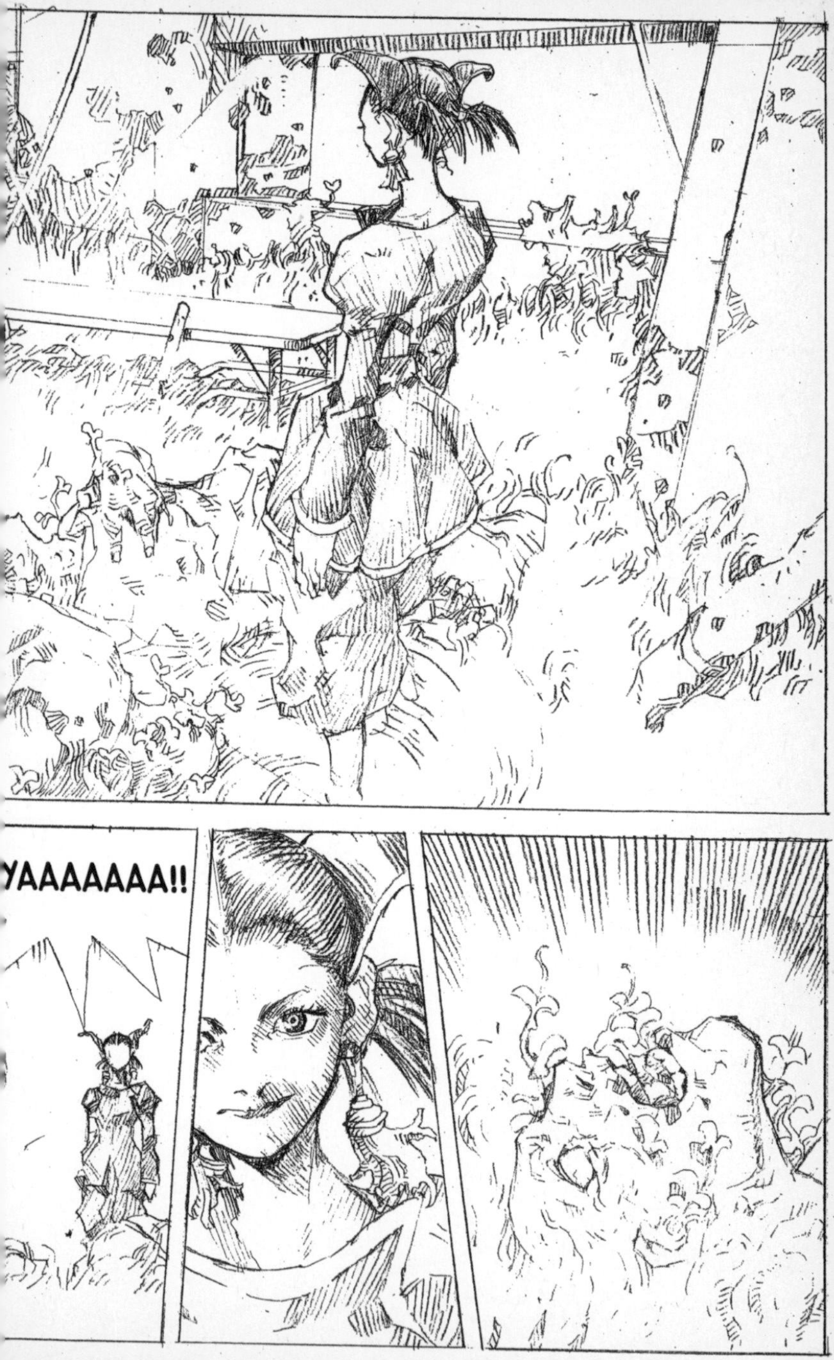
YAAAAAAA!!

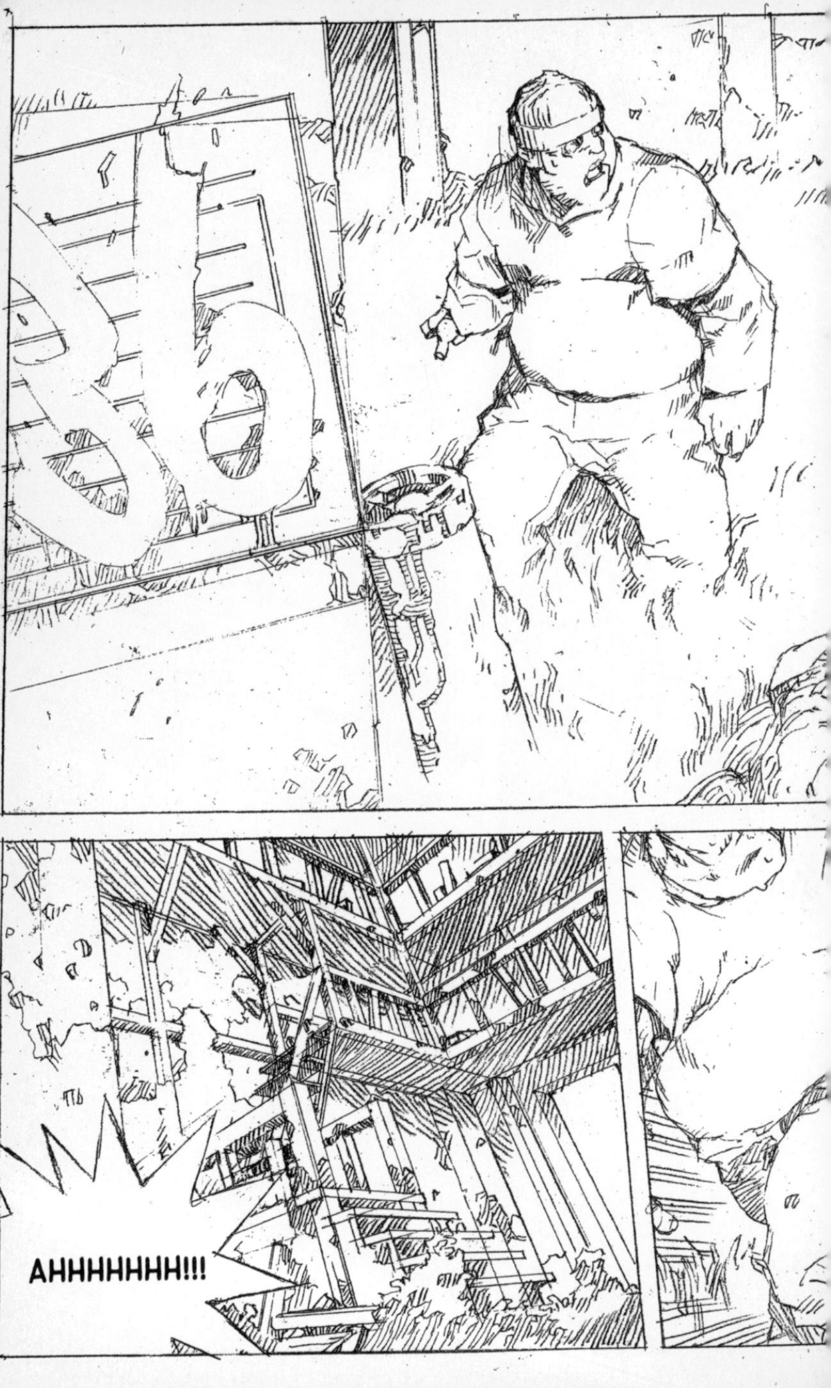
AHHHHHHH!!!

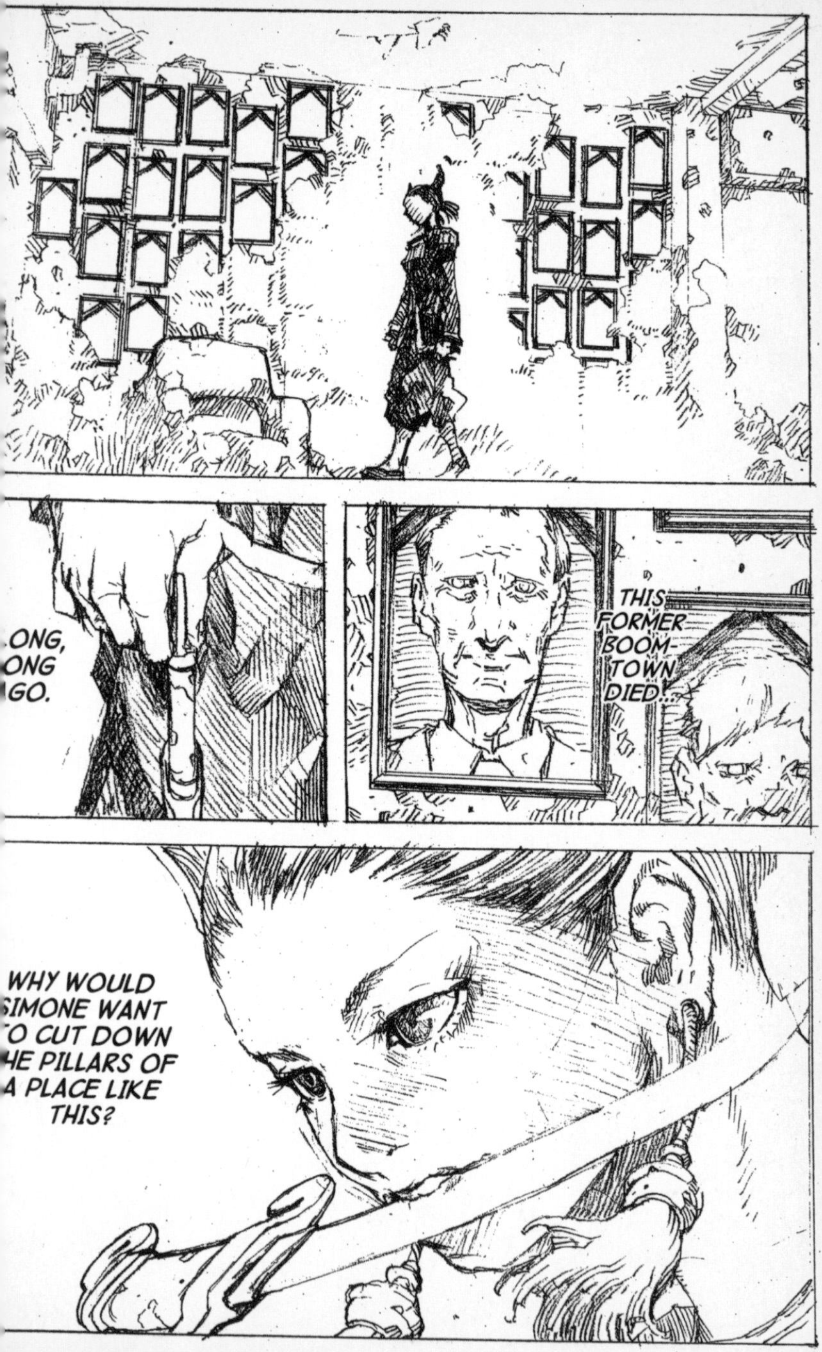
THIS FORMER BOOM-TOWN DIED...
ONG, ONG GO.
WHY WOULD SIMONE WANT O CUT DOWN HE PILLARS OF A PLACE LIKE THIS?

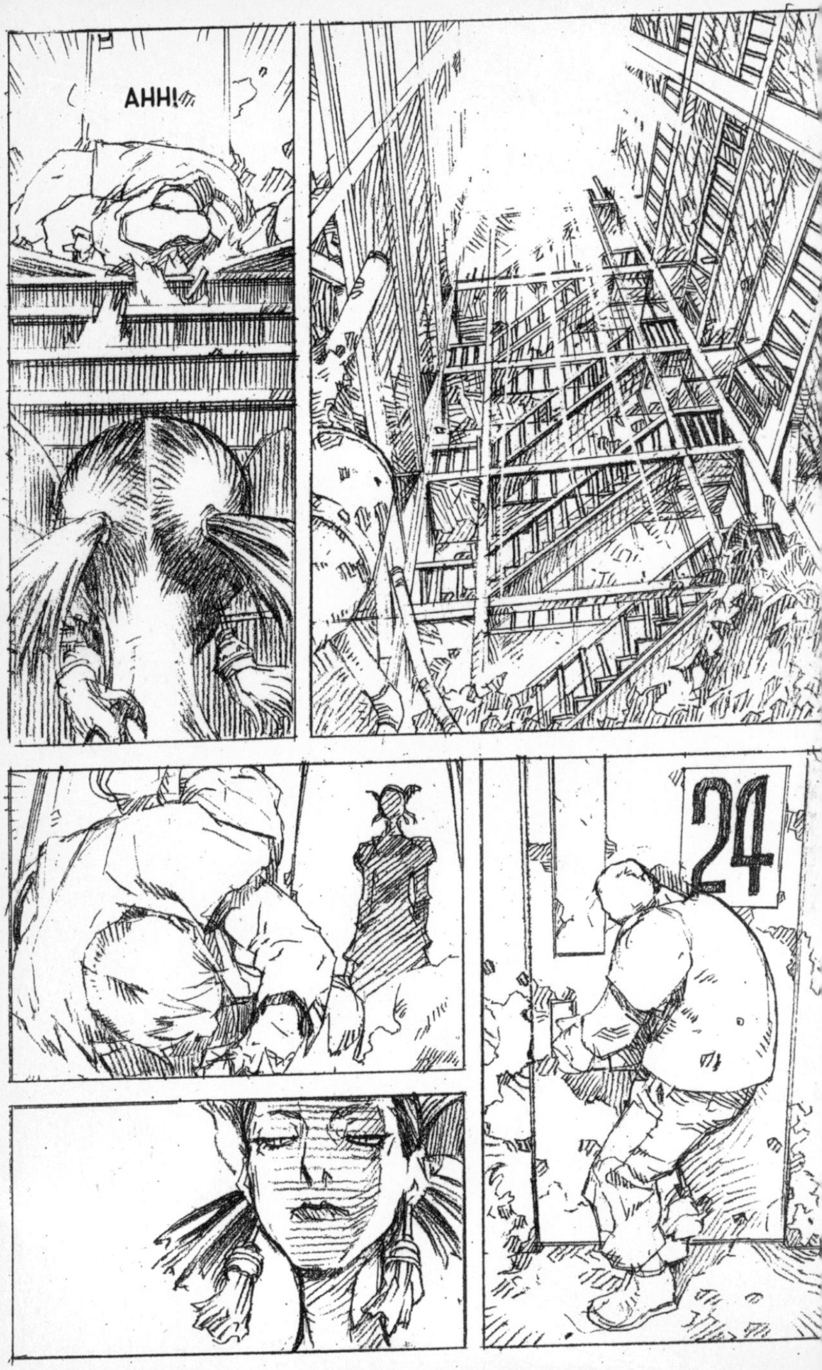
24
AHH!

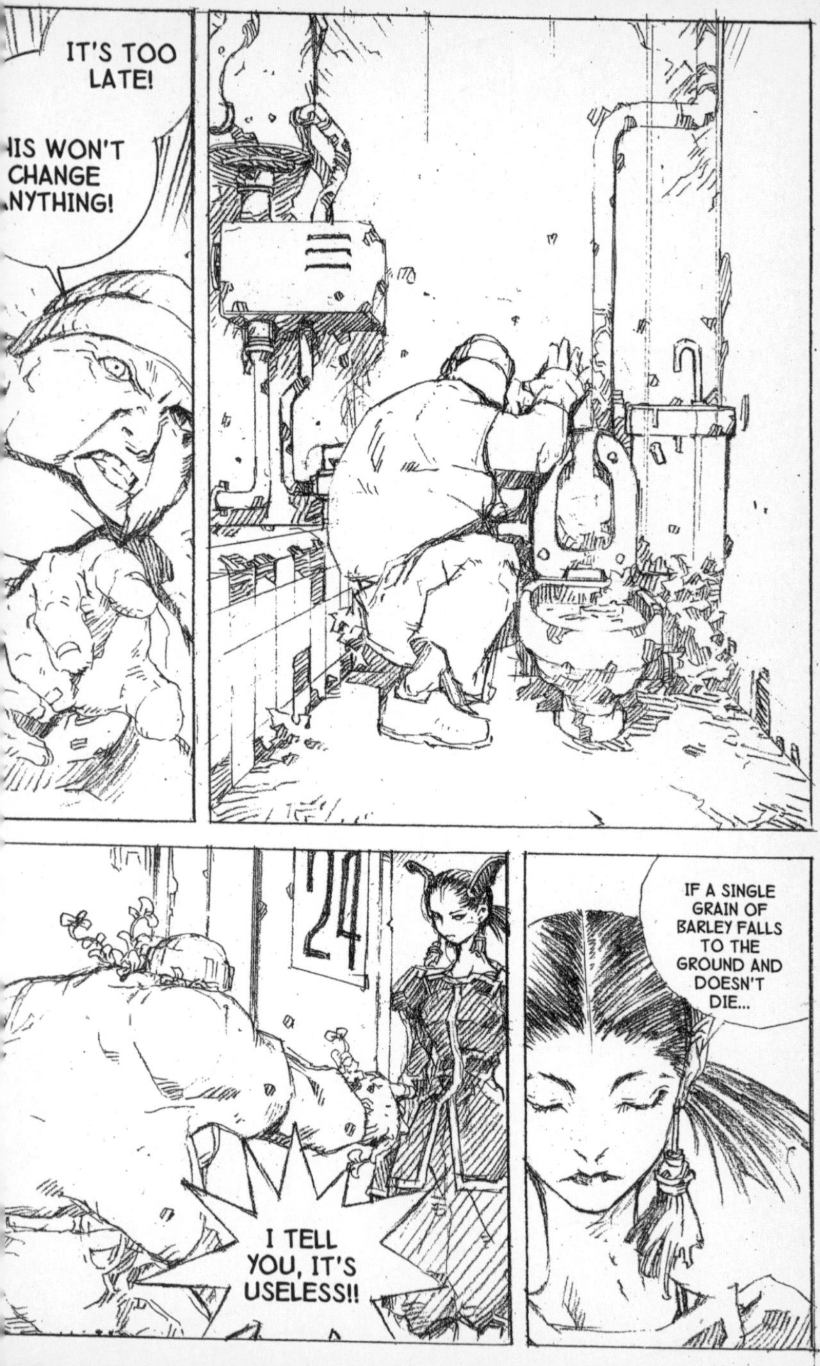
IT'S TOO LATE!
IS WON'T CHANGE NYTHING!
IF A SINGLE GRAIN OF BARLEY FALLS TO THE GROUND AND DOESN'T DIE...
I TELL YOU, IT'S USELESS!!

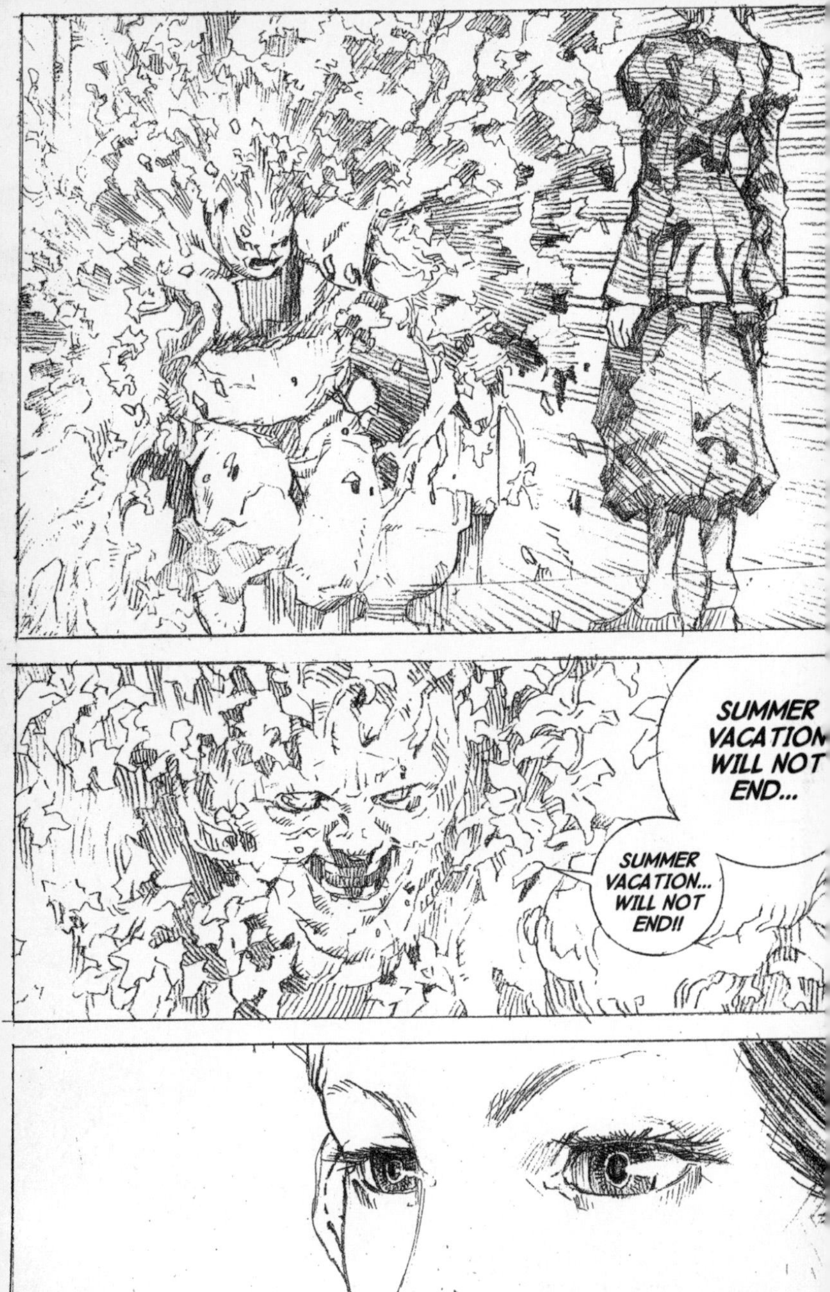
SUMMER VACATION WILL NOT END...
SUMMER VACATION... WILL NOT END!!

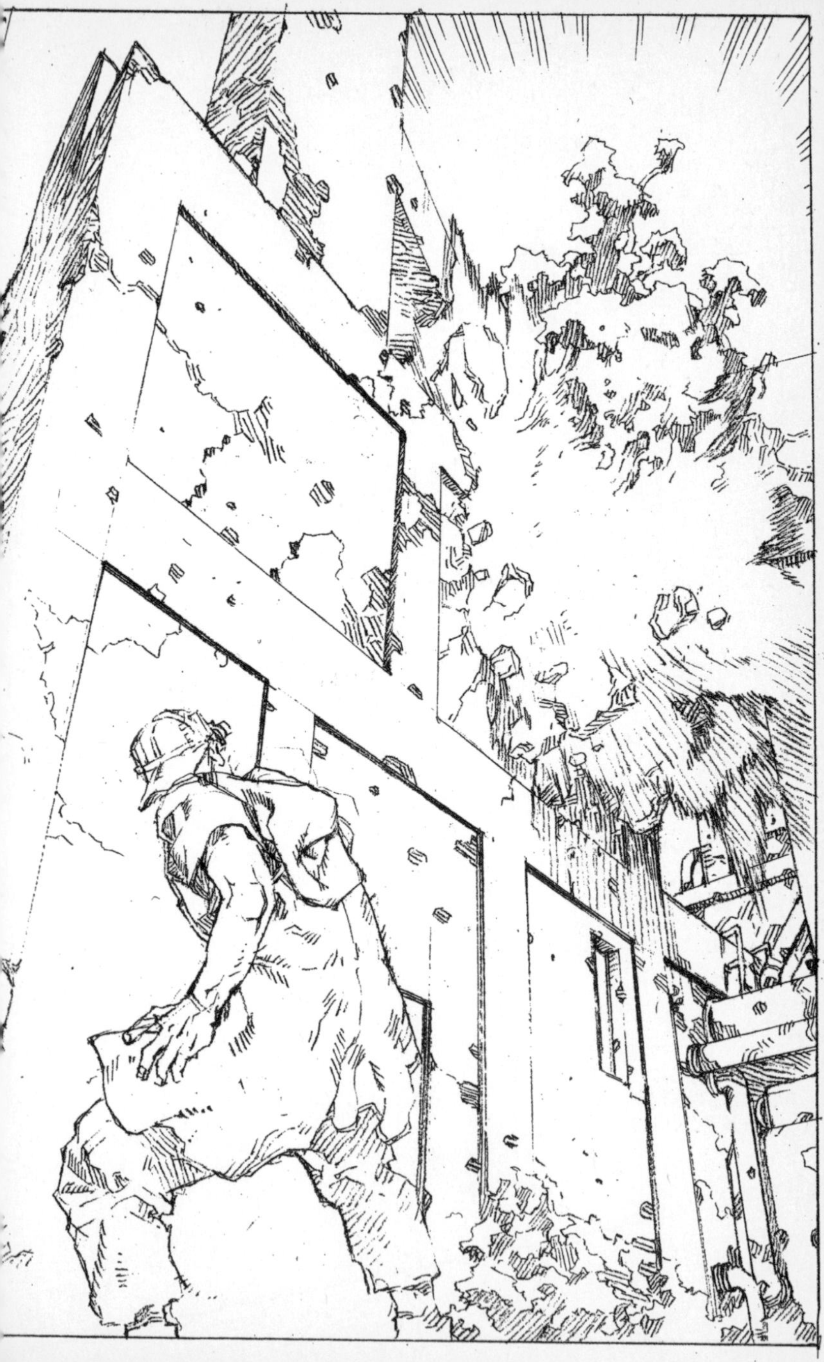

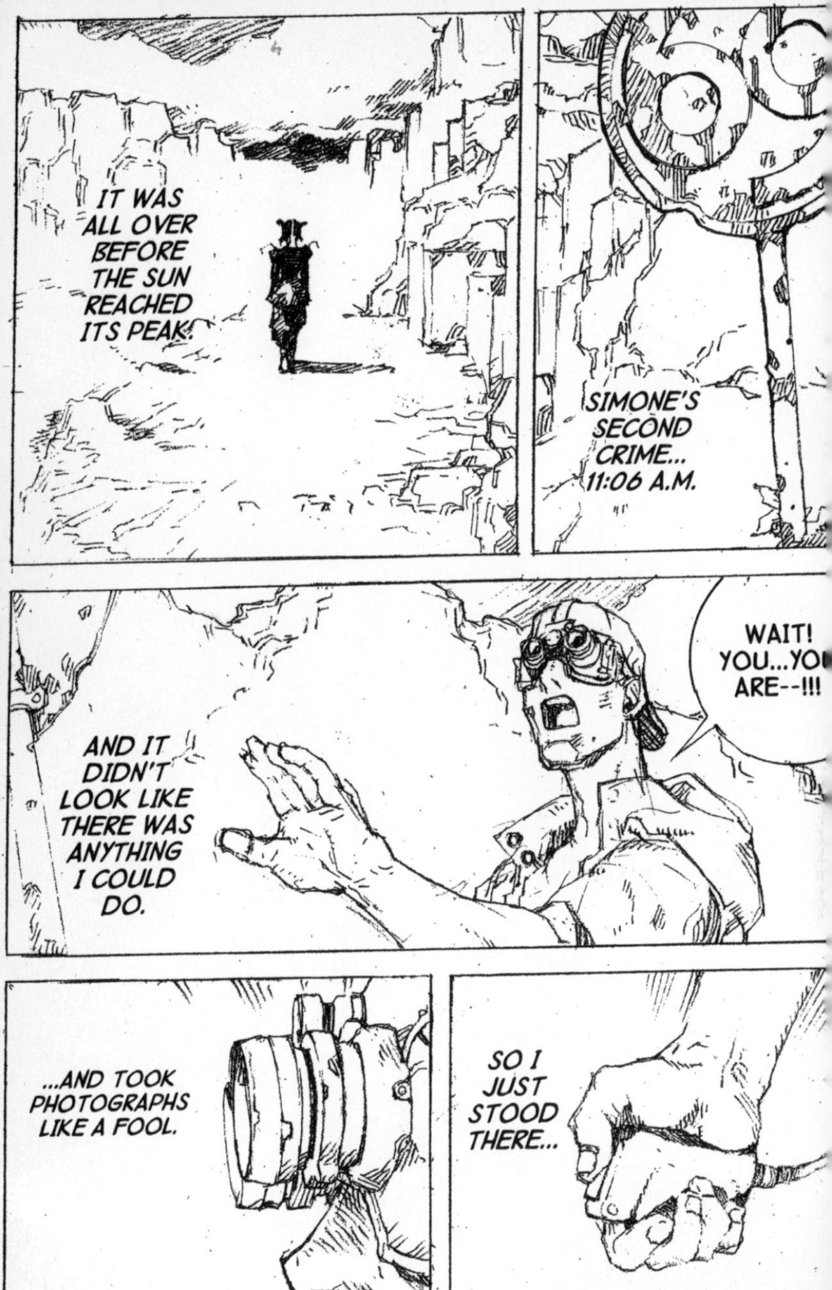

SIMONE'S SECOND CRIME... 11:06 A.M.
IT WAS ALL OVER BEFORE THE SUN REACHED ITS PEAK.
WAIT! YOU...YO ARE--!!!
AND IT DIDN'T LOOK LIKE THERE WAS ANYTHING I COULD DO.
SO I JUST STOOD THERE...
...AND TOOK PHOTOGRAPHS LIKE A FOOL.

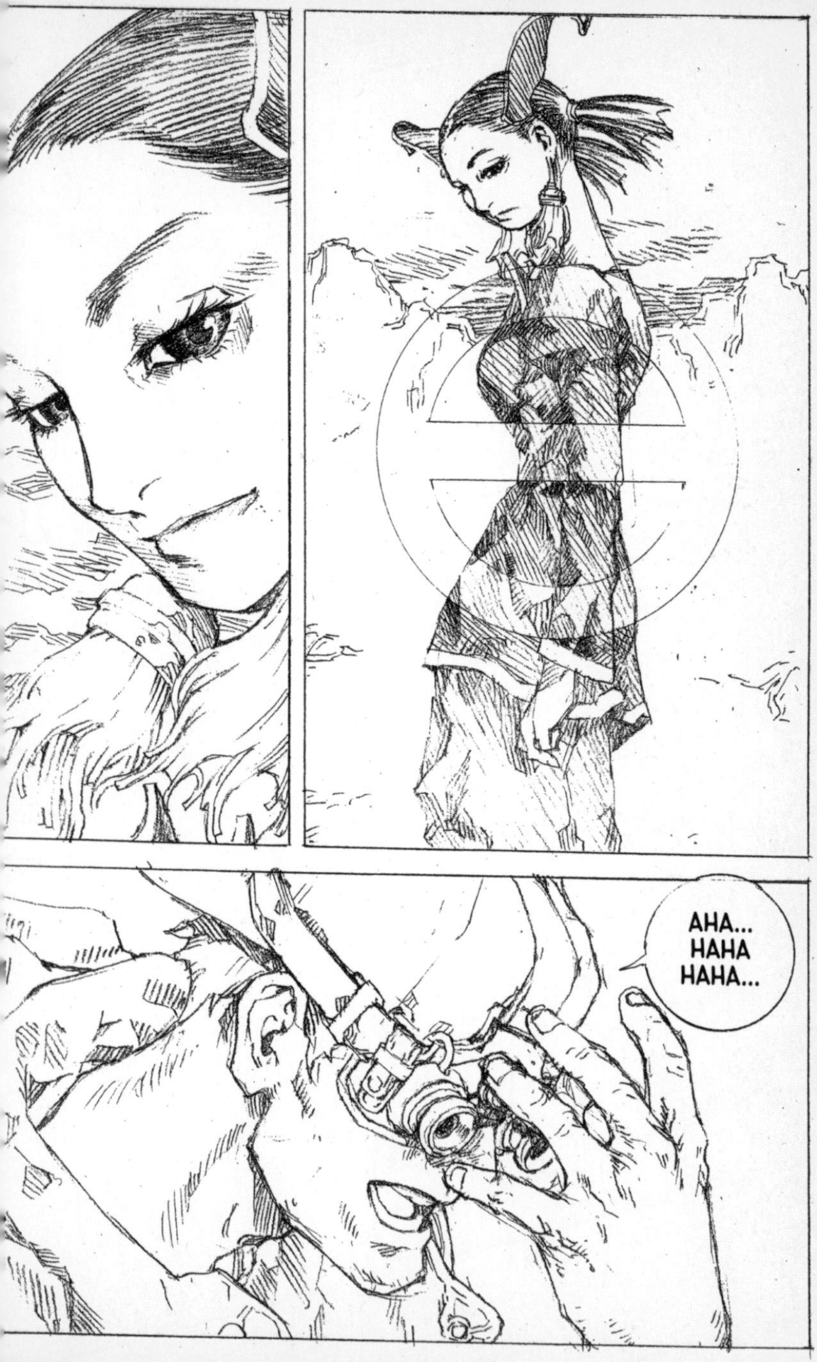
AHA... HAHA HAHA...

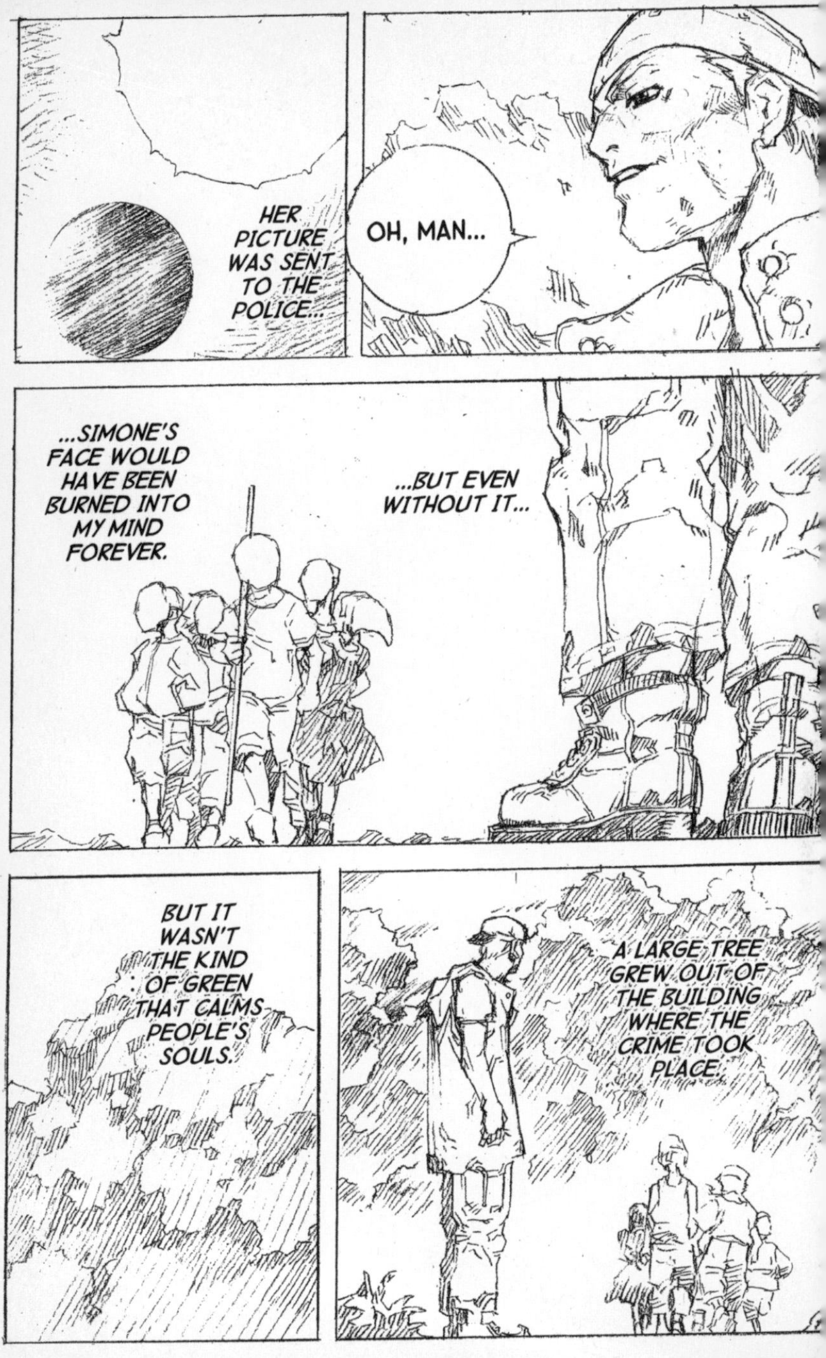
OH, MAN...
HER PICTURE WAS SENT TO THE POLICE...
...BUT EVEN WITHOUT IT...
...SIMONE'S FACE WOULD HAVE BEEN BURNED INTO MY MIND FOREVER.
A LARGE TREE GREW OUT OF THE BUILDING WHERE THE CRIME TOOK PLACE.
BUT IT WASN'T THE KIND OF GREEN THAT CALMS PEOPLE'S SOULS.

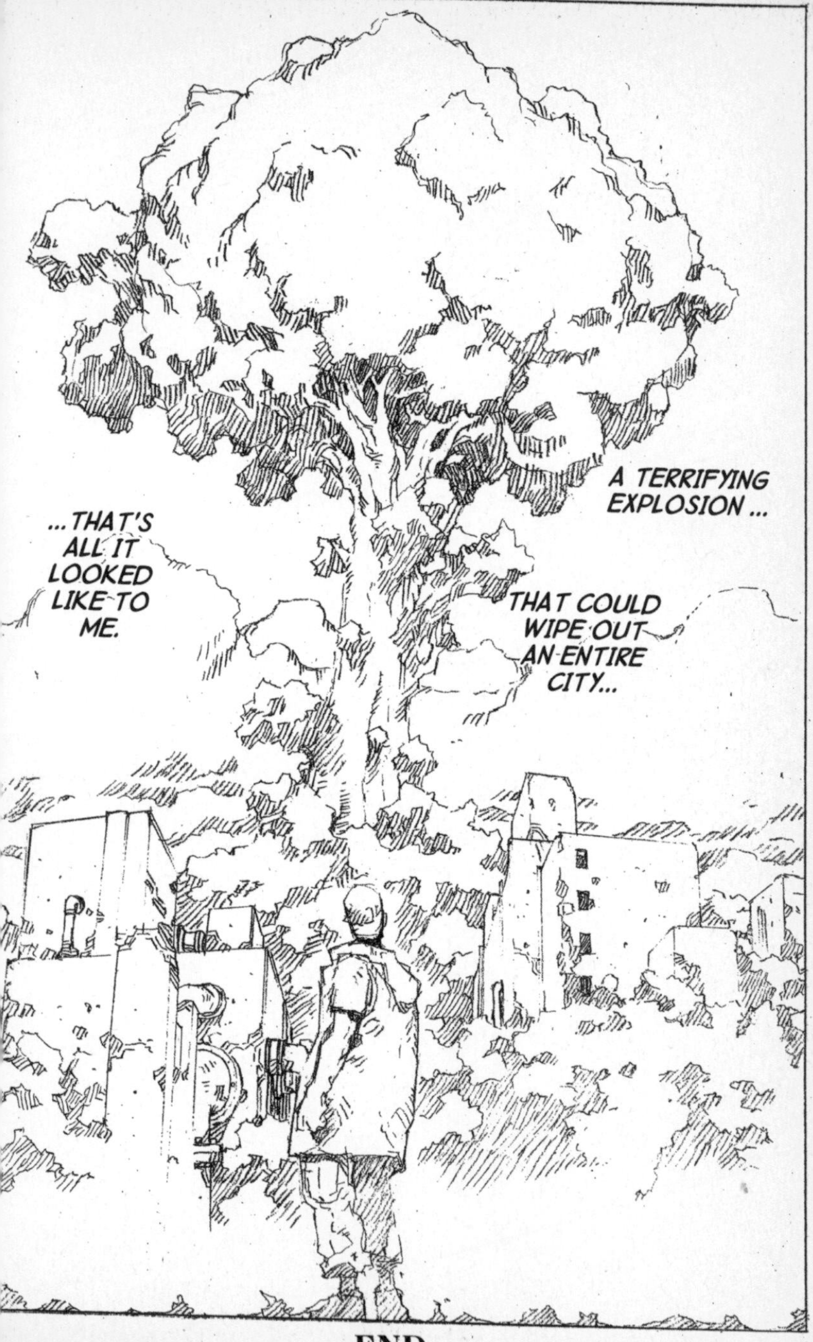
A TERRIFYING EXPLOSION ...
THAT COULD WIPE OUT AN ENTIRE CITY...
...THAT'S ALL IT LOOKED LIKE TO ME.

END

GAMEBO

SOFT

KING of

BANDIT

JiNG

GRAFiC

GBソフト王ドロボウJI

設定画集

ChibiPoru (1)

A BABY PORVORA WITH A CUTE, INNOCENT EXPRESSION. EVEN AT THIS SIZE, ITS EXPLOSION IS QUITE DESTRUCTIVE. (SEE *JING: KING OF BANDITS*, VOL. 2)

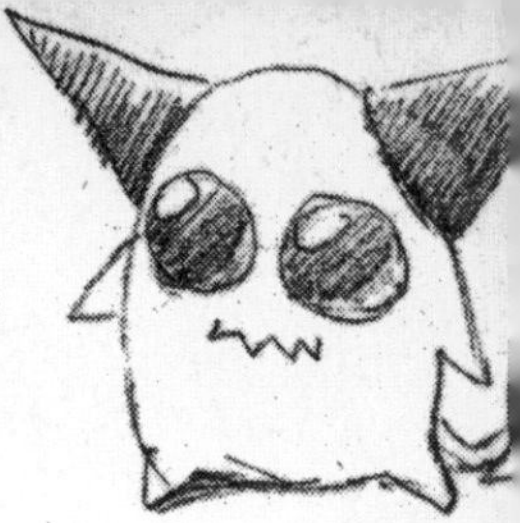

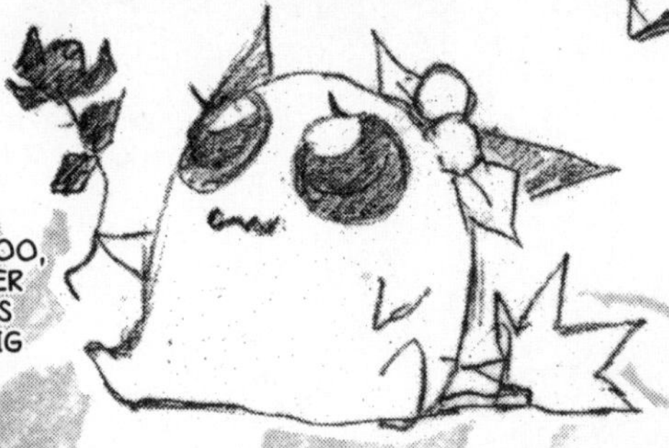

HimePoru

ONE IS SMALL, TOO, T FEMALE. THICKER PS AND EYELASHES TUALLY MAKE A BIG DIFFERENCE.

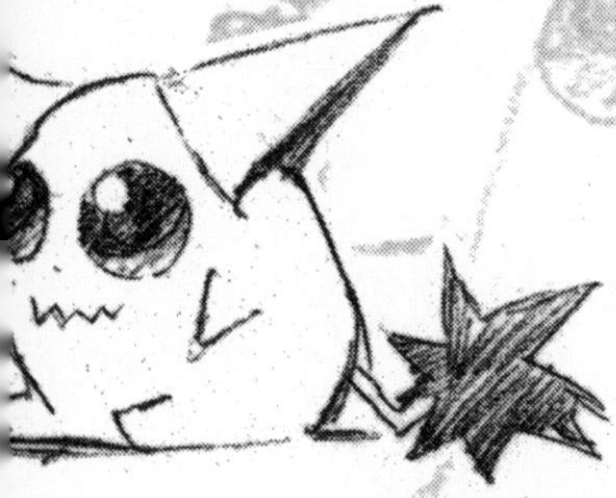

ChibiPoru (2)

AN ALTERNATE DESIGN FOR CHIBIPORU THAT DIDN'T APPEAR IN THE GAME. I LOVE HOW HE'S SIT-TING SO STILL. BUT CAN HE ATTACK FROM THIS POSITION? IT DOESN'T LOOK LIKE HE'S PREPARED TO ATTACK...DOES IT?

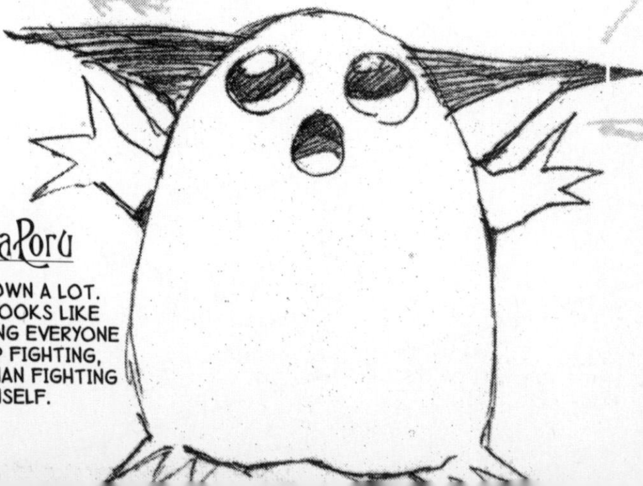

DekaPoru

E'S GROWN A LOT. UT IT LOOKS LIKE S TELLING EVERYONE O STOP FIGHTING, THER THAN FIGHTING HIMSELF.

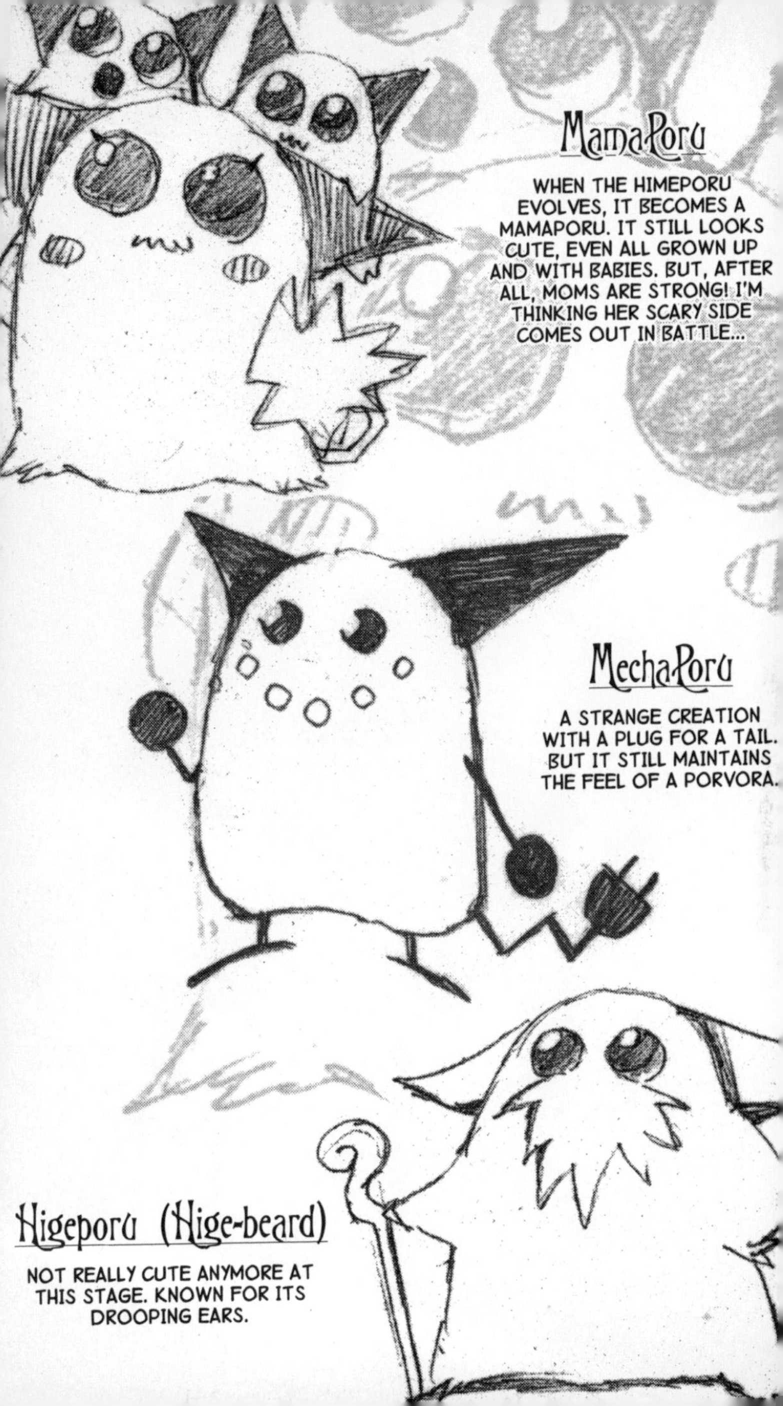
MamaPoru
WHEN THE HIMEPORU EVOLVES, IT BECOMES A MAMAPORU. IT STILL LOOKS CUTE, EVEN ALL GROWN UP AND WITH BABIES. BUT, AFTER ALL, MOMS ARE STRONG! I'M THINKING HER SCARY SIDE COMES OUT IN BATTLE...
MechaPoru
A STRANGE CREATION WITH A PLUG FOR A TAIL. BUT IT STILL MAINTAINS THE FEEL OF A PORVORA.
Higeporu (Hige-beard)
NOT REALLY CUTE ANYMORE AT THIS STAGE. KNOWN FOR ITS DROOPING EARS.

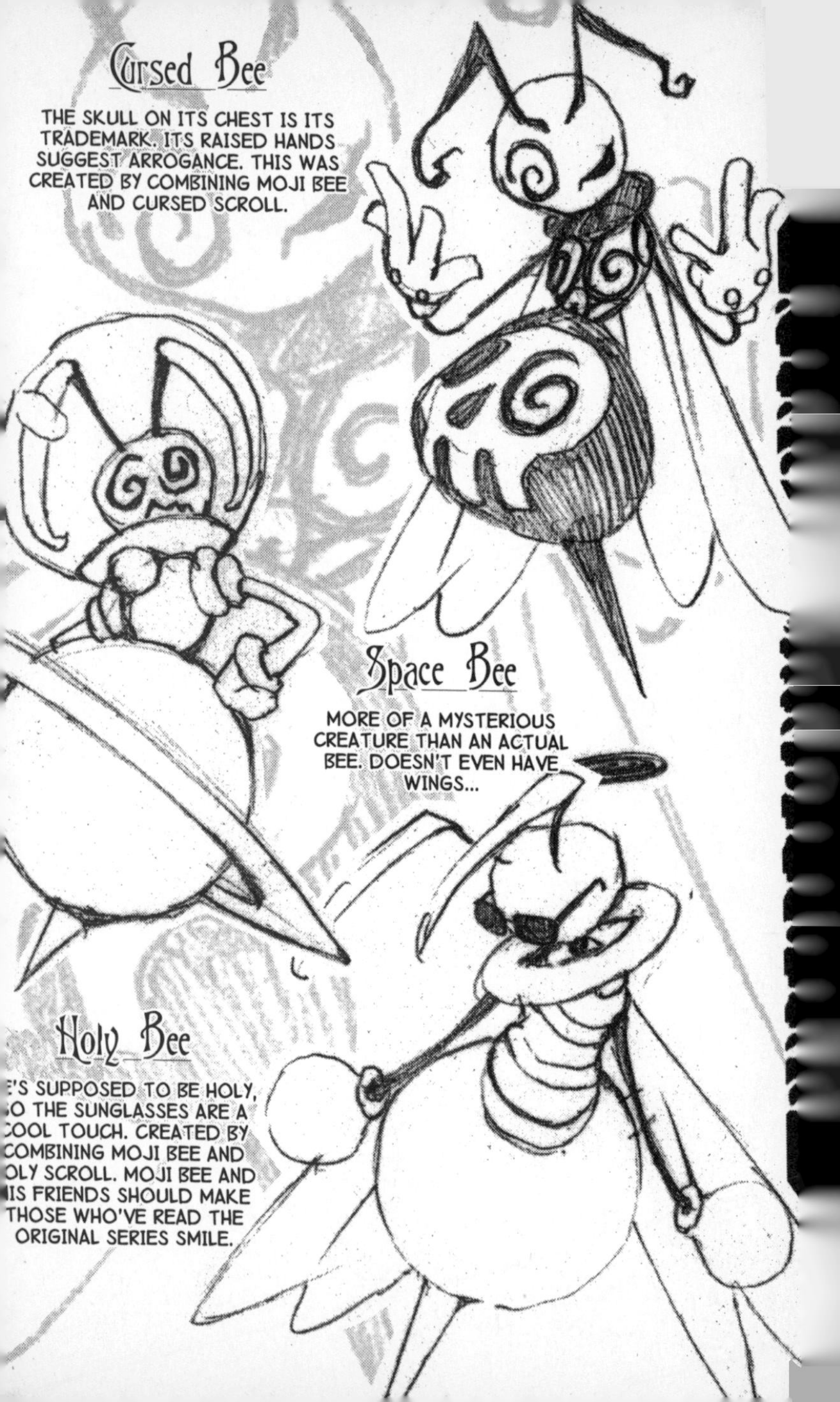
Cursed Bee
THE SKULL ON ITS CHEST IS ITS TRADEMARK. ITS RAISED HANDS SUGGEST ARROGANCE. THIS WAS CREATED BY COMBINING MOJI BEE AND CURSED SCROLL.
Space Bee
MORE OF A MYSTERIOUS CREATURE THAN AN ACTUAL BEE. DOESN'T EVEN HAVE WINGS...
Holy Bee
E'S SUPPOSED TO BE HOLY, O THE SUNGLASSES ARE A OOL TOUCH. CREATED BY COMBINING MOJI BEE AND OLY SCROLL. MOJI BEE AND IS FRIENDS SHOULD MAKE THOSE WHO'VE READ THE ORIGINAL SERIES SMILE.

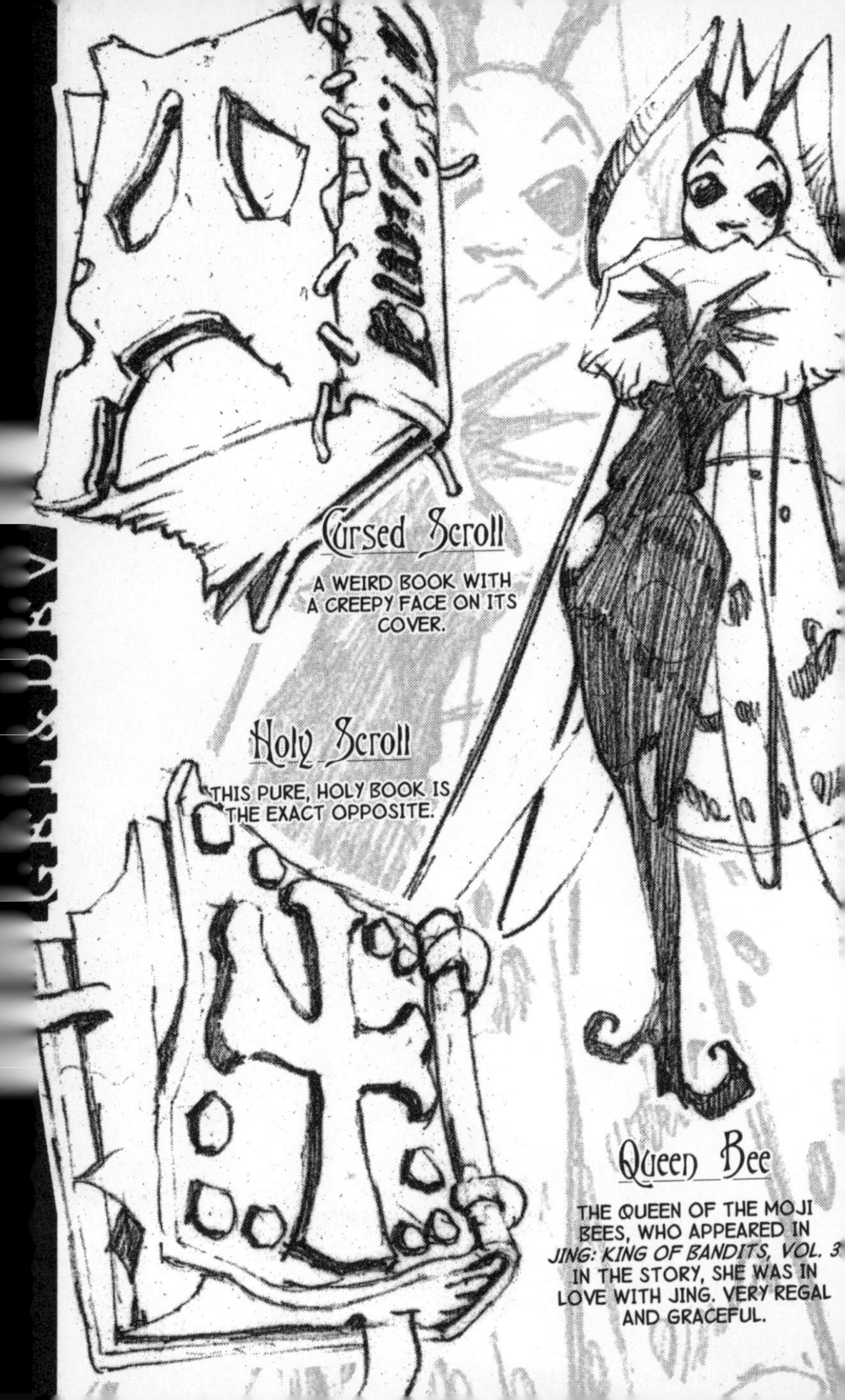
Cursed Scroll
A WEIRD BOOK WITH A CREEPY FACE ON ITS COVER.
Holy Scroll
THIS PURE, HOLY BOOK IS THE EXACT OPPOSITE.
Queen Bee
THE QUEEN OF THE MOJI BEES, WHO APPEARED IN *JING: KING OF BANDITS, VOL. 3*. IN THE STORY, SHE WAS IN LOVE WITH JING. VERY REGAL AND GRACEFUL.

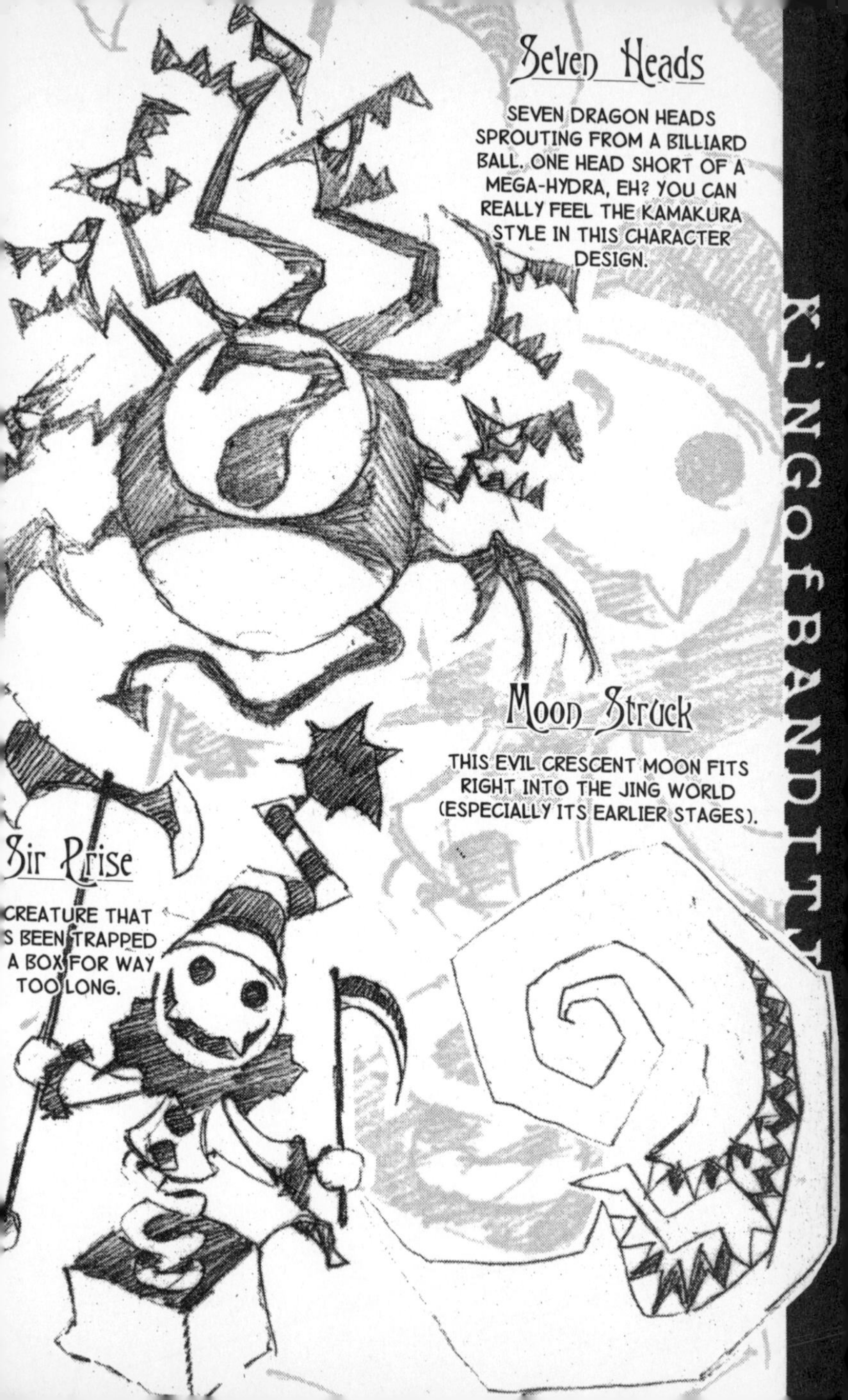
Seven Heads
SEVEN DRAGON HEADS SPROUTING FROM A BILLIARD BALL. ONE HEAD SHORT OF A MEGA-HYDRA, EH? YOU CAN REALLY FEEL THE KAMAKURA STYLE IN THIS CHARACTER DESIGN.
Moon Struck
THIS EVIL CRESCENT MOON FITS RIGHT INTO THE JING WORLD (ESPECIALLY ITS EARLIER STAGES).
Sir Prise
CREATURE THAT
S BEEN TRAPPED
A BOX FOR WAY
TOO LONG.
KiNG of BANDIT

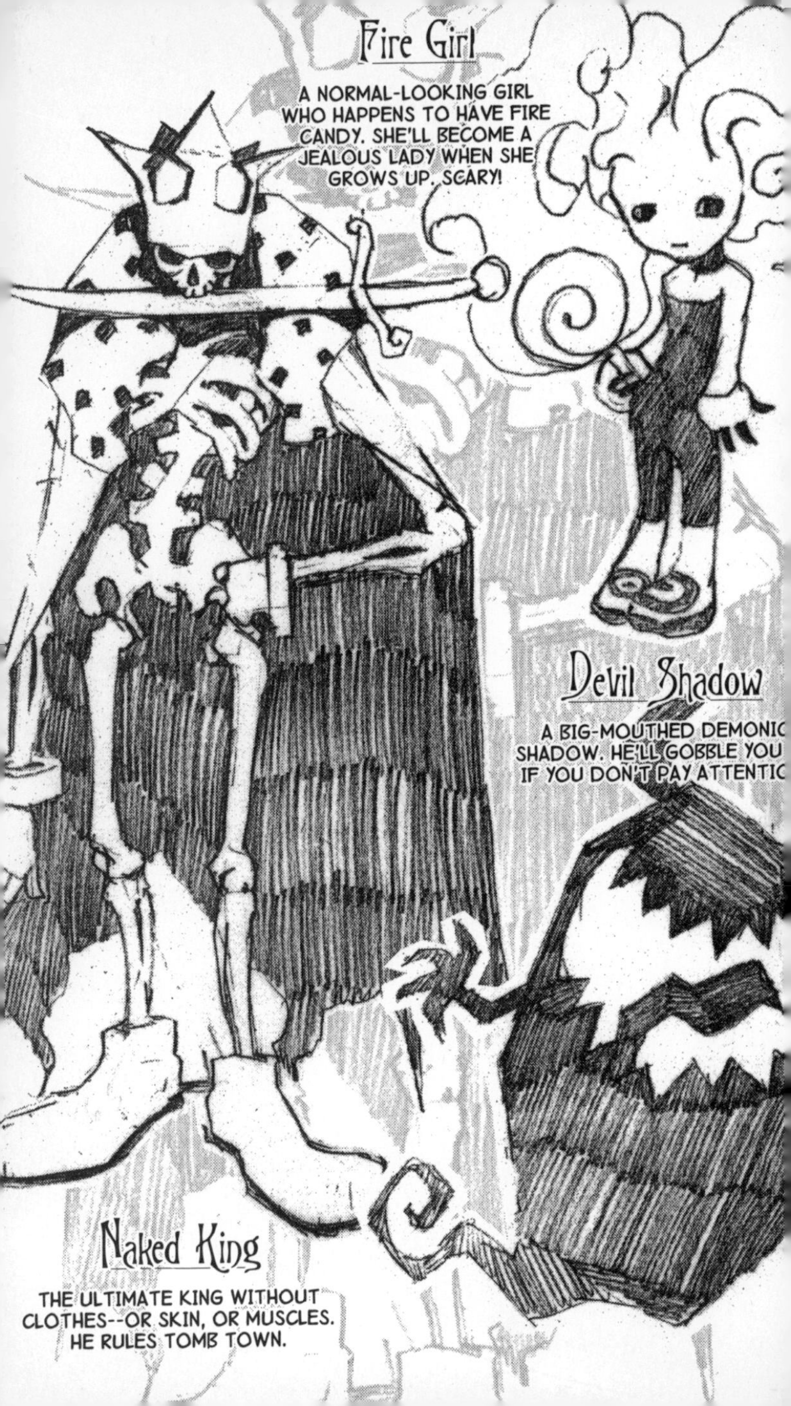
Fire Girl
A NORMAL-LOOKING GIRL WHO HAPPENS TO HAVE FIRE CANDY. SHE'LL BECOME A JEALOUS LADY WHEN SHE GROWS UP. SCARY!
Devil Shadow
A BIG-MOUTHED DEMONIC SHADOW. HE'LL GOBBLE YOU IF YOU DON'T PAY ATTENTIC
Naked King
THE ULTIMATE KING WITHOUT CLOTHES--OR SKIN, OR MUSCLES. HE RULES TOMB TOWN.

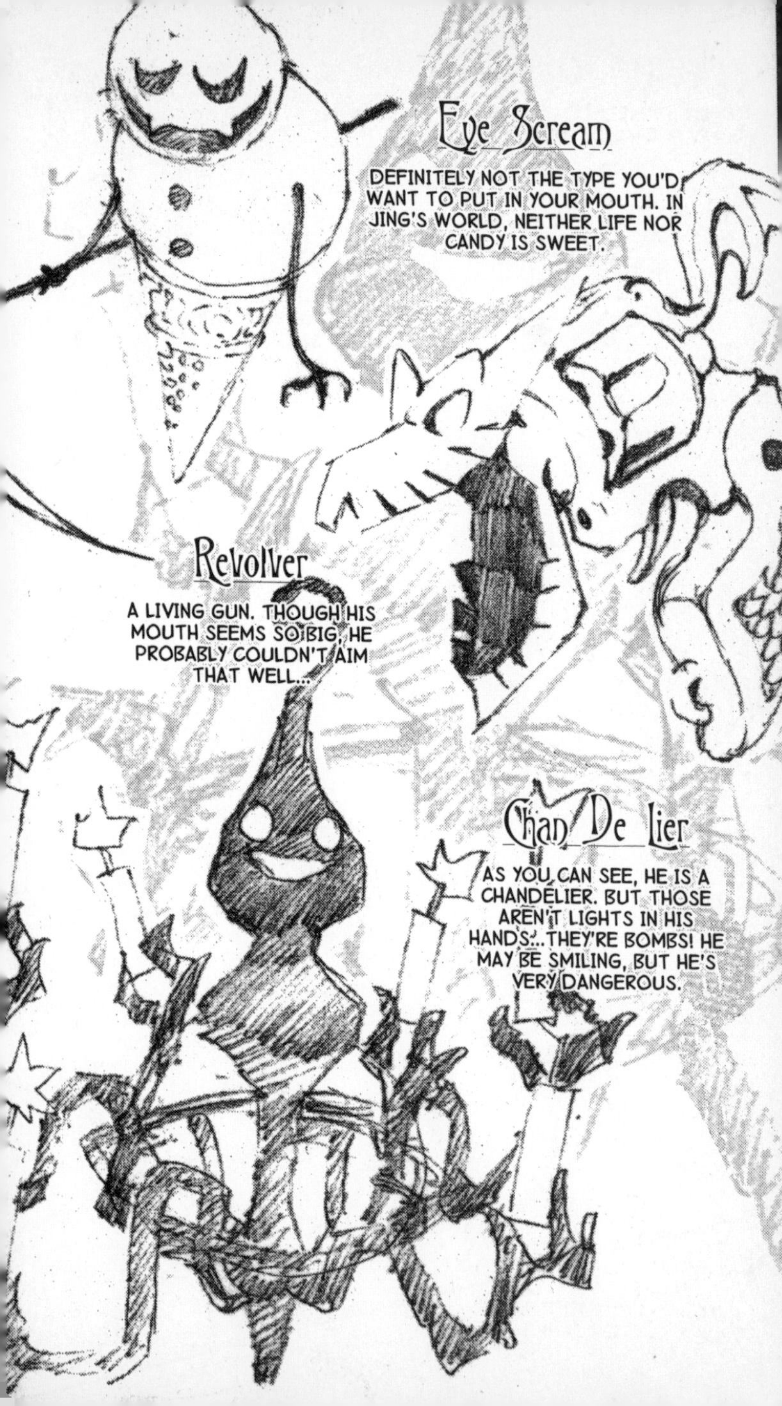
Eye Scream
DEFINITELY NOT THE TYPE YOU'D WANT TO PUT IN YOUR MOUTH. IN JING'S WORLD, NEITHER LIFE NOR CANDY IS SWEET.
Revolver
A LIVING GUN. THOUGH HIS MOUTH SEEMS SO BIG, HE PROBABLY COULDN'T AIM THAT WELL...
Chan De Lier
AS YOU CAN SEE, HE IS A CHANDELIER. BUT THOSE AREN'T LIGHTS IN HIS HANDS...THEY'RE BOMBS! HE MAY BE SMILING, BUT HE'S VERY DANGEROUS.

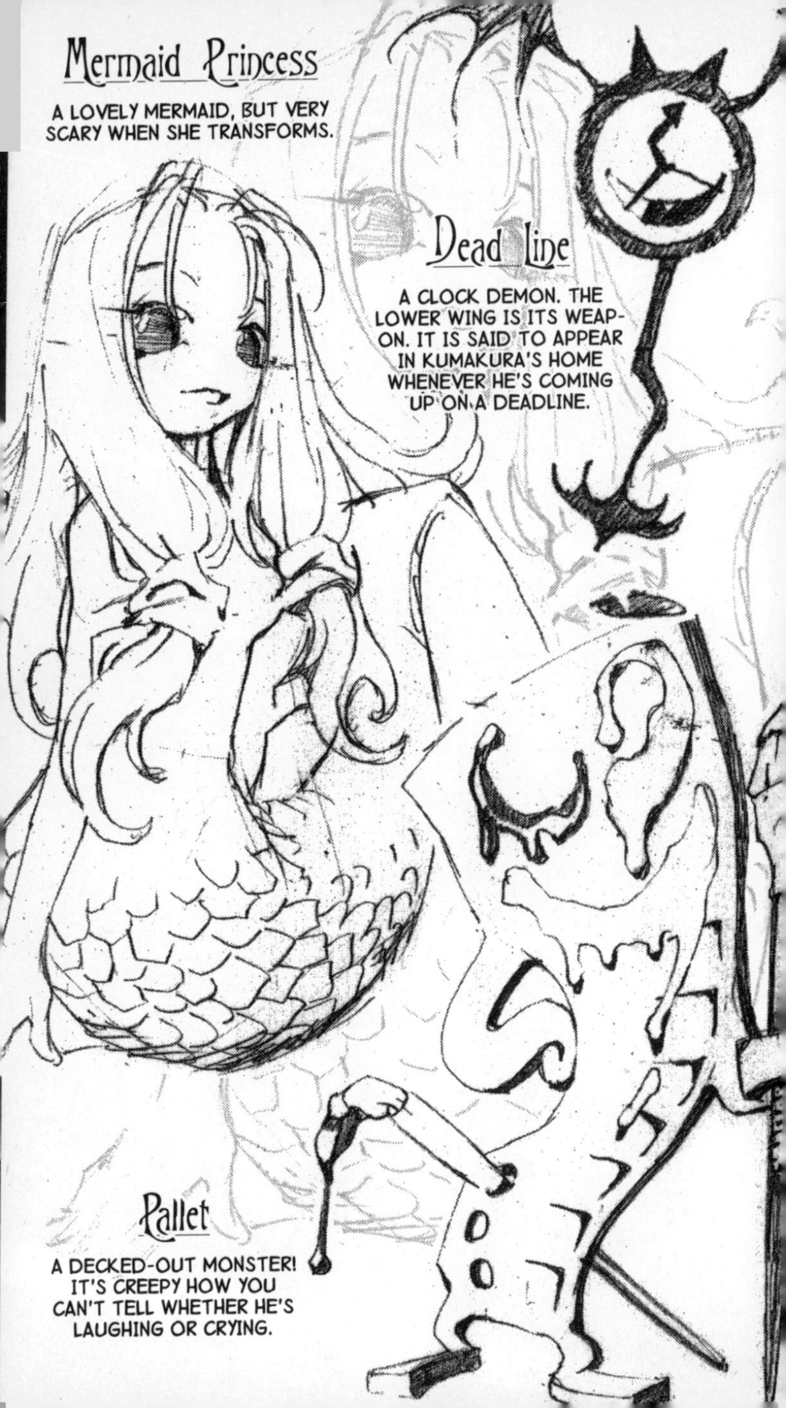
Mermaid Princess
A LOVELY MERMAID, BUT VERY SCARY WHEN SHE TRANSFORMS.
Dead Line
A CLOCK DEMON. THE LOWER WING IS ITS WEAPON. IT IS SAID TO APPEAR IN KUMAKURA'S HOME WHENEVER HE'S COMING UP ON A DEADLINE.
Pallet
A DECKED-OUT MONSTER! IT'S CREEPY HOW YOU CAN'T TELL WHETHER HE'S LAUGHING OR CRYING.

KING OF BANDITS

王ドロボウ JING

TWILIGHT TALES

Volume 3 Preview

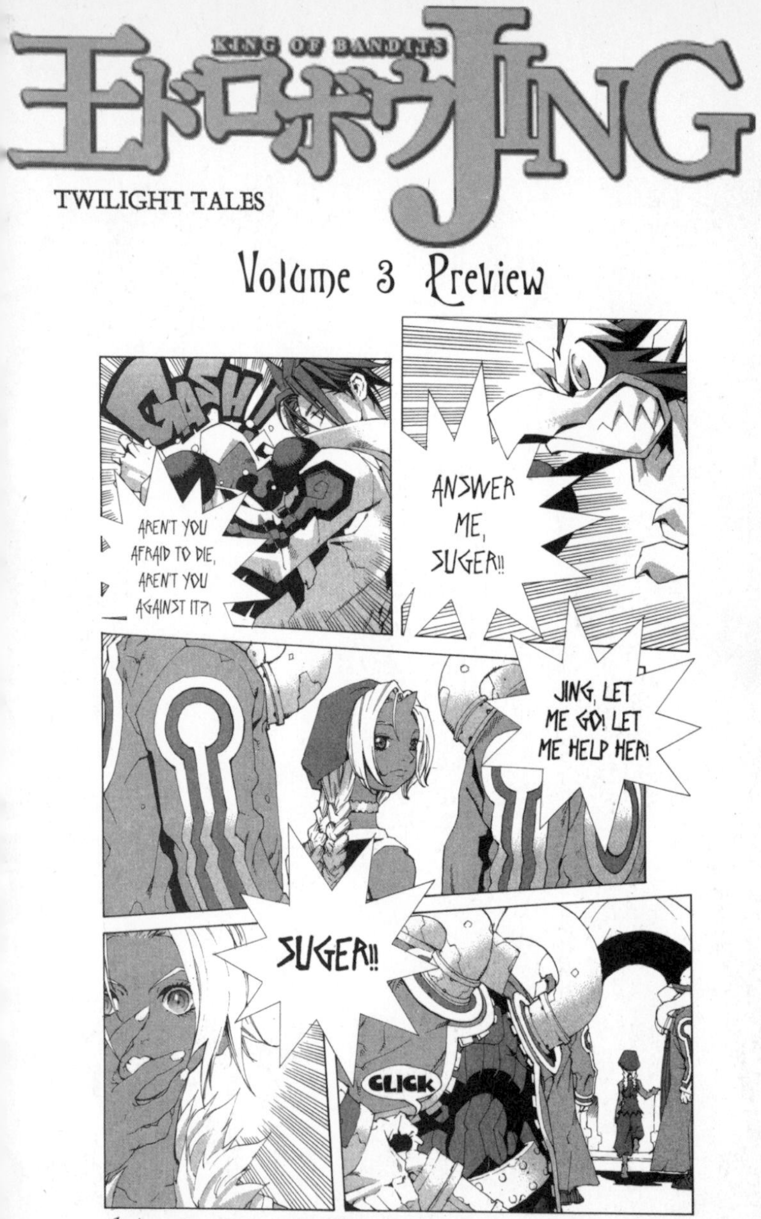
ANSWER ME, SUGER!!
GASH!!
AREN'T YOU AFRAID TO DIE, AREN'T YOU AGAINST IT?!
JING, LET ME GO! LET ME HELP HER!
SUGER!!
CLICK

Jing's on the prowl for the Lost King, who only appears when there is a coronation... and a sacrifice! Unfortunately, that sacrifice is to be Suger. This shocking news ruffles Kir's feathers, and Jing's avian associate refuses to let her go without a fight–because Suger is Kir's future bride! Will Jing help out his fine-feathered friends, or abandon them for the treasure of the Lost King?

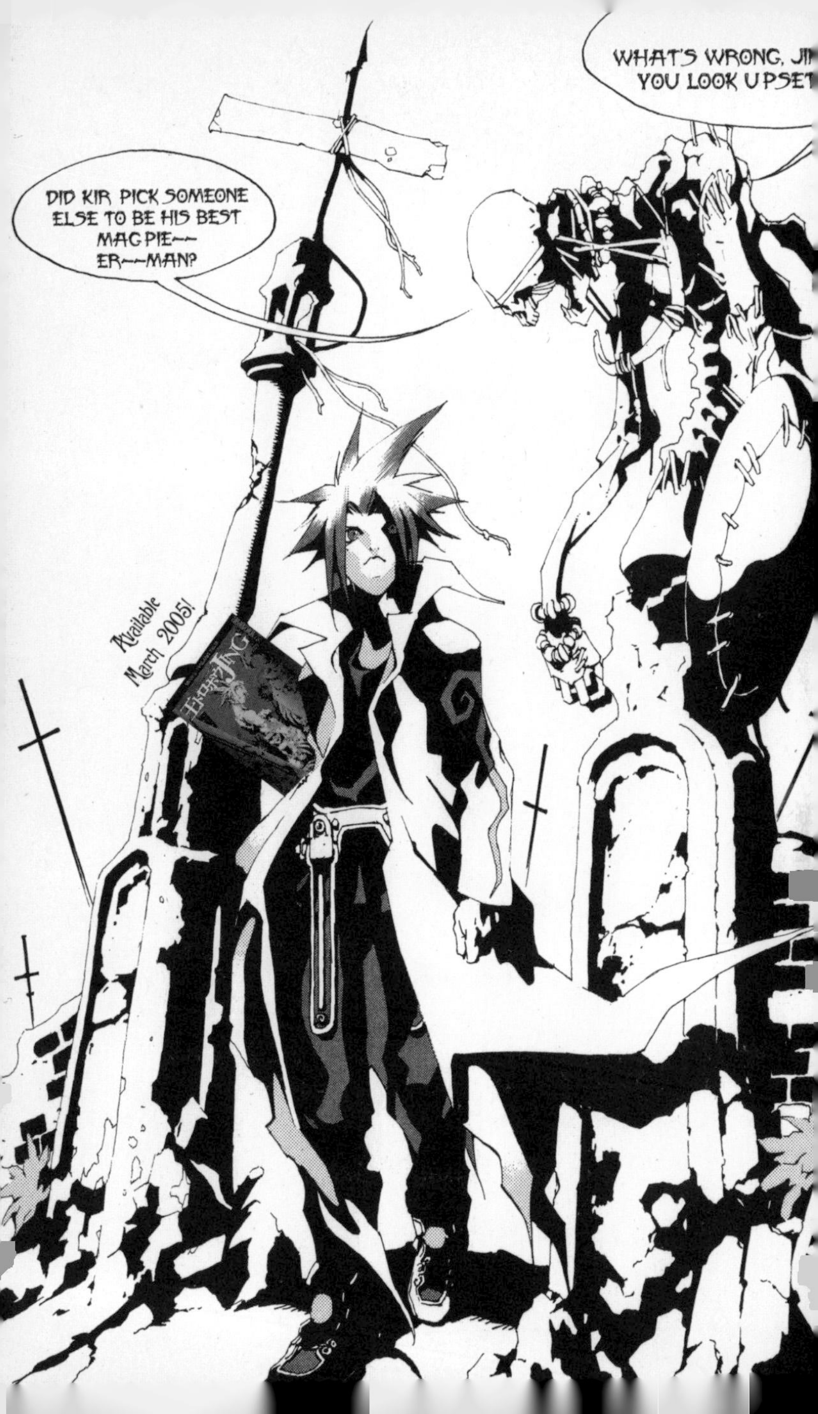
WHAT'S WRONG, JI
YOU LOOK UPSET
DID KIR PICK SOMEONE ELSE TO BE HIS BEST MAGPIE-- ER--MAN?
Available March 2005!

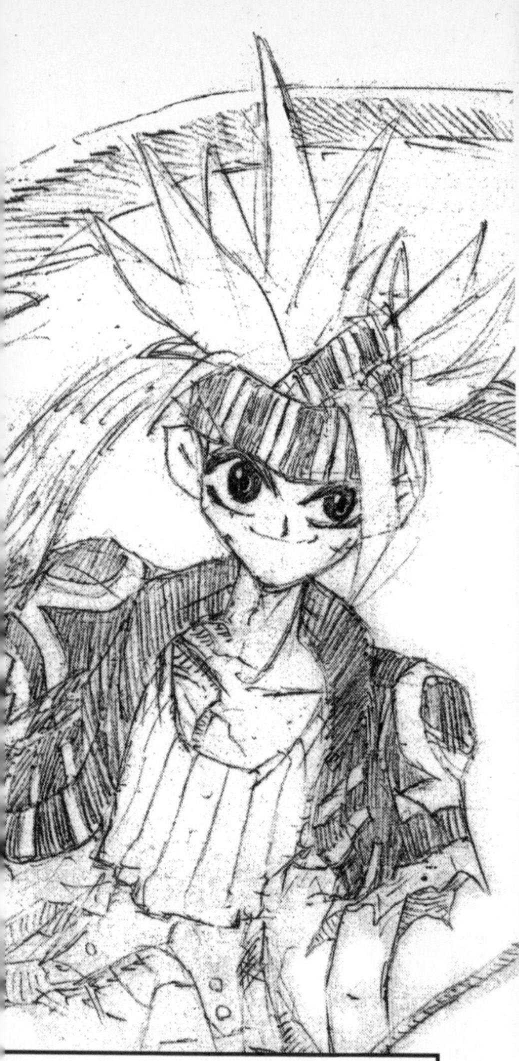

this your first fantastical foray into the world of ? Did he completely steal your heart? Well, you've to the party late, my friend! Oodles of fans have dy fueled their hunger for filching by reading Jing's t series. That's right! There are 7 volumes of the ous *Jing: The King of Bandits* series just waiting to fall into your eager fingers!

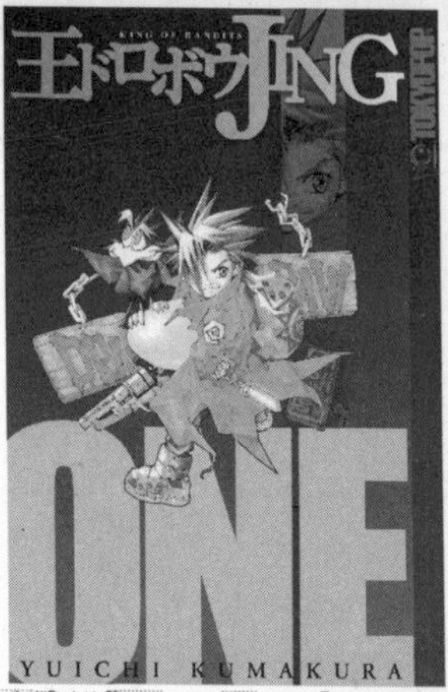
王ドロボウJING
TOKYOPOP
ONE
YUICHI KUMAKURA

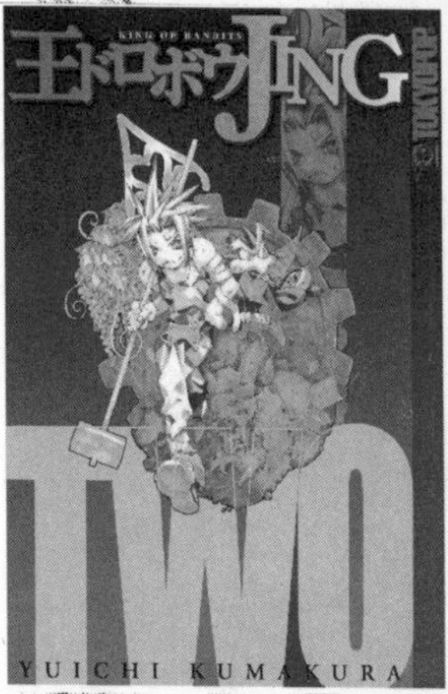
王ドロボウJING
TOKYOPOP
TWO
YUICHI KUMAKURA

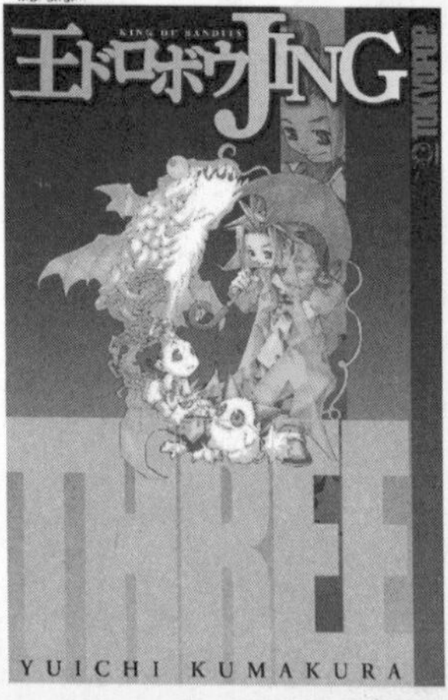
王ドロボウJING
TOKYOPOP
THREE
YUICHI KUMAKURA

COLLECT THEM ALL!

But don't steal them like Jing. Please, BUY them at a retailer near you!

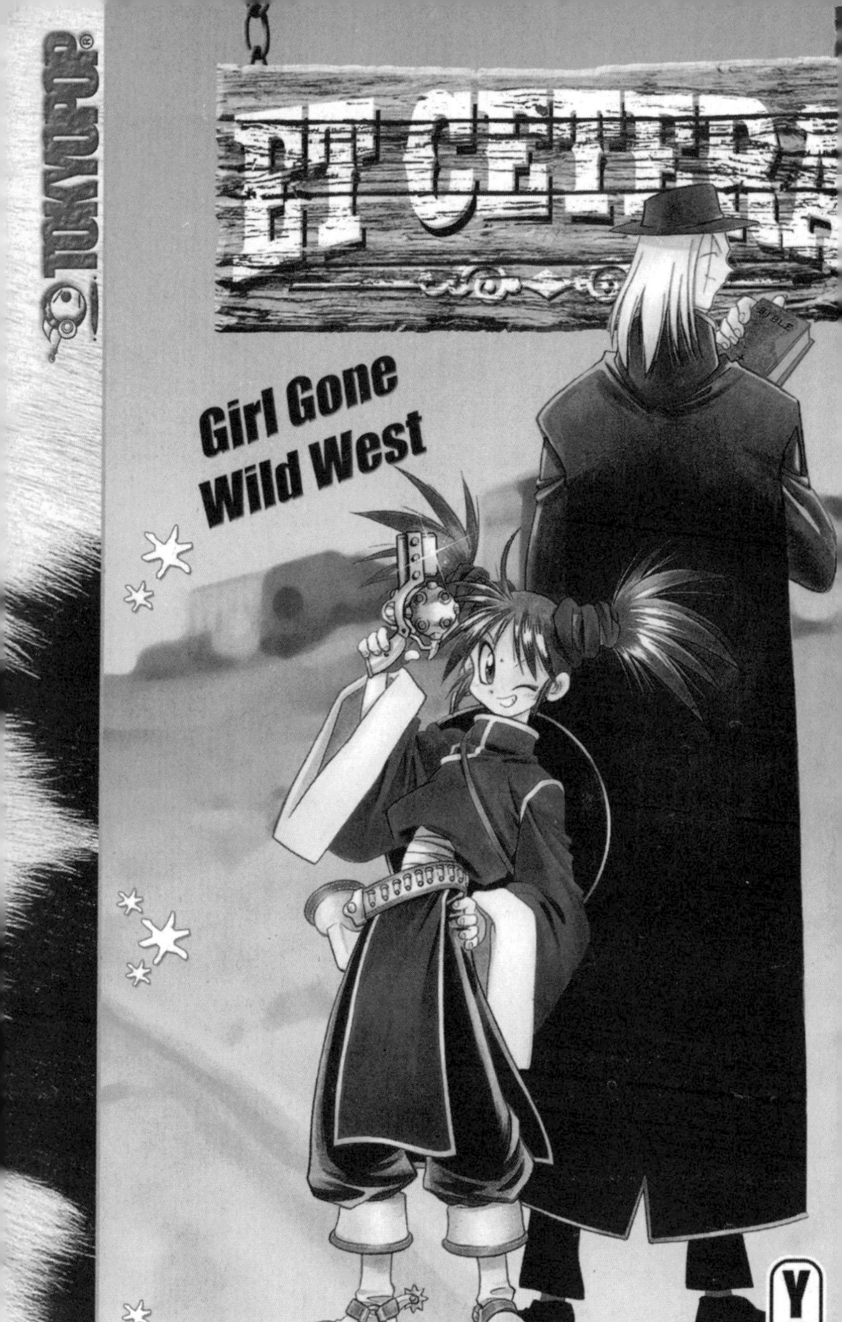
TOKYOPOP
Girl Gone
Wild West
BIBLE
Y
YOUTH
AGE 10+

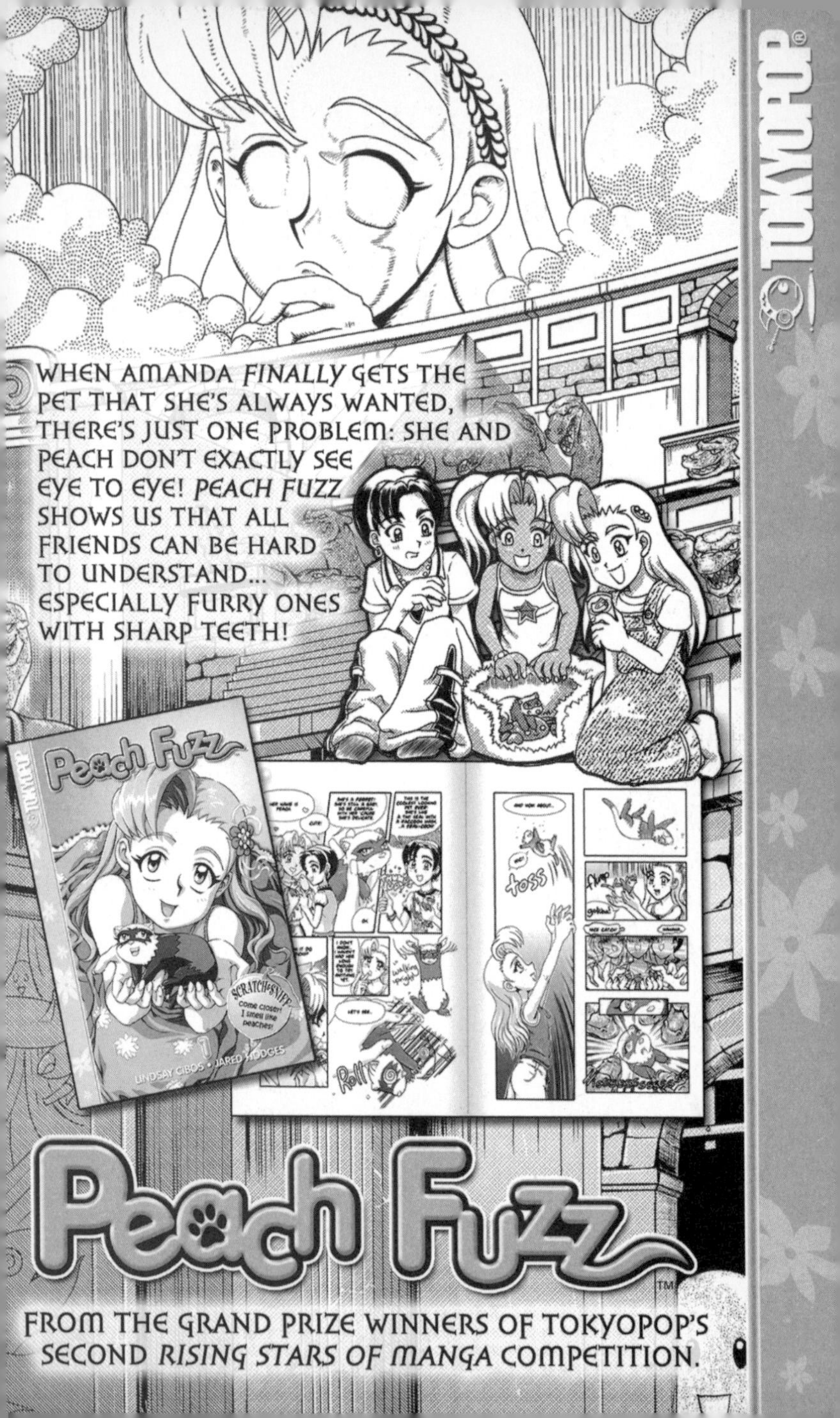
TOKYOPOP
WHEN AMANDA *FINALLY* GETS THE PET THAT SHE'S ALWAYS WANTED, THERE'S JUST ONE PROBLEM: SHE AND PEACH DON'T EXACTLY SEE EYE TO EYE! *PEACH FUZZ* SHOWS US THAT ALL FRIENDS CAN BE HARD TO UNDERSTAND... ESPECIALLY FURRY ONES WITH SHARP TEETH!
Peach Fuzz
SCRATCH & SNIFF
Come closer! I smell like peaches!
1
LINDSAY CIBOS • JARED HODGES
toss
Roll
Peach Fuzz™
FROM THE GRAND PRIZE WINNERS OF TOKYOPOP'S SECOND *RISING STARS OF MANGA* COMPETITION.

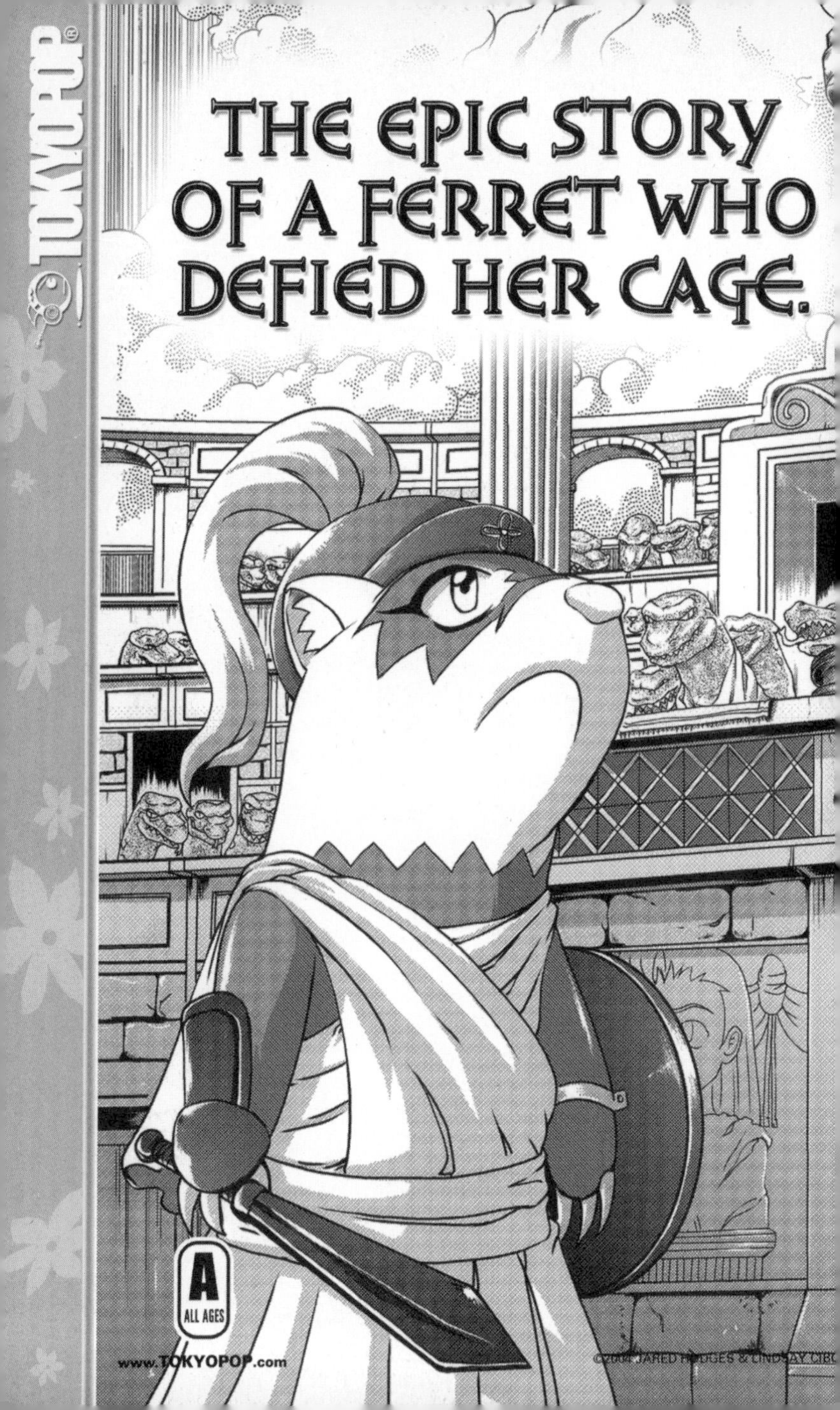
TOKYOPOP
THE EPIC STORY OF A FERRET WHO DEFIED HER CAGE.
A
ALL AGES
www.TOKYOPOP.com
©2004 JARED HODGES & LINDSAY CIB

ETERNITY

TOKYOPOP

Not all legends are timeless.

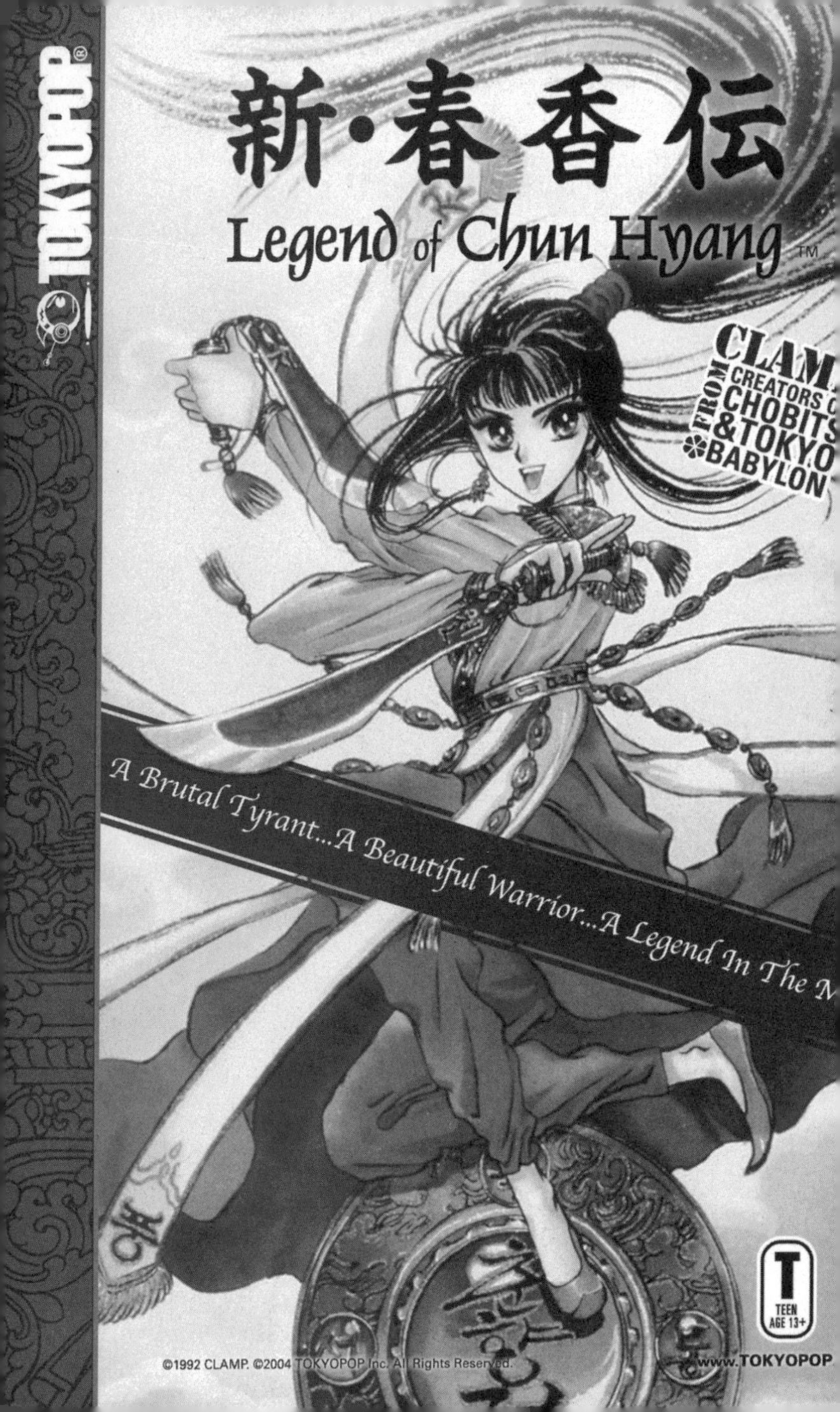
TOKYOPOP®
新·春香伝
Legend of Chun Hyang™
FROM CLAM
CREATORS O
CHOBITS
&TOKYO
BABYLON
A Brutal Tyrant...A Beautiful Warrior...A Legend In The M
T
TEEN
AGE 13+
©1992 CLAMP. ©2004 TOKYOPOP Inc. All Rights Reserved.
www.TOKYOPOP

ALSO AVAILABLE FROM 🐱 TOKYOPOP®

MANGA

.HACK//LEGEND OF THE TWILIGHT
@LARGE
ABENOBASHI: MAGICAL SHOPPING ARCADE
A.I. LOVE YOU
AI YORI AOSHI
ALICHINO
ANGELIC LAYER
ARM OF KANNON
BABY BIRTH
BATTLE ROYALE
BATTLE VIXENS
BOYS BE...
BRAIN POWERED
BRIGADOON
B'TX
CANDIDATE FOR GODDESS, THE
CARDCAPTOR SAKURA
CARDCAPTOR SAKURA - MASTER OF THE CLOW
CHOBITS
CHRONICLES OF THE CURSED SWORD
CLAMP SCHOOL DETECTIVES
CLOVER
COMIC PARTY
CONFIDENTIAL CONFESSIONS
CORRECTOR YUI
COWBOY BEBOP
COWBOY BEBOP: SHOOTING STAR
CRAZY LOVE STORY
CRESCENT MOON
CROSS
CULDCEPT
CYBORG 009
D•N•ANGEL
DEARS
DEMON DIARY
DEMON ORORON, THE
DEUS VITAE
DIGIMON
DIGIMON TAMERS
DIGIMON ZERO TWO
DOLL
DRAGON HUNTER
DRAGON KNIGHTS
DRAGON VOICE
DREAM SAGA
DUKLYON: CLAMP SCHOOL DEFENDERS
EERIE QUEERIE!
ERICA SAKURAZAWA: COLLECTED WORKS
ET CETERA
ETERNITY
EVIL'S RETURN
FAERIES' LANDING
FAKE
FLCL
FLOWER OF THE DEEP SLEEP, THE
FORBIDDEN DANCE
FRUITS BASKET

G GUNDAM
GATEKEEPERS
GETBACKERS
GIRL GOT GAME
GRAVITATION
GTO
GUNDAM SEED ASTRAY
GUNDAM WING
GUNDAM WING: BATTLEFIELD OF PACIFISTS
GUNDAM WING: ENDLESS WALTZ
GUNDAM WING: THE LAST OUTPOST (G-UNIT)
HANDS OFF!
HAPPY MANIA
HARLEM BEAT
HYPER RUNE
I.N.V.U.
IMMORTAL RAIN
INITIAL D
INSTANT TEEN: JUST ADD NUTS
ISLAND
JING: KING OF BANDITS
JING: KING OF BANDITS - TWILIGHT TALES
JULINE
KARE KANO
KILL ME, KISS ME
KINDAICHI CASE FILES, THE
KING OF HELL
KODOCHA: SANA'S STAGE
LAMENT OF THE LAMB
LEGAL DRUG
LEGEND OF CHUN HYANG, THE
LES BIJOUX
LOVE HINA
LOVE OR MONEY
LUPIN III
LUPIN III: WORLD'S MOST WANTED
MAGIC KNIGHT RAYEARTH I
MAGIC KNIGHT RAYEARTH II
MAHOROMATIC: AUTOMATIC MAIDEN
MAN OF MANY FACES
MARMALADE BOY
MARS
MARS: HORSE WITH NO NAME
MINK
MIRACLE GIRLS
MIYUKI-CHAN IN WONDERLAND
MODEL
MOURYOU KIDEN: LEGEND OF THE NYMPHS
NECK AND NECK
ONE
ONE I LOVE, THE
PARADISE KISS
PARASYTE
PASSION FRUIT
PEACH GIRL
PEACH GIRL: CHANGE OF HEART
PET SHOP OF HORRORS
PITA-TEN
PLANET LADDER

ST💥P!

This is the back of the book.

You wouldn't want to spoil a great ending!

This book is printed "manga-style," in the authentic Japanese right-to-left format. Since none of the artwork has been flipped or altered, readers get to experience the story just as the creator intended. You've been asking for it, so TOKYOPOP® delivered: authentic, hot-off-the-press, and far more fun!

DIRECTIONS

If this is your first time reading manga-style, here's a quick guide to help you understand how it works.

It's easy... just start in the top right panel and follow the numbers. Have fun, and look for more 100% authentic manga from TOKYOPOP®!